— SECOND EDITION —

MASTERING THE ART OF
Presence-Based Leadership

Partnering with Christ to Discern His Wisdom

KEITH E. YODER, Ed.D.
with Patricia Tillman

Trust in the Lord with all your heart and lean not on your own understanding; in all your ways acknowledge Him, and He shall direct your paths. —PROVERBS 3:5-6

For information concerning consultation, training, workshops, seminars, or speaking engagements, contact:

ttwm.org | mail@ttwm.org

Copyright ©2020 by Teaching the Word Ministries

ISBN: 978-1-7349313-0-3

First Edition Cover Photo: ©Petrasalinger | Dreamstime.com

First Edition: Design and editing by Patricia Tillman

Second Edition: Design by Jason Deller, editing by Katie Weeber

All rights reserved. No portion of this book may be reproduced without the permission of the publisher.

Unless otherwise noted, all Scripture quotations in this text are taken from the New King James Version®. Copyright © 1982 by Thomas Nelson, Inc. Used by permission. All rights reserved.

Scripture references marked NIV are taken from THE HOLY BIBLE, NEW INTERNATIONAL VERSON® NIV®. Copyright © 1973, 1978, 1984 by International Bible Society®. Used by permission. All rights reserved worldwide.

Scripture references marked The Message are taken from THE MESSAGE: THE BIBLE IN CONTEMPORARY ENGLISH™. Copyright © 1993, 1994, 1995, 1996, 2000, 2001, 2002. Used by permission of NavPress Publishing Group.

Scripture references marked NASB are taken from the New American Standard Bible®. Copyright © 1960, 1962, 1963, 1968, 1971, 1972, 1973, 1975, 1977, 1995 by The Lockman Foundation. Used by permission. (www.Lockman.org)

Scripture references marked NRSV are taken from the New Revised Standard Version Bible. Copyright © 1989, Division of Christian Education of the National Council of the Churches of Christ in the United States of America. Used by permission. All rights reserved.

This book is the magnum opus of Keith Yoder's lifetime of living, leading in, and teaching Presence-Based Leadership.

Keith mines biblical truth with fresh, rich insight and provides a solid foundation for leaders to progress in oneness with God and their teams. Personal examples, stories from other leaders, and practical action steps are masterfully woven together to inspire, challenge, enrich, and equip leaders.

Far from a fad or a flash in the pan, this book presents a timeless paradigm that is simultaneously life-changing, life-giving, kingdom-advancing, and God-honoring. You'll want to read it again and again, recommend it to your entire team, and live it out together.

—*Lisa Hosler* serves as president of Align Life Ministries, formerly Susquehanna Valley Pregnancy Services, Lebanon and Lancaster Counties, PA.

Dedication

With joy, we dedicate *Mastering the Art of Presence-Based Leadership* to God and in honor of all those who seek to live and lead in and from the presence of Christ.

Acknowledgments

By God's design, the cultivation of Presence-Based Leadership (PBL) has become a life message. The Lord orchestrated several formative influences to entrust this stewardship in me:

- Anabaptist reformers modeled Christ-centered discernment.
- In the 1970s, renewal advocates highlighted the value of being filled and led by the Holy Spirit.
- In the 1980s, intimacy with God as Father impacted me deeply.
- In the 1990s, ministry among leaders engendered convictions regarding organizational leadership for congregations, non-profits, and businesses.
- In the first decade of this century, worship, prayer, and the pursuit of societal transformation among leaders in various cultures and streams of Christian faith honed the practice of PBL.
- In this decade, the Holy Spirit is disclosing that Jesus modeled PBL in a relationship with His Father, rooted in the eternal fellowship among the Godhead!

While so many persons deserve acknowledgment for their contribution to this work, Patricia Tillman applied her talents as a researcher, wordsmith, teacher, and artist to the first edition. For this second edition, coordinated by Jay McCumber, Jason Deller created the visuals, and Katie Weeber edited the text.

—Keith Yoder

Table of Contents

Dedication...4
Acknowledgments 4
Passcode for Online PBL Resources..............................8
Foreword: Larry Kreider 9
Introductions: Keith Blank, Stephen Weaver 10

PART ONE: DISCERNMENT
The Act of Presence-Based Leadership 13

CHAPTER ONE: A Story of Presence-Based Discernment...............15

CHAPTER TWO: The Act, Attitude, and Art 33
    Presence-Based Leadership 33
    How Does This Work in Real Life?............................. 36
    Carl and Amber—A Pastor's Story 37

CHAPTER THREE: Leadership and Discernment 42
    Is There Another Way?.. 42
    The ACT of Presence-Based Leadership 43
    The ART of Presence-Based Leadership 46
    Pastoring the Marketplace 50

CHAPTER FOUR: Jesus' Radical Idea of Discernment as "Church"....... 54
    Ecclesia.. 54
    Gates..59
    Keys of the Kingdom of Heaven 61

CHAPTER FIVE: Keys of the Kingdom:
Christ-in-the-Midst Discernment 66
    In the Midst. 66
    Peter Gets It Wrong This Time 70
    Can Unbelievers Discern God's Will? 72

PART TWO: TOWARDNESS
The Attitude of Presence-Based Leadership 76

CHAPTER SIX: Towardness: The Nature
of the Triune Presence. 77
    Towardness 77
    Presence Stripped; Presence Returned 82
    Like a Dance: Perichoresis 84
    Designed to Thrive in His Triune Presence 86

CHAPTER SEVEN: Sonship: Responsibility and
Authority to Discern in Union with God. 91
    Characteristics of Sonship 91
    The Essence of Sonship. 93
    Why Not "Sons and Daughters"? 95
    Union 96
        Image-Bearing. 99
        Inheritance 103
    Responsibility and Authority 105
    Orphans (Slaves) or Sons? 107

CHAPTER EIGHT: Authority to Take Responsibility
in Your Metron 111
    What is Authority?. 111
    Submitted Authority #1: Aligned with the Measure of Truth 116
        How Do We Know What is True? 118
        Scriptural Truth and Spirit Interpretation .118
    Complementary, or Balanced Truth 120
    Submitted Authority #2: Entrusted by the Father 124

    Submitted Authority #3: Discern and Enact Christ's Will 125
    Submitted Authority #4: Spheres of Authority—Metron 126
    The Balance of Authority and Responsibility. .129

CHAPTER NINE: Authority and Responsibility as Kings and Priests 131
    Commissioned to Serve as Kings and Priests. .131
    Forgiving and Retaining Sin 135
    Kingdom Mindset 137

PART THREE: PRESENCE
The Art of Presence-Based Leadership 140

CHAPTER TEN: Our Presence Transformed by Christ's Presence. 141
    Our Presence. 141
    What is Presence?. 142
    Transforming Our Presence into Christ's Presence. 144
    The Holy Spirit Within Us 147

CHAPTER ELEVEN: Hearing the Shepherd. 151
    The Shepherd's Voice Filtered Through Our Hearts 151
    Issues of Life that Spring from the Heart 154
    Hearing Christ-in-the-Midst of Community 159
    Vulnerability and Transparency 160
    Hearing God is a Lifestyle 162

PART FOUR: COMMUNITY DISCERNMENT
IN PRACTICE 172

CHAPTER TWELVE: Building Discernment in Ecclesia. 174
    Community Discernment 174
        Unity or Oneness? 175
    Community Building 177
    Ecclesia with Christ-in-the-Midst Reprised 178
    Consolation and Desolation. 181
    Speaking Truth in Love 182

CHAPTER THIRTEEN: Cultivating a Culture of Prayer and Honor 189
    Presence-Based Leadership Culture of Prayer .189
    Intentionally Cultivating a Culture of Prayer 191
    Presence-Based Leadership Culture of Honor .194
    Scriptural Ways to Honor Four Types of Authority 196

CHAPTER FOURTEEN: Practical Elements of a Discernment Meeting . . 202
    Where Theory Becomes Practice. 202
    Template for Presence-Based Discernment. 204
    Meeting Preparation 209
    Leadership Discernment 213
    How to Recognize Wisdom from Christ. 214
    Practical Principles for Board or Team Discernment
        in Presence-Based Culture 216
    Lasting Legacy 223

Presence-Based Leadership Assessment 226
Glossary of PBL Terms. 229
General Index 232
Scriptural Reference Index. 238

ACCESS FREE PBL RESOURCES ON OUR WEBSITE!

Use the passcode: **PBL**

Tools for integrating PBL principles into your leadership or team:
- All of the charts and illustrations in this book and more
- Self-assessments and surveys
- Resources for activity ideas, training, and practice

Go to our website: ttwm.org
"**PBL Resources**" under the tab Store.

Foreword

I first met Keith Yoder in the early 1980s. As a young pastor, I sat under his teaching at a leadership conference and have admired him ever since. Ten years after we met, during a season of deep discouragement, I asked Keith to mentor me. He believed in me when I did not believe in myself. Keith has been a true spiritual father to me for almost twenty-five years.

One of the many things I have learned from Keith is the significance of Presence-Based Leadership. I am so grateful to the Lord and to Keith for this book, and I highly recommend it to you. Whether you serve in leadership in the church, in your community, or in the marketplace, the truths contained in these pages serve as a leadership-mentoring tool that will train you toward becoming a presence-based leader. Keith teaches us to hear Christ in a practical way, individually and in the midst of transparent community.

Keith has and is training a host of leaders throughout North America, India, Myanmar, Africa, and beyond. Join a growing team of leaders whose leadership capacity has been dramatically enhanced to lead like our Master, our Lord Jesus Christ.

—Larry Kreider
Author, International Director, DOVE International

Introductions

Leadership, in today's world, is not for the faint of heart. I recall many times in my thirty years of leadership where the Free Dictionary's definition of faint of heart was palpable for me:

> *People who are squeamish; someone who is sickened or disturbed by unpleasantness or challenge (i.e., the pathway around the top of the volcano near the crater, is not for the faint of heart).*

In some ways, church leadership is even harder than walking near a volcanic crater, because we come with assumptions and expectations about how we will love, honor and respect each other; but when discernment becomes intense, we often fall into patterns of interaction and response that fall far short of our Christian commitments and ideals.

It is into this challenging vacuum that the concepts of *Mastering the Art of Presence-Based Leadership* have provided me with fresh insight, new postures, and increased faith as I seek to honor God in my leadership.

At its core, this book is about "towardness"—facing, seeking, and yielding to the presence of Jesus Christ in **all** that we do, including in our responsibility of leadership. I've been challenged to increasingly acknowledge Christ's presence in our midst when we gather for discernment as the people of God. How can I surrender all my conversations, my discernment, my attitudes, my plans, and my reputation to Christ's authority each and every day?

Built on the solid foundation of Christ's presence in our midst is the conviction that God has given decision-making authority to every believer. Together, with our hearts submitted to God and turned toward each other, we are enabled to discern God's will in any situation, no matter how difficult the circumstances!

Reading this book has buoyed my faith and leadership. I still feel the "faint of heart" tremors rising at times, but because I acknowledge Christ's presence, often, these tremors no longer have power over me.

May God use this book and the concepts found on its pages to reestablish simple but foundational truths in our walk with Jesus that enable us to love and lead with new courage and boldness!

— **Keith Blank** has served more than thirty years in parachurch organizations, pastoral leadership, and as a bishop in LMC, a network of congregations based in Lancaster, PA. He also models and inspires leadership and ministry in the marketplace.

The Book of Job quotes Job responding to his examiners, "No doubt you are the people, and wisdom will die with you!"[1] So we moderns have seen ourselves on what we consider the Pinnacle of Progress.

One would think that this hubris would not be in the Church, but it is. In spite of our wealth (some would say *because* of our wealth) and campuses, our corporate Christian witness is less than impressive to a watching world. Where is the compelling winsomeness of other generations of the Church?

Voices in and out of the Church are saying that ours is a Laodicean age. Dan White Jr., in his recent book *Subterranean*,[2] says that we have exchanged ancient, proven spiritual practices for information delivered by personalities:

> *Preaching harder and louder at people to practice what they hear will not resolve this issue; this is not an issue of volume. For the future of the church [we] must recalibrate how we learn, understanding that we are shaped by the techniques we employ…*

---

1 Job 12:2
2 White, Dan Jr. Subterranean: Why the future of the Church is Rootedness, 2015. Cascade Books, Imprint of Wipf and Stock Publishers.

INTRODUCTIONS

We would rather *talk* about Jesus, it seems, than live with Him.

Keith Yoder and Patricia Tillman are presenting here an art, a way of being before God. Twenty-five years ago, I trusted my matrix of education and experience, research, consulting with "experts," brainstorming with the team, etc. These modern leadership skills, underwritten by our inordinate wealth, may serve in some settings, but they are no comparison to the living *Christ in us, the hope of glory.*

Keith and Pat invite us to a lifestyle of guiding others by practicing sensitivity and submission to Jesus, treasuring each moment in the love of His person, surrendering the means of our leadership metrics to Christ's authority and purposes. In this presence-based way, *the mystery* of Christ Jesus, *hidden for ages and generations, is now revealed to His holy ones*. I invite you to turn the page and walk on this road traveled by those who have gone before.

Stephen Weaver serves several leaders and congregations in an apostolic role as bishop in LMC, a network of congregations based in Lancaster, PA.

— PART ONE —

Discernment

THE ACT OF PRESENCE-BASED LEADERSHIP

The Holy Spirit moves uniquely in each organization—many times despite us—in answer to our prayers. Presence-Based Leadership (PBL) moves beyond just asking and believing God for something. PBL is intentionally listening for what Christ is already doing in a situation and how He wants us to partner in it with Him

Presence-Based Leadership
Guiding others with a posture of submission to wisdom discerned from Christ's presence

The Art

PRESENCE
Leading from a posture of rest in and from the circle of Trinity fellowship

The Attitude

TOWARDNESS
Cultivating a culture of prayer and honor

The Act

CHRIST-IN-THE-MIDST DISCERNMENT
Stewarding the metron of sonship within the ecclesia

©2016 TEACHING THE WORD MINISTRIES

PART ONE DISCERNMENT

Mastering any kind of art is a journey and not something we'll ever actually accomplish. But, oh, how exhilarating the journey! Because Christ passionately loves us, He won't let us stay comfortable as status-quo leaders. He brings us to the place where our self-made resources have failed us. We begin to realize this truth: *in our own strength, we don't have what it takes to reach the fullest potential God designed for us.* Something is missing. The Presence of Christ is the only source of energy and wisdom for long-term growth and meaningful productivity. It's simple, but never easy. It entails a challenging but fulfilling journey of learning to fellowship with our Trinity God. Learning to hear the Holy Spirit's voice. To be transformed. To walk as ambassadors for Christ's government in our assigned sphere of leadership.

PBL is applicable to more than congregational and missionary leaders. From the time that He first established the church, Jesus has called all of His followers to serve as partners in building His church, whether in ministry, marketplace, or community.

The Presence-Based principles we present in this book are practical for any leader or leadership team. Congregational leaders can glean fresh insight from stories about business and non-profit leaders, and vice versa. In this way, all can resource and support each other for one purpose: re-creating the culture of Christ's government wherever He calls us to lead.

Though we target this book to those in positions of leadership, the Presence-Based principles also apply to any Christ-follower. As is often said, leadership is influence, and God has given everyone a sphere of influence. It's the way the Trinity originally designed us to thrive—fulfilling God's purpose for our lives in His Presence and as part of His eternal plan.

---

* *Please note that the text is written from Keith Yoder's perspective. Any second-person plural (we's) are from the perspective of the whole team at Teaching the Word Ministries.*

— CHAPTER ONE —

A Story of Presence-Based Discernment

To begin this journey of Mastering the Art of Presence-Based Leadership, *we invite you to observe the dynamics of discernment among the board members of Eden's Way.*

The story provides a context that will allow PBL principles to fall into place as you read through the book. These principles are applicable for business as well as congregational and organizational leaders.

Though Eden's Way and its members are fictitious, all actions, events, and discussions derive from actual leadership meetings. Enjoy!

....

Chloe pulled her car into her brother Jack's driveway. She steadied herself against anxiety with a moment of rhythmic breathing, determined to remain composed. She assumed that the car with out-of-state tags belonged to Neam, the consultant they'd hired several months ago.

Before they hired Neam, they thought bankruptcy the only option for Eden's Way, the organic grains brokerage that her late parents started. Chloe and Jack now held the reigns—Chloe as president and Jack as CEO.

After a near-collapse into bankruptcy, their consultant, Neam, was helping the board put the pieces back together with an odd idea he called *Presence-Based Leadership*. So far, Neam's principles seemed to work, if it wasn't just luck or coincidence.

But would it take Eden's Way up the steep hill into the future?

PART ONE DISCERNMENT

Bennet, a longtime family friend and one of the original visionaries, parked his car beside Chloe's. As they greeted each other, they walked toward Jack's front door.

"I hear they're trying to tighten inspection standards," Bennet said.

"What good would that do?" Chloe sighed, already tired of the topic.

"I'm optimistic. I feel good about where we're headed…"

Chloe restrained her irritation. She appreciated his polite attempt at small talk, but Bennet wanted to purchase Jampa, another organics brokerage. Chloe did *not* want to buy Jampa.

At their last meeting—the first time in months that Neam wasn't there to facilitate—a heated argument erupted with no resolution. They needed to make a decision today, but neither had changed positions. To make matters worse, Jack leaned on Bennet's side.

Does Neam have any idea what he's in for today?

Jack greeted them at the door. Quiet worship music played on his stereo. Neam had suggested that Chloe, Jack, and Bennet meet half an hour early—*to pray.*

Neam offered a lot of practical business wisdom in walking through things, but Chloe hadn't expected a "spiritual" approach for a "secular" business. As a devoted Christian, however, worship music helped to calm her nerves. And she had nerves that needed calming.

Less than a year ago, two of their largest farmers and a grain processor, one after the other, lost their organics certification. Two of them were prosecuted for fraudulence and illegal stock negotiations. It hit national news.

As a result, several customers left Eden's Way, and Jack had to lay off a lot of employees. Chloe ached for the vision her parents had worked so hard to achieve. She wished she could muster up optimism, but the hurdles loomed too high.

Then she saw Helena, a spirited woman with soft white hair. She was a new member of the Eden's Way prayer team, and they had invited her to attend. Chloe thought the scene surreal—not only preparing for the board meeting with worship and prayer, but appointing a prayer team to cover a secular business.

"It's good to see you," Chloe greeted Helena as they hugged.

CHAPTER ONE A STORY OF PRESENCE-BASED DISCERNMENT

"I'm glad to be here!" she answered. "You know how much I loved your parents, and now you all. I'm glad to serve in prayer."

The five of them sat around the long dining table where the whole board would soon meet.

"Thank you for coming early," Neam began. "Helena, we're honored that you joined us."

"Honored to be here!"

Neam smiled at her. "We value your prayer investment and recognize its importance in rebuilding Eden's Way."

Then Neam turned to the others and briefly explained why they were there. As the original visionaries, they needed to cultivate the spiritual environment of the board meeting by preparing with prayer and worship. They would center on Christ's presence and maintain that attitude throughout the rest of the meeting.

Neam's words reminded Chloe of the two board members who quit when they discovered his "religious" approach. That discouraged her at first, but when the dust settled, she realized the two needed to leave. Their time had run itself out.

In the meantime, they gained Ida, the new CFO, who brought a wealth of experience. And they were in the process of interviewing other quality board candidates. Everyone on the board now followed Christ except their attorney, Maya. But she was deeply passionate about their vision and didn't seem to mind the prayer and talk about God.

As Chloe closed her eyes to soak in the worship, Neam opened with prayer. "Jesus, we honor Your presence with us and how You're already working Your purpose for Eden's Way. We submit our decisions into alignment with Your plan."

Then Jack prayed, "Jesus, we have no idea what to do. We're in a mess, and we need Your wisdom. We have some major decisions today. Show us Your way of peace."

Chloe agreed. They didn't know what to do. They desperately needed God's wisdom. They each proceeded to offer prayers or thanksgiving. The half-hour sped by.

Soon enough, Jack was greeting the other board members at the door, Maya, Ida, and Eli. Maya engaged everyone with her usual

PART ONE DISCERNMENT

chatter—something about the new health standards. The others joined with small talk.

Eli greeted Chloe with a nod. As VP of production, Eli felt especially responsible for the problems, but none of the current board members blamed him.

While she waited for everyone to settle, Chloe reviewed the list of discernment questions she and Jack had developed. Her eyes settled on the most pressing: *Should we purchase Jampa?*

Anxiety gripped her again at the thought of Jampa. Some considered the purchase as God's answer to prayer. Others believed it would ruin them.

"Let's get underway," Chloe called the meeting to order, trying to recapture the peace she'd felt in worship only moments ago. "We welcome Helena, who's joining us for the first part of the meeting. She has accepted our invitation to serve on the prayer team."

Each introduced themselves to Helena. "You just go ahead and do your thing," she said. "I'll pray for you as you go along."

After approving the minutes and agenda, Chloe introduced the next item, "Worship Focus." It was an item that Neam suggested they adopt as a permanent part of the agenda. Eli had volunteered to prepare and lead the Worship Focus this month.

He drew their attention to several red-print scripture passages where Jesus punctuated His message with *"He who has ears let him hear."* Eli invited the group to ponder the phrase and share what they sensed God revealing to them through it, especially about what it means to have "ears that hear."

Chloe almost chuckled. *Hearing God speak through scripture at a board meeting?*

"It seems Jesus used the phrase when He had something difficult for them to understand," Jack offered. "It happened when He challenged everything they formerly believed."

"It makes me wonder about my own ability to hear God," Ida's voice broke the lingering quiet. "When something challenges my beliefs, I turn my ears off. I know God wants me to think about business in a different way. I've served on a number of boards, but never in this

CHAPTER ONE A STORY OF PRESENCE-BASED DISCERNMENT

Presence-Based Leadership way. It's hard to get used to thinking about business as a tool for ministry—more than just providing finances, but as a ministry in its own right. I like the change. I think God's exposing some pretty big stoppers in my ears. I want them out so I don't miss anything He wants to do!"

"Same here," Jack said. "God has been melting a wad of wax out of my ears."

Several more commented, and then Maya said, "You know I believe different than all of you, so I see this in a different light."

"Please share," Eli encouraged.

"I respect that you all apply this to hearing God, but I'm thinking about our ability to listen to *each other*. I know I'm guilty too, but this ear-stopping happens too often in our meetings. We could get more done if we focused on hearing each other rather than pushing our own opinions."

"Ouch!" Jack said. "I'm certainly guilty of that."

"We all are," Eli said, "except maybe Ida."

"I have my moments," Ida quipped. "But seriously, I think we should apply this to last month's meeting. Did you tell Neam what happened?"

"Yes," Chloe and Jack nodded.

Bennet's voice surprised her. "I know I need to work on that too—hearing."

"You can say that again," Chloe noticed her own sarcasm. "I'm just ribbing you," she said to cover herself.

"No, you're right. Just ask my wife."

"I'm guilty, too," Chloe admitted. "That seems to be a norm for us, interrupting each other, going in circles not getting anywhere."

"Some of us are worse than others," Maya smiled.

"Now that we admit we're sabotaging progress, what are we going to do about it?" Jack asked.

A few others commented, but they said nothing that qualified as an effective answer. Then Neam challenged them. "Let's stand back and look at what's happening as objectively as possible. What is the Lord doing, right now, in this discussion?"

That took the group off guard.

PART ONE DISCERNMENT

"I know one thing," Eli said. "When I prepared this devotion, I didn't know it would go in this direction. I thought we'd talk about hearing God, but we're talking about hearing each other."

"God's telling us to listen to Him *and* each other," Ida agreed.

"Apply it to what happened last month," Neam challenged. "How is God dealing with that, right here and now?"

"He's helping us get to the heart of the mess," Eli said.

Neam smiled. "Yes. You're reflecting on the choices you made last month, and that's preparing your attitude for this month."

Chloe's irritation toward Bennet had waned somewhat. She still dreaded the impending Jampa discussion, but she was glad this conversation helped set the stage for a different attitude.

For a few more minutes, they discussed how the "ears that hear" scriptures applied to their situation and attitude. Before they moved on to the next agenda item, Eli asked Ida to close in prayer. She thanked Jesus for guiding their conversation and asked Him to continue unstopping their ears.

Chloe transitioned the group to "Equipping," another item Neam had suggested they add to the agenda. For this, she drew their attention to their copies of the new Core Values.

"Could I have one?" Helena asked. "I'll pray over it at home."

"Certainly," Chloe handed her a copy.

"That's a good idea," Ida said. "I'll go ahead and make copies for all the intercessors."

"We've been working hard on these over the past few months," Chloe began. "Let's review them in light of strengths and weaknesses. How are we already applying them well, and where do we need to grow?"

"*Honor God in All We Do*," Ida referred to the Core Value listed first. "I've known only one organization that had a value like that, and it was a church. It's a joy to see it in a business."

Maya pointed out another value, "*Giving Time, Talent and Treasure to Serving Those in Need*. Any business can give money, but allowing employees to take company time to volunteer? That shows where our heart is."

"It fits with our value for *Holistic Nurture*," Jack said. "Not just with organic food, but with whole lives."

CHAPTER ONE A STORY OF PRESENCE-BASED DISCERNMENT

Others made comments until Bennet said, "We do well with *Value and Respect for Customers and Employees*. Even with everything that has happened, and when customers haven't exactly shown respect for us, our people are always respectful."

"I vouch for that," Jack agreed. "After they go through the training, I rarely deal with disrespect."

"We could do better, though," Eli said. "Maybe not as much for customers, but for employees. Sometimes I get so caught up in daily tasks and putting out fires that I neglect my team. I forget to show that I value them. I'm not rude, but it's the listening thing again. Sometimes I just sweep over people."

"We can't babysit them," Bennet said.

"I wasn't talking about babysitting. I just know we could function better if we more intentionally valued staff—actually applied our *Collaboration* value. Maybe we could prevent things like being blind to vendor fraudulence."

"We couldn't have helped that," Bennet countered. "Sometimes things just happen."

Here we go again, Chloe thought.

"Maybe we could have helped it. Maybe Neam's trying to get us to a healthy place where we can prevent things like that. I think there were red flags—some of them big flags."

Bennet leaned back in his chair. "Give me an example of a 'red flag.'"

"Remember the particles of wheat in the gluten-free section?" Maya interjected. "We should have investigated that."

"We had no reason to believe it wasn't a fluke," Bennet said. "They hid it too well. It took an insider to uncover it."

"We also had the missing deliveries," Maya countered. "It all adds up."

"Nothing happened big enough to register major concern."

"I don't mean we could have prevented anything *then,*" Eli said. "But we can learn from that and build a tighter team *now*. We didn't have what it takes—what would you call it? Mutual trust? Collaboration?"

"We had a tight team," Bennet said. "We can't prevent what we have no way of knowing."

Ida jumped in. "Are we *listening* to each other right now?"

PART ONE DISCERNMENT

"I am," Bennet said.

Maya rolled her eyes.

Before anyone else could chime in, Chloe asked Neam, "What do you say? You're the consultant."

Neam nodded and spoke quietly. "It's good to reflect on the past—not to rehash everything, but to discern how we might do better. For now, the agenda item is to assess our strengths and weaknesses in implementing the new Values. Let's go back to Eli's sense of building a culture of value and collaboration."

Ida responded. "I can comment on that. You all know I've taken time recently to visit the offices, just to get to know our people and what they do, and I think there's plenty of room to grow in collaboration and valuing. For that matter, we should ask ourselves, *do* we value them? There seems to be a sort of disconnectedness."

"That's a result of what happened," Bennet interrupted. "We had good communication before that."

"That could be so," Ida said. "I wasn't here then. But right now, we need to empower them to grow, take ownership, and collaborate. Affirming their value would enable that."

Before Bennet could counter, Chloe said, "I think it would be very helpful, Ida, if you, Eli, and I set up a time to talk more about what you gleaned on your visits. The Core Values team is meeting next week. Could we get with you before then so we can find out more about your observations?"

They set a date, and the group continued to discuss Core Values for a short time until Chloe announced time to pray for Helena in her new position on the prayer team. Neam, Ida, and Jack prayed for God's blessing over Helena and sent her out with the sense of a special bond.

Chloe moved the meeting on to Reports.

When Ida shared how their financial debt had decreased for the first time since the fallout, they clapped and cheered. They were also pleased when Jack reported how the interviews with board candidates progressed well. Maya explained how stricter environmental and health standards would cost the company more time and money.

CHAPTER ONE A STORY OF PRESENCE-BASED DISCERNMENT

After a few other reports and comments, Jack took the floor as the agenda moved on to Discernment. *The dreaded discernment*, Chloe sighed. She wondered how Neam would handle the Jampa question.

"I'm not expecting to get through all these issues this afternoon," Jack said. "But we need to decide about the Jampa purchase today, so let's start there."

He summarized the points of discussion from last month. Those who argued for the purchase thought they should take the risk to increase cash flow and bottom line. Those against considered it too expensive, the risk too high, and that Jampa's reputation for underhanded business tactics would negatively impact the brand Eden's Way was trying to rebuild.

After the group tossed around a few thoughts, Bennet said, "We're putting so much energy into working on Core Values, but in real life, it's too soon for all of that. If we don't have money, the company folds, no matter what the values are. That's why this purchase is so vital. It would get us rolling again and secure our bottom line. Then we could move on to the abstract stuff."

Chloe turned to face Bennet squarely. "On the contrary, we need to secure our bottom line *before* we make any purchase."

"Right now, we don't have much of a bottom line to secure," Bennet scoffed.

"We discussed this before. Jampa would divide us. Their vision is nothing like Mom and Dad's—anything but industry standards and holism."

"Is their reputation any worse than ours? Jampa was never accused of scandal on national news."

This statement struck Chloe hard. "We didn't earn the reputation the media gave us."

"So you're saying they're just better at ducking the media?"

"They're *trying* to duck the media—"

"They're just good at covering their tails."

"—we're trying to honor God by working with integrity."

"Chloe, I know it's important to you that we stick to your dad's vision. It's important to me, too. But with no customers, there won't be a vision. No cash flow, no company. Jampa has what we need."

PART ONE DISCERNMENT

"*If* the vendors decide to stay," Chloe countered. "The transition would give them a convenient opportunity to leave. Everything's up in the air, and we don't have the finances or stability to make such a major purchase."

"Most vendors will stay. They're too invested. And you saw my projections. We'd make it up in three years and raise that at least twenty percent every year after. The market's wide open for growth. To get out of the slump, we need to take a risk."

Bennet turned to Jack. "You're the CEO. What do you think?"

Chloe fumed. *Buddying up to Jack again! If Jack takes Bennet's side and ignores me, I'll quit.*

"Some people need to *listen*," Maya muttered.

Jack raised his hand. "Okay, guys. Let's take a breather." He turned to Neam. "You have permission to jump in any time. You're the consultant. Where should we go from here?"

Neam smiled, but then remained quiet for a few moments.

More silence. With this Presence-Based thing, we certainly have a lot of silence. Chloe glanced at Neam. *I wonder if he has ever had clients in such an impossible situation.*

Finally, Neam said, "I appreciate Chloe's heart to honor the founding vision and Bennet's heart to discern a plan for moving forward financially. Remember what we said about the different perspectives of an issue? What's the word we used?"

"*Complementary*," Ida answered without hesitation.

"Go ahead and review that for us," he gestured to give Ida the floor.

"Instead of looking at differing opinions as 'opposites,' we see them as complementary sides of the same issue. It's not one against the other, but how they influence each other and work together—like that box you used to illustrate Presence-Based Leadership."

"I liked that box," Eli said.

"Remind us," Neam said.

"It represented God's wisdom for the situation," Eli began. "Christ-in-the-midst of us. When you put it in the middle of the table, none of us could see the colors on every side—only the one or two facing us. To know what the whole box looked like, everyone needed to share what they saw."

"And we trust Christ to 'build the discernment' in our discussion so we can see the whole picture," Ida added.

"Good. Now how would that apply to this situation?"

"Chloe sees one color and Bennet another," Ida said. "To understand the whole issue, we need to listen for how Christ works the parts together."

"Good," Neam glanced around the table. "Any other insights?" he asked.

"I don't see how that can work," Bennet said. "It's nice to use words like 'complementary' and 'build discernment,' but in real life, Chloe's opinion is directly opposite mine. I want to buy. She doesn't. How can we ever make that complementary?"

"Good question," Neam said. "Does anyone have an answer?"

After some thought, Ida said, "We're not trying to *make* things fit together. It's about Christ showing us the whole picture. Remember, we need to trust that He's speaking in-the-midst of us. As we listen, He'll orchestrate our discussion. I believe He already knows the best answer. We just need to listen for what He's saying."

"And we don't have to think in terms of only two options," Eli intercepted. "What if there's another way to go about this—I don't know, negotiate, or merge with a different company—or something else?"

All eyes followed Neam as he stood and grabbed a folded chair that leaned against the wall. He opened the chair and sat it in the middle of the tabletop.

"I've never seen that done in a board meeting," Ida quipped.

"Here's a visual," Neam explained. "The chair represents the seat of Christ, His presence in our midst. As we go on, this chair can remind us to keep focused on what He's doing and saying—to *hear* Christ's Spirit and how He orchestrates the discussion."

Neam then asked, "Does God really care about what happens to Eden's Way?"

"Yes, of course," Jack said.

"Then we have to trust that He'll show us the way of peace, the way that will bring His wisdom and life to Eden's Way."

Neam sat back down and waited for this object lesson to sink in. "What is Christ impressing you to speak right now?"

"That we give up our preconceived notions," Ida said.

PART ONE DISCERNMENT

"Please elaborate."

"We come to the table with no personal agenda or diehard opinion, but simply with a motive of wanting to hear what Christ is speaking. We have a posture that says, whether we purchase Jampa or not, we're looking for God's wisdom on it."

"But we need to use our heads," Bennet interjected. "We have facts and projections and reports—"

"Yes, and Christ can use them to help show us the answers," Ida said. "But we don't trust in them. We trust Christ to build the discernment in our discussion. He might use reports, experience, or research, but He does the building."

"God gave us brains and wants us to use them," Bennet persisted.

"Maybe that's the problem," Eli said. "We're all using our brains, but we're all thinking in different directions."

"We have a CEO," Bennet gestured toward Jack. "He should just take all the information and make the decision."

There he goes again, Chloe fumed. *Ignoring me just because I disagree with him.*

Jack adjusted his seat, flicked his pen, and laid it back down. "Bennet, Neam isn't telling us to stop using our minds," he said. "But we can use them in a better way if we hear Christ's wisdom. He's the only one who knows the future and all the factors. We have no idea what will work. We need to hear *Him.*"

After a pause, he continued. "I think I can speak for Chloe as well as myself. I don't want to go back to the old way. Chloe and I could make decisions on our own, but we don't know everything. Collaborating and hearing God's answers has opened our eyes to a lot that we missed before. It's so much better now."

"He's right," Chloe said, appreciating Jack for intentionally acknowledging her position. "Everyone's far more involved in sharing now that we're given the opportunity, and we've benefited a lot from that. I *know* we would have gone into bankruptcy if not for working with everyone on this."

CHAPTER ONE A STORY OF PRESENCE-BASED DISCERNMENT

"And remember. We're committed to building collaboration with the employees," Ida added. "If we don't do it here in the board room, how can we expect the staff to do it?"

"Let me make a suggestion for continuing," Neam said. Everyone turned toward him, waiting as he took his time.

"Let's adjust our original question to more accurately reflect our position in a Presence-Based way. Instead of asking, 'Should we purchase Jampa?', we directly ask Christ, 'What is Your wisdom and direction in the Jampa decision?'"

Brilliant, thought Chloe. *Such a simple adjustment, but it changes everything.*

"Before we say anymore," Neam continued, "let's take a few minutes to quiet ourselves and listen for the perspective Christ is showing each of us."

After Neam gave some basic guidelines for focus, they waited quietly for three or four minutes, with some jotting down notes of how they sensed the Lord's direction.

When Neam called them back into discussion, Maya started. "It might help if I shared some new information that concerns this decision." She went on to give evidence, not only about Jampa's sub-standard practices in customer relations, but the immoral behavior of Jampa's owner and CEO.

As the report penetrated their thoughts, Eli said, "Bennet, I appreciate how much work you put into these projections. You spelled out the risk factor, and I agree we need to take risks sometimes, but I think Maya's report bears a lot of weight. I'm trying to say that I don't—what's the new lingo? —I don't have 'peace' about moving forward with this purchase. It doesn't fit who we are."

Bennet's jaw tensed, but he said nothing.

"They've set a precedent of immorality and sub-standard policy that infiltrates that whole company," Eli continued. "As I see it, if we make the purchase, we'll inherit that baggage."

"We may have to deal with the baggage *at first*," Bennet corrected. "But we can change it, teach them to do it our way."

"But we haven't even learned 'our way' ourselves yet!" Maya said.

Everyone batted their opinions about for a time, the tension in the room heating from a simmer to almost a boil, but Chloe didn't hear them.

PART ONE DISCERNMENT

So much for listening to Christ-in-the-midst, she thought, and wondered if Christ really was among them. And Neam's silence irritated her. *Why doesn't he say something? We're getting nowhere, just like last month, and he just sits there.*

Finally, she heard herself interrupt Bennet on a particularly pointed comment. "Neam," she said. "We're still not getting anywhere with this. Please give us a clue how to work this out."

Even though she tried to hide it, she heard the irritation in her tone. But at least her comment put the lid on the pot, cooling the boil back down to a simmer. Everyone stared off in various directions. Ida reached for her water bottle and took a sip.

Then Neam said softly, "Let's look to the center, where Christ is actively engaged in this discussion."

Bennet chuckled under his breath. His arrogance provoked Chloe, but she had to admit, the notion that Jesus was engaged in this argument was somewhat forced.

Neam reminded them that Christ was always speaking His wisdom, and they needed to listen for it. He recognized a point of value in each of their perspectives and said that they should submit those perspectives to Christ. With a gesture, he symbolically placed each perspective in the center of the table where the chair represented Christ's place.

Then he prayed, "Lord, as we submit our perspectives to You, we trust You, that You'll lead us to the purpose You've already established for us. We surrender the government of Eden's Way to Your shoulders. We yield our cares and questions to You because only You are worthy to carry them."

Neam's firm, steady voice gently nudged the group. "What is Christ speaking for Eden's Way? What is His wisdom for the Jampa purchase? Let's listen for what He is saying."

Chloe stared at the chair on the tabletop, trying to push her irritation away so she could listen with her spirit. She didn't expect to hear anything, but before she realized what was happening, she grew conscious of a picture emerging in her mind. *Where did that come from?* She saw a tree dying from rotten roots. *What a perfect illustration. Could it be from God?*

CHAPTER ONE A STORY OF PRESENCE-BASED DISCERNMENT

Before Chloe could talk herself out of it, she shared her vision. "Think of it like a tree," she began, amazed that her tension level remained low. "If the roots are rotten, then the whole tree will rot. From the beginning, Jampa had deeply engrained unhealthy values, and if we purchase them, we'll be getting those rotten roots. It would take a lot of time, money, and energy to remove the rottenness and regrow them—and we haven't even regrown ourselves yet."

They sat silent, again, for an extended time. Then Bennet took a deep breath and sat back in his chair.

"I get the message," he said.

Chloe braced herself. *What "message" did Bennet "get"?*

"Well? Let us hear it," Maya urged.

"I need to start listening more to God."

That stunned Chloe and everyone else. They stared at Bennet until Jack chuckled, "I think his wax is melting."

How did he do it? Chloe wondered about Neam as a penetrating peace settled in the room. *He didn't say that much. Maybe that's the point. Neam didn't do it. Jesus really is here, leading this discussion. We just need to let Him do it.*

"It just so happens," Bennet explained, "that over the weekend, we had a dead tree taken out. The man said it was planted too close to the pond. It didn't like the moisture, so its roots rotted."

Maya laughed out loud. Everyone else smiled.

Chloe sat amazed and humbled as she realized that the picture of the tree really had come from Christ. He really did lead the discussion as they submitted themselves to hear Him.

"We value your input," Chloe said to Bennet. "I haven't forgotten that you're the main reason why the company grew like it did, and we need you now."

Silence ensued, and Chloe welcomed the thick peace that lingered. *Lord, You are good.*

"I don't often say these words," Bennet said. "Just ask my wife! But I'll say them. *Forgive me.* I know I can be arrogant."

Chloe's attitude against Bennet melted into forgiveness as he spoke.

PART ONE DISCERNMENT

"Don't get me wrong," Bennet continued. "Though the rotten tree picture hits home, I'm still not sure that it automatically means letting go of Jampa. But I've got the point—what my wife and God have been trying to tell me for almost thirty-five years: I need a better attitude."

"We forgive you, Bennet," Neam said. "God's doing deep work here. *Father, thank You for Your care, for guiding us…*"

After a full minute of sitting quietly, enjoying the deep peace of God's presence, Neam asked, "What else is Christ saying?"

They pitched several more comments, and Jack admitted, "On a business note, I agree with Bennet that the purchase would open up a lot of potential to rebound. But I also see that it would probably hurt us in the long run, put us back where we don't want to return."

"The point is," Ida said, "we'd be merging with a brand that doesn't honor God. We'd be breaking our new Core Value before we've even got it incorporated."

"I hear what you're saying," Bennet said, "and I'm trying to process it. Putting so much weight on the moral baggage—not ours, but *theirs*—is new to me."

"It's new to all of us," Ida said.

"I *know* Jampa is rotten. But we're not. We don't have to let them pull us down. We can lift them up. I could understand letting this opportunity go if we had an alternate plan, but we don't."

"Not a short-range plan," Maya said, "but long-range. Last month I also thought we should take the risk, but now we're stabilizing with no reason to believe it won't continue. Rushing things would be a mistake. And I'm passionate about our value of holistic growth. We need to rebuild in a holistic way."

"Can't we work out how to do both?" Bennet asked.

"Both what?"

"Both buy Jampa *and* incorporate our values?"

No one spoke until Neam asked, "When do you need to finalize the decision?"

"Friday of next week," Bennet answered.

"May I suggest a plan for moving forward?"

"Suggest away," Jack said.

CHAPTER ONE A STORY OF PRESENCE-BASED DISCERNMENT

"Next Friday gives us nine days. We can take the rest of this week to pray about it, consider any other pathways the Lord may be showing us, or if there's peace in making the purchase or not. Ida can give the appropriate details to the prayer team so they can cover it in prayer and give us any insights they receive. Then, if possible, can we reconvene on Tuesday to share and discern the Lord's wisdom?"

"Sounds like a plan," Jack said.

"What if we still can't agree?" Bennet asked.

"I trust the Lord to show us His way of peace as we keep an attitude of submitting to Him. Of course Chloe and Jack need to make a final decision before the deadline. But often the Lord surprises us with His wisdom. For now, let's focus on listening."

Jack and Chloe moved through the rest of the agenda items that had an immediate need and made plans to address the remaining items later. All but the last item: Reflections. When Neam first suggested they include Reflections as a regular conclusion to their meetings, Chloe thought it frivolous. But since then, she has realized how much it reinforces team coherence and collaboration.

"I'm understanding it more," Bennet said. "I still don't completely get this *Presence-Based* thing—but thanks for your patience."

"Before today," Chloe said, "I honestly thought we'd never pull out of this mess. I don't know how you do it, Neam, but I have hope now. God's not going to let us go."

"More and more, I realize this is the only way we can survive," Ida added. "Not just survive, but *thrive*. I always knew Christians should serve God at work, but it's more than that. We're 'doing church' right now just as much as we do on Sunday mornings."

....

We'll unpack the principles illustrated in the story throughout the rest of the book. Read on for more true stories, guides, charts, teachings, and challenges.

PART ONE DISCERNMENT

CHALLENGE

At the end of each chapter, we list questions and activities to challenge and assist you in applying PBL principles. You may complete the exercises individually, but we suggest you share the process with a partner or group. Each person brings another perspective of God's truth and builds the texture of truth we glean. You may also wish to journal your responses and what you sense God teaching you during this process.

ACTIVITY

Before reading further, write out a list of qualities you believe would characterize someone as an effective leader. In the Challenge sections throughout the book, we'll occasionally refer back to your list to consider how your understanding of leadership may develop.

— CHAPTER TWO —

The Act, Attitude, and Art

PRESENCE-BASED LEADERSHIP

How is Presence-Based Leadership different than any other team leadership? Any group may use good techniques to make decisions, and any of these methods may also play a part in Presence-Based discernment. But, as illustrated in the story, PBL has one major difference.

Instead of depending only on human wisdom, we acknowledge that Christ alone has the perfect wisdom for any situation. Beyond that, He has given us the honor of His presence among us so we can hear His wisdom.

Instead of taking the weight of making decisions on ourselves, we partner with Christ as our Head. We discern and align with His plan.

As God uses the minds, abilities, and experience that He gives us, we collaborate with one goal: hearing Christ and allowing Him to build discernment. For the rest of the book, we unpack what this means and how to develop PBL in our own lives and leadership.

When my colleagues and I introduce PBL to a group of leaders, we often give participants a bookmark, similar to the image on page 34, that displays the whole definition:

> *Guiding others by practicing sensitivity and submission*
> *to the presence and direction of Jesus;*
> *Abiding moment-by-moment*
> *in the strength, peace, wisdom, life,*
> *and love of His person;*

PART ONE DISCERNMENT

> *Surrendering all discernment, conversations,*
> *attitudes, opinions, plans, actions,*
> *reputation and authority*
> *to Christ's authority and purpose.*

Every word calls for engagement, not only in leadership discernment, but in all areas of life. In PBL workshops, we try to make this definition easier to process by reading it aloud together while keeping our hearts open to sense the Spirit's guidance.[1]

You may take time to do the same right now, noting the word or phrase that stands out most in your mind. *What significance may it have in your life? What is God showing you through it?* This activity often stirs a deeper realization: *this is what it means to partner with Christ in real life and leadership.*

---

[1] *Use the passcode "PBL" to access a color, printable version of this image on our website. Find access information on page 8.*

PRESENCE-BASED LEADERSHIP

Guiding others by practicing sensitivity and submission to the presence and direction of Jesus; abiding moment-by-moment in the strength, peace, wisdom, life, and love of His person; surrendering all discernment, conversations, attitudes, opinions, plans, actions, reputation, and authority to Christ's authority and purpose.

©2016 TEACHING THE WORD MINISTRIES

CHAPTER TWO THE ACT, ATTITUDE, AND ART

The chart below shows the overall structure of the model with a brief definition:

*Guiding others
with a posture of submission
to wisdom discerned
from Christ's presence.*

Presence-Based Leadership
Guiding others with a posture of submission to wisdom discerned from Christ's presence

The Art

PRESENCE
Leading from a posture of rest in and from the circle of Trinity fellowship

The Attitude

TOWARDNESS
Cultivating a culture of prayer and honor

The Act

CHRIST-IN-THE-MIDST DISCERNMENT
Stewarding the metron of sonship within the ecclesia

©2016 TEACHING THE WORD MINISTRIES

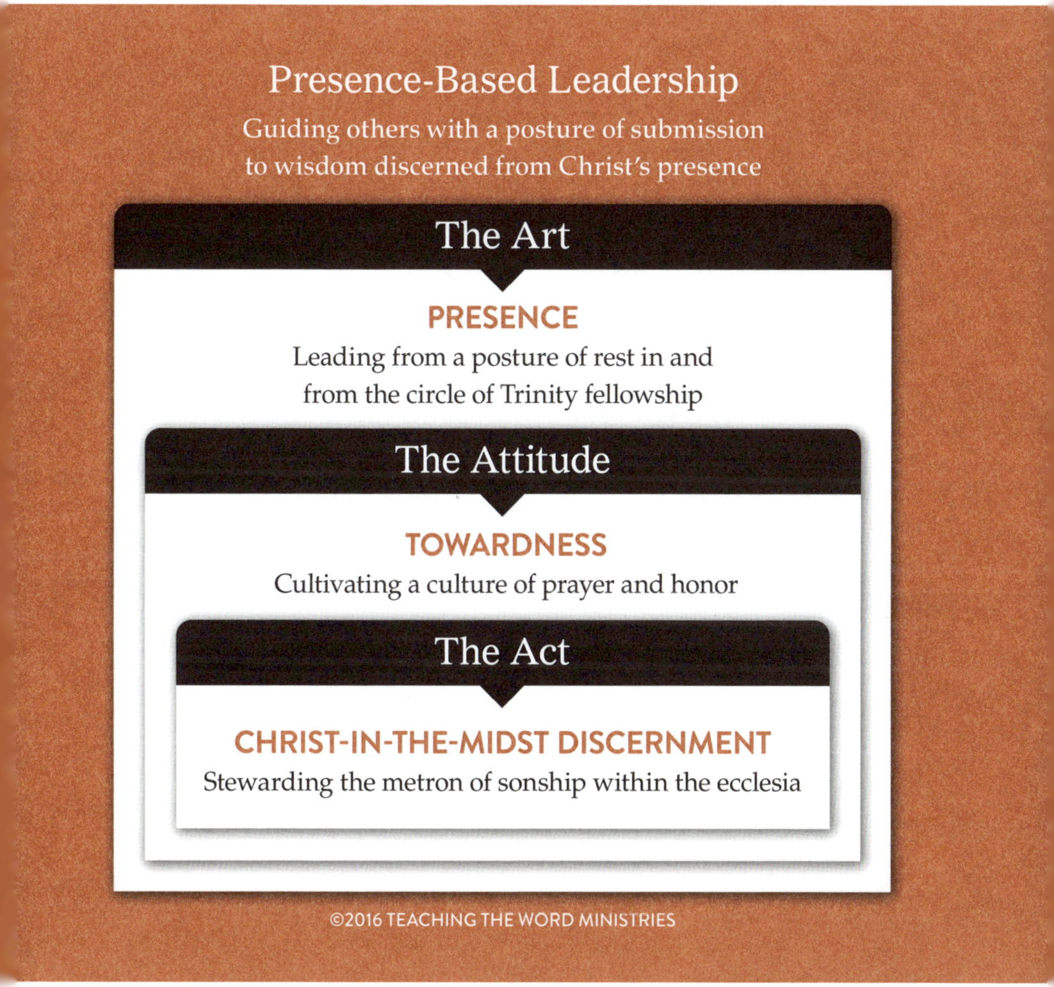

PART ONE DISCERNMENT

Starting with the smallest, inner box, we define the **Act** of PBL: Christ-in-the-midst discernment. To make decisions, we steward, or manage, the sphere of authority Christ entrusted to us. We do this not with our wisdom, but by discerning Christ's wisdom.

Learning the practicalities of the Act is probably the real purpose for reading a book like this. *Why don't we skip Attitude and Art and get down to this immediate need—how to practically make leadership decisions that work?*

Hearing God's direction, however, is not a "five-step" remedy to plug in and expect immediate results. We cultivate the Act only as we also nurture the Attitude and Art.

As you witnessed in the Board Story in Chapter One, the Act of PBL works best when exercised with the **Attitude** of PBL, represented by the middle box in the chart. We call this attitude *"Towardness,"* and explore it more fully in Part Two. For now, understand that towardness means the passionate, mutual honor among the members of the Trinity. We reflect that Trinity attitude to the best interest of others.

The Act and Attitude of PBL, then, thrive when practiced in the framework of the **Art**, which we call *"Presence."* It's a process of allowing Christ's presence to become our presence. We lead as one with Christ as He is one with the Father[2]—Presence-to-presence, Life-to-life.

If you have followed Christ for more than a few years, you already know that what may seem easy to write on paper or with pixels has complex twists and difficult turns in real life. That's where PBL becomes an art. It's not easy, but it is good—and effective, fulfilling, productive, increasing life and peace.

HOW DOES THIS WORK IN REAL LIFE?

We'll examine the Act, Attitude, and Art in Parts One to Three. In Part Four, we'll build the practical framework for implementing PBL in your leadership teams. For now, we look again at the definition of Presence-Based Leadership:

---

2 John 17:21-24

CHAPTER TWO THE ACT, ATTITUDE, AND ART

*Guiding others with a posture of submission
to wisdom discerned from Christ's presence.*

We can learn brilliant leadership techniques and apply sage advice from excellent leaders. But leadership involves people. Every person is different. Every situation is different. Rarely can we use any piece of advice, no matter how proven, across the board. What works one time may not work another time. Leadership, in general, is an art: sensing where-to-do-what and when-to-speak-or-not, or when to wait and when to move.

In Presence-Based Leadership, we understand that as we rest in Christ, we have His mind[3]—His leadership genius. We depend on His wisdom to discern what to do each moment. We cultivate the Art of PBL through practice: sensing the Spirit's leading, hearing the beat of our Shepherd's heart, or stepping in time with the Father's will. We lead from a posture of rest and wisdom within the circle of Trinity fellowship. Eugene Peterson put it this way:

> *So come on, let's leave the preschool finger-painting exercises on Christ and get on with the grand work of art. Grow up in Christ.*[4]

To "grow up" means we own our calling to leadership as part of the eternal government of Christ.[5]

CARL AND AMBER–A PASTOR'S STORY

"If you don't slow down your schedule, you're going to kill us!" Amber confronted her husband.[6] "We'll end up like those pastors' families you read about who fell apart or had moral issues. You can't keep dragging us like this."

---

3 1 Corinthians 2:16
4 Hebrews 6:1a, The Message
5 Isaiah 9:6-7; Luke 17:21; 1 Peter 2:4-5
6 Amber and Carl are pseudonyms for a pastoring couple, and this is their true story.

PART ONE DISCERNMENT

Amber paused to measure Carl's reaction. He appeared closed to any suggestions, but she decided to press her request anyway.

"Could you take a sabbatical? At least three months?"

Carl looked at her in shock. "I might be able to slow down some," he answered. "But I can't just stop. I'm doing what God called me to do. We have plans. We have a vision. We can't just go on vacation for three months."

"Will you at least *consider* a sabbatical?" Amber asked.

"No."

"Then could you at least pray about it?"

"No." Carl didn't understand why he should pray about something when he already knew the answer.

> "If it's God's best for you, then it's also God's best for the church."

"Well, I'm going to talk to Keith about it," Amber resolved.

Carl wasn't worried. He was confident that I would agree with him.

At our next mentoring meeting, Carl and Amber sat across from me. I had worked with them for several years through some difficult situations. I was already waiting for Carl to realize he couldn't keep up his current pace. He needed to take an extended period to wait in the Lord's presence and seek His heart and will. When Amber suggested he take a sabbatical, I agreed with a resounding "Yes!"

"But how can the church survive?" Carl asked.

"If it's God's best for you, then it's also God's best for the church," I responded.

In my experience, when leaders take a well-planned and focused sabbatical, not only do they mature, but the people they influence also mature in numerous ways.[7]

With prayerful consideration, the elders of Carl's church also said "yes" to the sabbatical.

"*We* need a sabbatical from *you*," they told Carl.

---

7 For more specific details on discerning a successful strategy for a sabbatical, see Keith's booklet, Navigating Your Sabbatical: Purpose, Plan and Support *from our website:* ttwm.org.

"I had built a leader-centric church," Carl admitted, "with everything centered around me, my vision, and my preaching. They needed the chance to catch their breath and regroup."

For several months, I worked with Carl and church leadership to prepare them and the congregation for the six-month sabbatical. Carl had his assignment to rest and reflect, and the ministry leaders stepped up to their new responsibilities with God's grace and love. I mentored them through the sabbatical and helped to facilitate Carl's transition back into ministry. God brought renewal and deep growth for all involved.

"Our picture of church was consumeristic, please-me, and program-oriented," Amber said. "We weren't real. We weren't relevant. The only thing that makes church relevant is Jesus. People need to have relationship with Christ and each other."

"During the sabbatical, I changed—or I should say, God changed me."

In the first part of the sabbatical, Carl and Amber took a family vacation where they visited an ornate cathedral with intricate architectural design.

"They built that place to house the presence of God," Carl said. "We loved it. The kids loved it."

Later on, they went to another church, also known for its architecture. But this one seemed more like a museum than a church. They didn't sense much of the Lord's presence in its dark, musty interior, crowded with tourists and attractions. Carl's six-year-old son started crying and said he wanted to go back to the first church.

That's when Carl sensed God showing him that the church he pastored was more like the second cathedral. It was a museum for spectators to observe God, rather than a house for the Spirit's relational presence. Carl realized that he had built the congregation on programs that gratified people to keep them coming, rather than challenging them to mature in their relationship with Father God.

"After that realization, I went into depression for a while," Carl admitted. "But God encouraged me. I heard Him say, 'You're My son. I love you. This is going to be fine. Just lean toward Me.'"

The Lord set Carl in a new direction of helping people fellowship in Trinity Presence. Helping them accept their responsibility and honored place as sons and daughters in God's household.

PART ONE DISCERNMENT

"Now when I preach, I realize that the Holy Spirit knows what these people need, not me. Who am I to assume the topic of the sermon I preach is what everyone needs? It's my job to esteem Christ, to lift up God and His word with as much wonder and awe as possible. As people see Jesus and the power of God, Christ will draw them in.[8] Then I leave them in the hands of the Holy Spirit. He speaks to them and takes care of them Himself. The people see Christ, not me."

Christ led them to develop a teaching team. Rather than Carl preaching for all the services, a group of gifted teachers rotated Sunday services. They opened the congregation to different perspectives and understandings of Christ and scripture.

"The change was wonderful," Amber said, "but it also brought some grieving. It was hard for a lot of people. They were attached to Carl. They wanted things to stay the same."

"It's like when Amber took over the staff meetings," Carl explained. "She led in the Presence-Based Leadership way. We covered a lot less, but we made a lot more impact. What we did get done had an infusion of power."

"We moved to the heart of things, to Christ, to relationship," Amber explained. "'Life-to-life' we like to say. We took time to reflect and time for listening prayer. We centered on Christ and His presence. We found a different pace. People didn't push back as much because we connected to the heart. It took time to move into this. For the longest time, we kept having to remind everyone to focus on God's heart."

As Carl continues living his story of partnership with Christ, God has more recently called him to fully release the leadership of his congregation into the capable hands of other leaders. Through much prayer, we've discerned God drawing him into regional leadership.

If not for Carl's transformation, he might have missed this transition, or found it harder to accept. The Lord helped him find his significance in Christ, rather than in his role as a pastor.

---

8 *John 12:32*

CHALLENGE

1. List ways that Carl and Amber's story is similar to your own. *In what ways might their story challenge you?*
2. Re-read the full definition of Presence-Based Leadership. *Which words or phrases linger in your mind after you're finished? How do those words relate to your leadership? What might the Lord be showing you through them?*

LOOKING AHEAD

In Chapter Three, we begin with the *Act of Presence-Based Leadership*, the inner box on our chart. We explore how the reality of leadership boils down to making quality decisions.

To help illustrate PBL principles, I tell stories of many leaders, three in particular:

- Jared (pseudonym), a business leader
- Pastor Erick (pseudonym), a congregational leader
- Lisa Hosler (her real name), president of Align Life Ministries, formerly Susquehanna Valley Pregnancy Services in Lebanon and Lancaster Counties, Pennsylvania. She is currently publishing her own book on Presence-Based Leadership. It will equip leaders and their teams to be aligned with God, in agreement with one another, and advancing with God through prayer. We highly recommend Lisa's book.

Unless otherwise noted, we use pseudonyms and camouflage any details that may divulge identities, but all of the testimonies are true. The leaders convey how they embraced PBL and its impact on their ministries and workplaces. Through their examples, the Lord invites us to open our minds to the transforming truth of His wisdom, which lives in His presence.

— CHAPTER THREE —

Leadership and Discernment

IS THERE ANOTHER WAY?

"Are you in meetings where the discussion goes around and around, and you don't get anywhere?" I asked a group of elders at a large urban church.

"Yes!" Pastor Erick answered. "Almost every meeting."

This admission was significant coming from Erick, considering his background. If anyone wants to know anything about running an organization, ask Erick. As a former top leader of a renowned company, he traveled the world training teams in strategy, marketing, and product development. He knew how to make effective decisions and bring projects to completion.

After God called Erick into a full-time pastoral position, he applied the same business strategies to his church ministry. But instead of growth and advancement, most decisions resulted in division, confusion, and disappointment. In addition, several difficult changes in senior leadership brought increased frustration and a significant loss of church membership.

As students of the word of God, Erick and the other leaders prayed before their leadership meetings and dedicated their work to the Lord. Though they remained focused on the agenda, their evening discussions continued until eleven, twelve, or one o'clock in the morning, and often accomplished little.

Until Erick understood PBL, he had concluded that confusion, strife, and stagnancy were the inherent "baggage" of congregational leadership, something leaders simply had to accept as normal.

It's not that Erick dismissed the wisdom of methods he already knew or ignored his training and experience. He took every opportunity to build his skills. Erick applied the principles well, but with little progress.

We can pinpoint several highly successful leaders worldwide who have a knack of making brilliant leadership decisions. They model godly principles and attitudes of successful leaders for the rest of us. They've greatly enhanced our understanding of effective leadership, and we praise God they fulfill their purpose by serving us in this way. Our model of Presence-Based Leadership embraces this knowledge.

But for Erick, in an unstable world of continuous change and imperfect people, situations arose where none of his methods fully applied. They may have worked one day and not the next, or with one person and not the other. Even when one thing functioned smoothly at a good pace, something else blindsided him and forced him back to the original problem. Too often, leadership decisions caused congregational discord. Erick thought this hit-and-miss contention-juggling was a given.

Other leadership teams struggle in situations where the decision-making power rests on one or a few people. These people may or may not hold the position of chair, president, or CEO. They may not even have a position on the leadership team. But they maintain sway over the group's decisions.

Whether in a leadership position or not, what they say goes. It doesn't matter what anyone else says. These people get their way. We call them "perceived leaders." Such leadership stifles growth and breeds disillusionment and suspicion.

Many leaders wonder, *is there another way? Can we ever move past the perpetual task of "putting out fires"? Or stop the downward cycle of ingrown control issues? Or move from survival mode into an environment that thrives?*

THE ACT OF PRESENCE-BASED LEADERSHIP

We have many definitions of leadership. Often people define leadership simply as "influence," and it is. Let's move one step further to suggest that leadership is *influencing people to move from one point to another*. The next "point" may be financial growth, productivity, better service, security, fulfilled purpose, completed tasks, or deeper relationship. Whatever the course, good leaders empower people toward the fullest potential of a God-ordained "next point."

How do leaders influence people to move from one point to another? The bottom line: They make effective decisions—many, many decisions, large and small, throughout every day. Every decision affects the progress of their influence. Decision making not only impacts our leadership, but it's central to who we are.

Some decisions require an intense period of inquiry and team discernment. They involve risk that impacts a large number of people. Others are commonplace decisions, made in a moment. They will impact only one person or a small part of the overall progress: *Should I return the call now or an hour from now? What words should I use to make the email clear and respectful? What color markers will work best for the whiteboard diagram?*

Small decisions affect big decisions. They ultimately combine to determine our character, good or bad, which underlies the overall morale and focus of the team and community. A series of wise leadership decisions increases productivity, collaboration, and fulfillment. A series of poor decisions leads to low morale, dead ends, false starts, confusion, and discord.

So to build on our definition of effective leadership, we add one more phrase: Leadership is influencing people to move from one point to another *by making effective decisions.*

But is it enough just to make effective decisions?

A few of the decision-making methods leaders use include:

- Drawing from education or experience
- Researching known options
- Learning what others have done successfully
- Asking for advice from experts
- Brainstorming with a team
- Doing it the way we've always done it
- Relying on instinct

CHAPTER THREE LEADERSHIP AND DISCERNMENT

Any of these methods can bring what we consider success—or not. In reality, we have no idea if our decisions will succeed or fail, or how they will impact others. We don't know the full scope of factors, what roadblocks loom, or what the government might do to affect us. We don't even know what true success may look like. A decision may show positive or desired results but hold hidden pitfalls, energy leaks, a shift in the wrong direction, or disunity in another part of the system.

We could say, "We'll make the best decision we can at the moment, and then deal with any problems that might arise." But that brings us back to leading from a defensive posture, allowing circumstances to drive our strategy.

What we need is someone who knows the full scope of factors, the future, the hearts and minds of all people involved. Someone who has the government "on His shoulder."[1]

As leaders who aspire to follow Christ, we have access to the One who not only knows the future but has already orchestrated the future. Because the future belongs to Him and His government, He carefully selected a place for each of us in it. As well as a place for our businesses and organizations.

Wouldn't it be great if God would just tell us what decisions to make in every situation? Can we somehow tap into God's presence, His purpose and plan, and then partner with Him in what He's already doing? Is that possible? Is that scriptural?

That's what moves ordinary leadership to the level of Presence-Based Leadership. Mastering PBL involves accepting the responsibility to lead the way God originally designed us to lead. By moving far beyond just making decisions to *discerning wisdom* in the presence of the Trinity as partners with Christ.

In her book, *Pursuing God's Will Together*, Ruth Haley Barton writes:

> *Discernment begins when we acknowledge the fact that we lack the wisdom we need and that without divine intervention, the best we can do is stumble around in the dark. Discernment begins when we are in*

---

[1] Isaiah 9:6-7; Matthew 18:20

PART ONE DISCERNMENT

> *touch with our blindness and are willing to cry out from that place, "My teacher, I want to see."*[2]

God created us with the intention that we rule on earth and into eternity with Him in community and partnership.[3] Christ reestablished this core purpose for humankind in the institution of His *church*.

The Greek word *ecclesia* [ek-lay-SEE-ah], or "church," embodies the act of making decisions by discerning God's wisdom from heaven and establishing it on earth. We'll return to this concept of "church" as a decision-making body in the next chapter. For now, keep in mind that PBL concerns making decisions by discerning Christ's direction and purpose.

THE ART OF PRESENCE-BASED LEADERSHIP

"Do I seem *weary*?" Lisa Hosler asked her coworker.

We had prayed with Lisa during a seminar she attended with staff members from her Pregnancy Resource Center (PRC). As we prayed, the Lord helped us sense the weariness within Lisa. We affirmed her for her excellence and professionalism. But we also sensed God guiding her to lead from a posture of rest rather than busyness.

One of the prayer ministers sensed the weariness not only in Lisa but in her staff and board as well. It was God's desire for them to learn a different way of leadership—a way of inspiration and peace.

As a high-achieving, purpose-driven Christian, the idea of weariness offended Lisa at first. For thirteen years as director and team-style leader, she saw the ministry grow from one center to three, from one paid staff member to fifteen, and from thirty volunteers to one-hundred-fifty.

Lisa knew the Apostle Paul's exhortation: "…let us not grow weary while doing good, for in due season we shall reap if we do not lose heart."[4] She considered her work very "good," and it extended God's love to

---

2 Barton, Ruth Haley, Pursuing God's Will Together: A Discernment Practice for Leadership Groups. IVP Books, Kindle version, page 30. Copyright 2012, Ruth Haley Barton.
3 2 Timothy 2:12; Revelation 5:10
4 Galatians 6:9

CHAPTER THREE LEADERSHIP AND DISCERNMENT

numerous people in meaningful ways. *How could this all lead to weariness? Wasn't dependence on God enough to keep me going?*

But Lisa recognized the treadmill syndrome of running non-stop. She knew that taking a break from this pace would throw her further behind in her work. She yearned for the day when she could slow down, but it never came. Instead, her busyness accelerated, and the relentless schedule concerned her.

It wasn't that Lisa's organization didn't thrive, or that she failed as a leader, or that she made poor decisions. But there was a better way, a place beyond weariness, a supernatural strength that could overflow to empower others.

Without realizing it, Lisa longed for a place of peace and service beyond her own. With greater wisdom. With deeper community and support among staff. With more meaningful, effective growth and outreach. She needed to learn how to lead like Jesus—by resting fully in the moment-to-moment wisdom of His Father.

Many Christians are familiar with the acronym: WWJD (What Would Jesus Do?). That seems like a good, godly approach for making decisions, and it is. For those of you who may still wear WWJD bracelets, go for it! Let's look more closely at what the question implies.

Determining what Jesus would do if He were here in my shoes keeps the question on an intellectual level. Instead of going directly to Jesus and asking for His wisdom, we try to figure out what He would do. It's good, as it challenges us to search God's word for His principles, but we miss the here-and-now communion with God.

At first, Lisa made her decisions by going a step further. Rather than mentally trying to figure out what Jesus would do, Lisa used this approach: WDJWMTD (What Does Jesus Want Me to Do?).

For most of the major decisions she made, Lisa retreated somewhere by herself and prayed, "Lord, show *me* what to do." When she felt she had the answer, she shared it with her team, and together they implemented the strategy.

PART ONE DISCERNMENT

This method brought a level of success to her ministry, but something was missing. While her decisions resulted in growth and productivity, where was the flourishing peace that marks the true wisdom of God?[5]

What Lisa learned, as her story will illustrate throughout the rest of this book, is Presence-Based discernment. She and her team assemble and ask: *Lord, what are You doing in this situation, and how do You want us to partner with You in it?*

This approach takes them from the stance of "doing my job with God's help" to "serving in community as full partners with Christ in His government."

Think about that a moment. *Serving in community as full partners with Christ in His government.* As a phrase of fewer than 140 characters, we could post it on Twitter. Or engrave it on a plaque as an encouraging reminder of who we are in Christ when times get tough. But like the tip of an iceberg, the essence of this truth runs far deeper than a simple leadership quote.

Serving as a partner of Christ involves eternal purpose, the risk of transparency in relationship, the responsibility of sonship, the discipline of hearing and submitting to the Shepherd's voice, the risk of approaching an all-consuming God. "For who would dare risk his life to approach Me?" God asks.[6]

He might change things! Worse, He might change me! On the other hand, surrendering leadership to Christ ultimately means solid wisdom, deep-seated fulfillment, life-giving collaboration, wholeness, and eternal fruit.

This is what makes Presence-Based Leadership an *art*.

Consider the artwork of a master sculptor. What is it about the statue that overwhelms us with inspirational beauty that reaches beyond our senses? Where does the mystery of *meaning* come from? How does it speak a message to our souls without words?

Excellent technique is necessary, but many have learned the technique of sculpting without *mastering the art* of it. Using line, balance, tone,

---

5 James 3:17-18
6 Jeremiah 30:21, NASB

texture, shadow, and light in a synergistic way to create a "message"—a *presence*—of unity, beauty, and purpose.

Similarly, many have learned the techniques of leadership, but yearn to move to the next level of mastering the *art* of it. The *presence* of it. The synergy, the unspoken message of humble but solid spiritual authority. The vibrant, interdependent community of mutual honor and excellence.

Some philosophers have asked, "Can *art* be taught?" We can teach methods, but what about the *art* of it? If we analyze an art form, break it down into categories, and organize it into steps and techniques, chapters and paragraphs, will it still be an "art" when we're done, or only an impersonal system of patterns?

Throughout these decades, we've worked with Christ-following leaders, not only in our ministry circles, but in groups throughout the world. We've seen PBL reproduced, Presence-to-presence and Life-to-life—the process of mentoring, transparent relationship, one-to-one modeling among leaders and leadership teams.

We've found that seminars or "book-learning" situations, while they have their necessary place, don't alone produce the lasting, deeply-rooted value that one-on-one mentoring and real-life experience has. The art of PBL is "presence"—the essence of "relationship."

We've often asked ourselves the question, "Why are we writing a book? Can PBL be taught and reproduced through written words?" If "presence" is the essence of "Presence-Based Leadership," can we teach it without actually being present?

The main Hebrew term translated as "presence" in the Old Testament is the word for "face." "In the presence of the LORD," could literally be translated "In the *face* of the LORD."

New Testament Greek terms for "presence" also mean "face" or "in the eye of." These words suggest a sense of physical closeness and interaction. There's nothing "virtual" about biblical presence. To be present, we have to actually be there, not only with God but with each other.

So why write a book about a leadership model that can only be imparted through real-life, face-to-face interaction if a book can't substitute for that?

PART ONE DISCERNMENT

We recognize our dependence on Christ and our need to trust the Spirit for His Face-to-face closeness to our readers. So the purpose of this book is to:

- Challenge Christ-following leaders to intentionally deepen and increase their engagement as partners of Christ in His eternal government.
- Assist in forming alliances with others God is calling to master the Art of Presence-Based Leadership.
- Enhance the learning content and experience of leaders in current mentoring and leadership relationships.

Consider that fully embracing PBL by its own nature requires a community of hearts present with each other and in communion with the circle of Trinity fellowship. We invite you to surround yourself with a community while learning the Art. Whether with people in or outside your leadership sphere, we challenge you to discuss and process the principles presented in this book with others.

PASTORING THE MARKETPLACE

"There has to be a difference," Jared said just after becoming president of his company. "There has to be a difference in the way a Christian leads a business and the way someone runs a comparable business without Christ."

When Jared first contacted us, he was the new president and co-owner of a profitable business. As a man already committed to the Lord, he desired his company to honor Christ. His parents instilled in him the value of hard work and sacrifice.

But Jared also understood and sometimes fell prey to the danger of workaholism. He knew striving for success could become an idol in disguise rather than a means of serving the Lord.

Jared wanted to establish his business as a mission, not only as a means to provide funds for kingdom work, but as a way to help "pastor the marketplace." As Jared grew into a lifestyle of knowing and following Christ, he saw evidence of Christ's government extending into the lives of others that he contacted directly or indirectly through his business.

Through learning and living Presence-Based Leadership, Jared not only saw his company grow (even through hard economic times when finances appeared bleak), he watched God touch numerous people with transformation and miracles.

God has miraculously opened doors for Jared to meet politicians and leaders of broad influence, where he represented Christ and helped to establish the wisdom of Christ in the world of business. God moved in miraculous ways, even when Jared was oblivious to it, and sometimes even despite him!

Jared has also helped to build a community of business leaders whose hearts and companies are devoted to honoring Jesus—even fellowshipping with and supporting *competitors* in prayer!

"God's economy is different than the world's," Jared explained. "In the world, there's only one pie and only so much to go around. Everyone competes for the biggest piece of the pie. But in God's economy, His resources have no boundaries."

Not that Jared doesn't work for excellence and increased profits, but he trusts that God has plenty for all. "I watch my competition," Jared admits, "but I don't have to make enemies of them. We may compete with each other, but we're connected in God's Spirit and can also support each other in prayer."

According to Genesis 1, God created humankind with an assignment: to fill the earth, subdue it, and rule.[7] What does that mean, *to fill, subdue, and rule*? God commissioned us with authority to build community. To work, discover, organize, and produce. To bring into order the disorder of the world as its rulers and as partners with the Creator.

Take careful note that "rule" does *not* mean "dominate." God's rule doesn't oppress but empowers and releases others to also rule according to their purposes.

---

7 *Genesis 1:28*

PART ONE DISCERNMENT

> **To rule means to carry the government of the Trinity into an area that falls short of His design.**

To rule means to carry the government of the Trinity into an area that falls short of His design. God designed us to establish His government of peace in the specific business, ministry, or organization where He has placed us—into every environment, relationship, and conversation we encounter. This is not just a fairy tale or a theology meant for only a few exceptionally spiritual people. Jesus intends all of His followers to be His body of ambassadors in everyday life.[8]

CHALLENGE

1. List techniques you have used to make leadership decisions. Recall several decisions you've made and evaluate the long-term effectiveness of each.
   a. *How did it facilitate progress in your organization?*
   b. *In what ways did it affect the morale and engagement of your community?*
   c. *What challenges unfolded in implementing the decision?*
   d. *Looking back, how could you have made the decision more effective?*
2. List qualities or understandings you have in common with Pastor Erick, Lisa, or Jared. List any differences. *In what ways do you relate to their stories? How do their stories challenge you?*
3. Take a moment to focus on Christ and His presence in and around you. Ask Him to give you an impression, understanding, or picture of His perspective of your leadership. *In what ways have you extended Christ's government and attitude into your sphere of influence? How is the Lord investing in you to empower you to grow in your leadership?*

---

8   Matthew 5:13-16; Matthew chapters 5-7; Ephesians 5:8-10, 15-17; 2 Corinthians 5:20

CHAPTER THREE LEADERSHIP AND DISCERNMENT

LOOKING AHEAD

If you're looking for a leadership method that will bring ready-made solutions with easy, prescribed steps that work for everyone in every situation, then this book is not for you.

But if you're seeking to lead in a way that…

- Empowers you to establish God's governmental rule of love and truth in your occupation and ministry,
- Influences others in your leadership sphere with humble confidence, authority, wisdom, and growth,
- Influences other leaders to grow in God's presence,
- Partners with God toward long-lasting productivity in harmony with others,

…then keep reading!

Check your preconceived ideas of leadership. PBL requires the soul-searching dismantling of old mindsets to allow the knowledge, talents, and technique that you already have to transform into the art of discerning Christ's wisdom.

To understand how to walk in Presence-Based Leadership, you must grasp some key Biblical principles about how Christ established leadership for His followers. In the next chapter, we explore Jesus' radical, governmental act to give decision-making authority to every believer.

Get ready! His truth stretches our thinking, challenges us with new perspectives, and will always initiate transformation.

— CHAPTER FOUR —

Jesus' Radical Idea of Discernment as "Church"

ECCLESIA

Here's a quick quiz:

Which of these groups of Christ-followers do you consider to have "church" *as Jesus meant it* when He said, "On this rock I will build my church"?[1]

1. Six members of a business team discussing how much product to order
2. Three food pantry workers discerning how to expand their service through local churches
3. A congregation of people gathering to worship God and hear His word
4. A husband and wife discussing what to give their child for Christmas
5. A church benevolence committee deciding how to engage with a single mother who asked for help with her heating bill

Answer: All of the above, *except* number 3. Surprising?

---

1 Matthew 16:18

CHAPTER FOUR JESUS' RADICAL IDEA OF DISCERNMENT AS "CHURCH"

Many Christ-followers understand "church" as what we do on Sunday mornings (or Friday or Saturday) throughout the world. Not necessarily the building, but the people who gather in it. It's certainly vital that we meet regularly for corporate worship and to hear God's word through an anointed teacher. It's fine that we call this "church."

But as Matthew records Jesus' original use of the term *church*, or *ecclesia* in the Greek language, Christ had something else in mind.

In Greek society, *ecclesia* referred to governmental leaders, literally "called-out ones," who assembled to make civil decisions. The group included *all* leaders, not only synagogue or religious leaders. So what did Jesus mean when He used a civic term to say, "On this rock I will build My **ecclesia** [a body of decision-making leaders]"?

Consider this story from our business leader, Jared.

"You have no idea how exciting it is to walk with you in this," Jared's employee, Steve, said to him concerning the practice of PBL in his business.

Jared smiled as the conversation continued. Steve was not only a leader in Jared's business, but a leader in his local congregation. Instead of Steve taking his "church" training and applying it to his work life, he did just the opposite. He took the PBL principles he learned *in the business arena* and applied them to his participation in a local congregation. This is simply practicing *ecclesia* as Jesus first established it.

Over time in Western-World history, people developed a gap in their understanding of sacred and secular. Somehow things that were considered "sacred" or "religion-related" fell on one side of a divide, while things "secular" or "outside of religion" fell to the other side. Western-World culture makes sure the divide remains deep and wide—between religion and government, religion and marketplace, religion and entertainment, etc.

Even in our congregations today, some categorize our church work separately from our secular work. But long ago, people didn't separate the two. Life was simply religious. Religion was life. Everyday life was saturated with God or gods, and worshipping God or gods saturated everyday life.

This was the cultural context for most in New Testament times. Remember this context as we explore what Jesus meant by using the word *ecclesia*. He did not intend to build something separated from everyday life and work.

PART ONE DISCERNMENT

Scripture records only two situations where Christ used the term "church," both found in Matthew. The first occurred in Caesarea Philippi (Matthew 16:18), and the second occurred two chapters later and a few miles south in Capernaum (Matthew 18:17). In context and word choice, Jesus reiterates the function of the church as a body of people who make governmental decisions.

First, let's review the conversation at Caesarea Philippi. To set the context, carefully read the full passage:

> *He said to them, "But who do you say that I am?"*
>
> *Simon Peter answered and said, "You are the Christ, the Son of the living God."*
>
> *Jesus answered and said to him, "Blessed are you, Simon Bar-Jonah, for flesh and blood has not revealed this to you, but My Father who is in heaven.*
>
> *And I also say to you that you are Peter, and on this rock I will build My church [ecclesia], and the gates of Hades shall not prevail against it.*
>
> *And I will give you the keys of the kingdom of heaven, and whatever you bind on earth will be bound in heaven, and whatever you loose on earth will be loosed in heaven."*
>
> —MATTHEW 16:15-19

Caesarea Philippi sits in the shadow of a towering precipice that ascends from the edge of the town. The gaping mouth of a cave yawns from the side of the cliff. In Jesus' day, before an earthquake altered the tectonic plates beneath, a spring of water surged from the belly of the cave and fed the mouth of the Jordan River. As Josephus described:

> *...within which there is a horrible precipice that descends abruptly to a vast depth; it contains a mighty quantity of water, which is immovable; and when anybody lets down anything to measure the depth of the earth beneath the water, no length of cord is sufficient to reach it.*[2]

---

2 Josephus, Wars. Book 1. Chapter XXI.3; translated by Loughner from William Wiston.

CHAPTER FOUR JESUS' RADICAL IDEA OF DISCERNMENT AS "CHURCH"

Throughout millennia, pagans dedicated the site to a smorgasbord of gods, even offering human sacrifices that they tossed into the water. If no blood rose from the spring, it meant their god had accepted the sacrifice.

They carved thrones for their deities into the cliff and built temples to keep their "divine" statues from crumbling in the weather. By the time Jesus brought His disciples to the shrine, Herod the Great had erected a monumental white marble temple that straddled the mouth of the cave to worship and appease Caesar.

What name did the Israelites give the cave?

The Gates of Hades.

Jesus brought His disciples to this infamous place (Matthew 16:13-19). He had reasons. Near the *Gates of Hades*, Jesus asked His followers, "Who do you say that I am?"

Always the first to answer, Simon said, *"You are the Christ, the Son of the living God!"* Simon "got it"!

What is it he "got"?

As if in bold defiance of the Caesarea Philippi cliff that housed so many false gods, Simon understood that the rightful Son of God stood before him. The one Jewish Scripture declared would restore God's government to earth.

I'm sure Jesus' response caused a stir among the disciples, so important that He marked it by changing Simon's name to "Peter." The Greek word for *Peter* is *Petros*, which means a stone or piece of rock.

While *Petros* referred to a fragment of rock, Jesus next declared He would build His *ecclesia* on the "rock," using a slightly different Greek word, *petra*, which means *a cliff or mass of rock*.

In essence, the Scripture could be interpreted as: "I also say to you that you are Petros, a fragment of a large-cliff, and on the large-cliff I will build My church. "

What is this "mass of rock" upon which Jesus builds His church? *Peter's revelation of Christ.* Not on Peter. Not on a belief system. Not on a worship ritual, knowledge of Scripture, a building, or a governmental hierarchy. But instead on a Person: the Person of Truth, the Son of the Living God.

PART ONE DISCERNMENT

Christ established His *ecclesia* on the *petra* of this revelation of Himself, "the Head of the body, the church [*ecclesia*], the firstborn from the dead, that in all things He may have the preeminence."[3]

This revelation confirmed the plan of the Trinity, that through Christ, God would restore His people to His original purpose for them—to subdue and rule on earth as partners in leadership with Him.[4]

As believers, Christ must have preeminence in our decision-making—not our own reputations, intellects, or motives. That's what makes us "Christ-followers." We give Him preeminence.

We already mentioned that in New Testament times, *ecclesia* described civil assemblies. When a community needed to make a decision, the people of influence (called-out ones) would assemble, much like a city council, to represent the public. These respected persons would apply their wisdom to the matter, make decisions for the benefit of the whole, and then declare their decisions publicly.

When translating Old Testament Scripture into Greek, Hebrew scholars also used the word *ecclesia* in instances where the elders of Israel assembled to make decisions for the Hebrew people. In other words, Jesus used *ecclesia* to declare that He would build a *decision-making body* of believers.

"Church?" the disciples must have thought. *"Jesus builds a gathering of people who will make decisions in His government?"* To them, this was a new understanding—a radical vision. In other words, *"I will build your discernment—your understanding of the different elements involved—until you come to My wisdom, until you hear from heaven the will of the Father and can clearly state the truth that the Father is showing you."*

Jesus calls all believers as "called-out ones." Over the centuries, we've become so accustomed to differentiating "clergy" from "laity" that we often think Christ calls only certain ones into divine leadership. On the contrary, Jesus calls *all* believers to be leaders—decision-makers—in the circles of influence He has assigned to each one.

---

[3] *Colossians 1:18*
[4] *Genesis 1:27-28*

CHAPTER FOUR JESUS' RADICAL IDEA OF DISCERNMENT AS "CHURCH"

This doesn't mean we shouldn't have positional leaders in our organizations. God designs different people to fulfill different roles in His body according to the gifts, experiences, and personalities He gives them.

This book is geared to support those who serve in positional leadership. But keep in mind that when we refer to the *ecclesia*, we're not referring only to the governmental hierarchy of congregational leadership, but to *all* believers in *all* walks of life, in their spheres of influence, with no division between sacred and secular.

As Creator, God calls *all* to lead on earth—to fill, subdue, and rule by establishing Christ's government in their respective circumstances.

In understanding PBL, keep in mind that when Jesus first used the term *ecclesia*, He wasn't referring to meetings where we praise God and preach His word (though, again, the meaning of "church" has broadened over the centuries to include these wonderful and necessary practices). Jesus instead referred to our responsibility to gather as a governmental, decision-making body.

On the *rock* of Peter's revelation of Christ, Jesus would build His body of believers who would partner with Him in ruling—discerning His will to influence people—on earth.

GATES

As previously mentioned, Jesus led His disciples to a towering rock called "The Gates of Hades," where He introduced His intention to build His *ecclesia* on the Rock. He continued His object lesson by declaring that *"the Gates of Hades shall not prevail against you."* Imagine how this struck the disciples as they probably gazed upon the intimidating, majestic shrine devoted to false gods and the Roman emperor who oppressed their people. Jesus declares that these gates and their gods were no match for His followers. In the face of Christ, the Rock Himself, the enemy's power is no power at all.

PART ONE DISCERNMENT

The word "gates" ties into our "governmental decision-making body" theme. The Old Testament records instances where the elders assembled at the city gates to make leadership decisions.[5]

Governmental leaders (the *ecclesia*) held court, discerned wisdom, resolved issues, and made decisions at the city gates. With the object lesson of the Gates of Hades, Jesus illustrated His point: When the followers of Christ gather to discern His will, the wisdom they discern will rise superior to any strategies Satan might devise at the Gates of Hades.

> **When the followers of Christ gather to discern His will, the decisions they discern will rise superior to any strategies Satan might devise at the Gates of Hades.**

No strategy of devils can overcome the wisdom we discern from Christ. And with Christ's wisdom, we'll overcome any plan Satan devises to divide or destroy the work of God.

Consider our business leader Jared. One day he walked through his office building, glanced into a room, and found an employee sound asleep at his desk. Instead of waking him, Jared simply snapped off the lights and moved on, delaying His response to discern God's will for the situation.

Another employee said, "It's not the first time we've caught him sleeping on the job. I think we should let him go."

But Jared remained sensitive to the Lord's direction in His government of truth and grace. When He sensed the right timing, he sat down to talk with the man.

"What's going on in your life?" Jared asked.

The employee explained how his wife took their baby and left him with overwhelming financial difficulties.

Jared then sensed the Spirit's leading, "We're going to start over with you. We're going to forget this happened and give you the opportunity to improve as an employee."

Jared put guidelines around the man's responsibilities and continued to remain in touch with him concerning his situation. The man improved his work habits and proved to be a strong employee. Four years later, he

---

5 *Ruth 4:10-11, for example.*

decided to take another job opportunity, but expressed genuine appreciation for how Jared had provided a great working environment and helped him through that difficult season.

The Holy Spirit knew the man's heart. In other cases, the Spirit might impress Jared to release an employee from a position. But for this man, the best approach was to help him through his difficulty.

Because Jared waited to sense the leading of the Lord before reacting, God extended His eternal grace beyond the simple workings of the business.

As a member of Christ's *ecclesia*, Jared discerned God's will for the situation and followed through. Consider that the enemy also had a desire for Jared's employee. Satan desired to crush the man. But through Jared's submission, the discernment of Christ prevailed.

As the Lord's wisdom reigned for Jared, Christ's wisdom can reign in each member of His *ecclesia*. Through us, He rules among the ruins of a broken world controlled by deception, human understanding, or rebellion against God. *Nothing* Satan tries to do can prevail against us, unless we make a move outside of the wisdom of Christ.

KEYS OF THE KINGDOM OF HEAVEN

That day in Caesarea Philippi, Jesus gave this kingdom-building authority to His *ecclesia*, but He didn't stop there. He continued to explain His plan for His church:

I will give you the keys of the kingdom of heaven...

Keys symbolized authority to open doors. *Authority to open what doors?* Jesus explained what authority He meant:

> "... whatever you **bind** on earth will be bound in heaven, and whatever you **loose** on earth will be loosed in heaven."[6]

---

6   *Matthew 16:19*

PART ONE DISCERNMENT

Jesus charged His disciples with authority to "bind and loose," introducing the concept in Caesarea Philippi and reiterating it later in Capernaum.[7]

Over the years, we've heard teachings on "binding and loosing" based on our contemporary English understanding of the terms. But the disciples themselves were familiar with the terms as used in Jewish law. From Rabbinical writings, we learn:

- "To bind" meant to *forbid* someone from doing something, or to *withhold fellowship* from them.
- "To loose" meant to *permit* someone to do something, or to *forgive* them.[8]

Both terms concerned the authority rabbis had to make leadership decisions that dealt with issues in the synagogue. The "keys of the kingdom," then, symbolized the authority Jesus gave his followers to make governmental decisions that either forbid or permit.

In Matthew's record of Jesus' Capernaum discourse (Matthew 18:18), we also find that the context of "binding and loosing" concerns governmental authority.[9] Jesus discussed the appropriate way leaders should respond to a believer who falls into sin:

> ...*and if he refuses to hear them, tell it to the* **church** *[ecclesia]. But if he refuses even to hear the* **church** *[ecclesia], let him be to you like a heathen and a tax collector.*[10]

In other words, the church should withhold fellowship [bind] because the person refuses to honor the discernment.

---

7 Matthew 18:18
8 See Mishnah, Nedarim 6:5: "If one vows abstinence from milk, he is **loosed** [permitted] to eat whey... but Rabbi Yose **binds** [forbids] it."
9 Matthew 18:15-17
10 Matthew 18:17; Note: "Withhold fellowship" concerns disciplinary measures but remember that Jesus treated the "heathen and tax collectors" with radical love rather than rejection (Matthew 9:11).

CHAPTER FOUR JESUS' RADICAL IDEA OF DISCERNMENT AS "CHURCH"

Jesus continues by again using the words "binding" and "loosing":

> *...whatever you bind [forbid] on earth will be bound in heaven, and whatever you loose [permit] on earth will be loosed in heaven.* [11]

Jesus explained that in the case of believers falling into sin, the *ecclesia*—the believers who have the authority in that situation—will decide whether to forbid or permit, to forgive or withhold fellowship. In our above example, Jared used this authority in dealing with his employee. He sensed the Lord leading him, in this case, *to loose*, or *to forgive*.

Though not as evident in English translations as in the original Greek, a central point in Jesus' instruction to "bind" and "loose" is that we first discern God's will in heaven *before* establishing it on earth. It doesn't mean we can use human wisdom to create a solution and then expect heaven's blessing. The wisdom we discern can only come from His presence.

The original Greek text makes this more evident. We can't directly translate the grammatical structure of the Greek in this passage into English with a result that makes sense. The syntax simply doesn't exist in English. Consider this word-for-word translation of the Greek that Matthew records both times Jesus spoke the phrase:

> *Whatsoever you bind on earth shall have already been being bound in heaven, and whatsoever you loose on earth shall have already been being loosed in heaven.* [12]

---

11 Matthew 18:18
12 Matthew 16:19; 18:18

This literal rendering illuminates the kind of discernment Jesus established. The decision to bind or loose is dependent upon sensing what is already happening in heaven. We bind what has *already* "been being bound" by God, and we loose what has *already* "been being loosed" by God. We sense what God is already doing in the situation and partner with Him in it—the core principle of Presence-Based Leadership.

Jesus illustrated this principle when He taught his disciples how to pray:

...Your kingdom come, Your will be done on earth as it is in heaven...[13]

> **We sense what God is already doing in the situation and partner with Him in it—the core principle of Presence-Based Leadership.**

How profound! We grow so familiar with Jesus' words that we often miss the earthquake of new revelation that shook the tectonic plates of Jewish law. Until this time, only official authority figures who underwent rigorous training could serve as governors and make leadership decisions that concerned God's will.

But Jesus gave the "keys of the Kingdom"—the authority to discern and establish the Father's will—to ordinary people! Accountants, fishermen, or doctors could discern God's wisdom from heaven and proclaim it on earth. No wonder the scribes and Pharisees considered Jesus a threat to their authority!

---

13 *Matthew 6:10*

CHAPTER FOUR JESUS' RADICAL IDEA OF DISCERNMENT AS "CHURCH"

CHALLENGE

1. Review the list that you wrote at the end of Chapter One of the qualities of effective leaders. Edit or add any characteristics according to any new understanding you may have gleaned.
2. Name the last few times you worked with one or more people to make a decision. Consider how you made that decision and the decision's outcome. *Had you discerned Christ's will in the matter? In what ways might you have acted differently (or not) if you had considered the Presence-Based principle of discerning Christ's will in heaven and establishing that on earth?*

LOOKING AHEAD

Jesus didn't stop at "binding and loosing." The following chapter explores His next statement that ripped open the veil that separated heaven and earth: "For where two or three are gathered in My name, I am there in the midst of them."[14]

---

14 Matthew 18:20b
 For further understanding of ecclesia and binding and loosing principles, also read Keith's booklet, Binding and Loosing, Keys to the Kingdom of God. Find at ttwm.org.

— CHAPTER FIVE —

Keys of the Kingdom: Christ-In-the-Midst Discernment

IN THE MIDST

As Lisa Hosler and her team learned to practice Presence-Based Leadership, they learned to embrace their responsibility as the *ecclesia* in their PRC ministry.

At one point, the team assembled to discern the Lord's wisdom for a problem in the training arm of the organization. For several years they had devoted much time and energy to develop a substantive training program that supported and empowered the new mothers they served. They remained sensitive to the culture and real needs of their clients as they prepared for training sessions. They focused on building relationships rather than just dispensing information.

But why wasn't it working? When the mothers first heard about the program, they were excited and promised to come, but when class time arrived, "It was like pulling teeth to get them to come," Lisa said. "All that prep work for only a few attendees was frustrating. But then God shifted us into discernment mode."

Lisa and the team gathered to pray and ask the Lord for His strategy. After a time of listening for the Lord's wisdom, each shared what they sensed the Spirit saying. Through the discussion, they discovered God's brilliant wisdom for an incentive program. They developed a system that allowed the participants to earn points toward purchasing baby-care

CHAPTER FIVE KEYS OF THE KINGDOM: CHRIST-IN-THE-MIDST DISCERNMENT

products that ministered to their real needs, while at the same time motivating them to attend the sessions.

The attendance rate, and therefore the fruitfulness of relationship-building and ministry opportunities, increased significantly. Moms learned responsibility and received resources, not as handouts, but as rewards for their hard work. Lisa and her team didn't find the answer in human wisdom. The answer came from Christ's presence among their assembly.

This leads to Jesus' amazing proclamation in Matthew 18:19-20. After declaring His Gates-of-Hell-defying church and imparting the authority to bind and loose, Jesus then said:

> ...*if two of you agree on earth concerning anything that they ask, it will be done for them by My Father in heaven. For where two or three are gathered together in My name,* **I am there in the midst of them**.[1]

Two or three who gather in His name—under His authority—is a picture of Christ's presence among His *ecclesia*, His wisdom among His decision-making body.

Christ gives His discernment for His governmental purposes, even if only two people together recognize His authority and active presence in their discernment.[2] And, I like to say, if there's no one else with whom to pray and discern, then you and Jesus make two.

But we find synergy in more than one coming together to honor the Lord, as He, Himself, exists in a relationship-oriented leadership of Three. When we join in group discernment, we reflect His image and the authority of oneness in community.

Christ's promise that "anything they ask will be done for them" is possible *because* we submit to the presence and authority of Christ-in-our-midst. We discern together what is already happening in His presence and join Him as His partners.

---

1 Matthew 18:19-20, bold mine.
2 Note the next verse (Matthew 18:21). Peter asked questions about how to forgive, in line with our "body of discernment" theme because to "bind or loose" means "to forgive or to withhold fellowship."

PART ONE DISCERNMENT

Carefully ponder this: God the Son, Preeminent Eternal Creator-King, promises His presence in *our* assembly! *"What is man that You are mindful of him?"*[3] In Paul's words as paraphrased by Eugene Peterson:

> *"We look at this Son and see the God who cannot be seen.*
> *We look at this Son and see God's original purpose*
> *in everything created.*
> *For everything, absolutely everything, above and below, visible and invisible, rank after rank after rank of angels—*
> *everything got started in Him*
> *and finds its purpose in Him.*
> *He was there before any of it came into existence*
> *and holds it all together right up to this moment.*
> *And when it comes to the church [ecclesia],*
> *He organizes and holds it together,*
> *like a head does a body.*
> *He was supreme in the beginning and—*
> *leading the resurrection parade—*
> *He is supreme in the end.*
> *From the beginning to end He's there,*
> *towering far above everything, everyone.*
> *So spacious is He, so roomy,*
> *that everything of God finds its proper place in Him*
> *without crowding.*
> *Not only that, but all the broken and dislocated*
> *pieces of the universe—*
> *people and things, animals and atoms—*
> *get properly fixed and fit together in vibrant harmonies,*
> *because of His death,*
> *His blood that poured down from the Cross."*[4]

---

3   Psalms 8:4; 144:3; Hebrews 2:6
4   Colossians 1:15-20, The Message

CHAPTER FIVE KEYS OF THE KINGDOM: CHRIST-IN-THE-MIDST DISCERNMENT

This is the same Son of God who promises not only to stand in the center of our gatherings, but to be an active participant! Imagine a session with your board or decision-making time with your spouse or coworkers. Now imagine Jesus standing in the center of your team, orchestrating the flow.

The fullness of His presence—all wisdom, authority, strength, and peace—manifests as we attend to Him. It's not that He *has* wisdom that He'll dispense like candy from a machine. But Christ *is* the embodiment of God's wisdom.[5] As we lead from the posture of His presence, we will prevail. Hell's gates will not.

By practicing Presence-Based Leadership, we **honor** Christ in our midst, **discern** His will, **harmonize** with each other in declaring the discernment, and **implement** His will. We will further develop these concepts later, but here we summarize:

- **Honor Christ:** Intentionally focus on His presence with an attitude that submits to His authority.
- **Discern His Will:** Intentionally take time to clear away our preconceived ideas and listen for His impressions—what He's already doing in the situation and His direction for how we partner with Him in it.
- **Harmonize:** In the community of two or three (or more), build a consensus of moving forward and declaring the discernment.
- **Implement:** Speak and pray His will with clarity to initiate and follow through with His direction.

Remember the quiz at the beginning of Chapter Four? The *ecclesia*, as Jesus established it, includes all believers, whether in business, congregation, family, or service. The food pantry workers needing creative discernment for expanding their services. The husband and wife discerning God's best for their child. The church benevolence committee deciding how to engage with needy individuals.

---

5 *1 Corinthians 1:24, 30*

PART ONE DISCERNMENT

As we discern and implement Christ's will, *we are "being church"!* Jesus established the church to shape and form the world around us according to His will. When we align with and declare something true about God and His will, it causes the world to transform.

PETER GETS IT WRONG THIS TIME

What happened? In Matthew 16:18, Jesus changes Simon's name to *Petros* and proclaims that He'll build His *ecclesia* on Peter's revelation. But only five verses later, Jesus rebukes Peter: "Get behind Me, Satan! You are an offense to Me, for you are not mindful of the things of God, but the things of men."[6]

Embarrassing for Peter, yes. But Jesus' admonishment didn't debase Peter. In reality, Jesus honored him (though Peter might not have understood that at the time!). Called as a leader in the *ecclesia*, Jesus needed to realign Peter's mindset.

What had Peter said that so offended Christ? He disputed Jesus' prophecy that He would suffer and die at the hands of Jerusalem's elders. Instead of discerning Christ's wisdom, Peter spoke from his own agenda, with a mindset contrary to Christ's truth. He didn't yet understand the practice of "casting down arguments and every high thing that exalts itself against the knowledge of God…"[7] His decision to forbid [bind] Christ was based on his human worldview.

Remember those shrines at the Gates of Hades? Peter still had shrines in his own heart (as we may all have)—voices from his limited knowledge of how the world was supposed to operate. *If Jesus died, how could He fulfill the rule of the Messiah to establish His kingdom on earth? This could not be!*

As Christ's decision-making body, we sometimes focus on the shrines of human knowledge, motive, and power, rather than Christ. Like Peter, we make wrong decisions. Scripture calls our human mindsets "strongholds:"

---

6 Matthew 16:23
7 2 Corinthians 10:5

CHAPTER FIVE KEYS OF THE KINGDOM: CHRIST-IN-THE-MIDST DISCERNMENT

> *"For the weapons of our warfare are not carnal*
> *but mighty in God for the pulling down of **strongholds**,*
> *casting down **arguments** and every high thing*
> *that exalts itself against the **knowledge** of God,*
> *bringing every **thought** into captivity*
> *to the obedience of Christ…"*[8]

Notice that the above passage says nothing about pulling down demonic strongholds or spiritual powers that are "out there" somewhere. It speaks of strongholds in our own minds. Our thoughts that are not aligned with Christ as the Truth (though the Devil certainly causes and thrives in deceptive mindsets).

The cultures and environments in which we live often engrave on our minds thoughts that run contrary to the way of God. We combat those strongholds by seeking, agreeing with, and acting on Christ's truth.

Usually, we can't see our own intellectual and emotional mindsets, just as Peter didn't see his at the time. But as we follow Christ, He exposes more and more of our false mindsets by shining the light of His Truth on the hidden places in our hearts.

He often accomplishes this enlightenment through other people or difficult circumstances. We don't always appreciate the exposure at first, but in reality, Christ honors us by cleansing and training us to handle greater responsibility and authority.

We know the truth, and the truth makes us free, with the fullness of "joy inexpressible and full of glory"[9] for those who experience the Spirit's truth after a mindset of deception.

At one time, I held a position on a church board of elders. The church librarian submitted a question to us that concerned policy/procedure for the library. Because I held a master's degree in library science, I subconsciously assumed I possessed all the professional knowledge necessary to resolve the issue. I thought the elders and I could quickly find a resolution.

---

8 *2 Corinthians 10:4-5, bold mine*
9 *John 8:32; 1 Peter 1:8*

PART ONE DISCERNMENT

On the contrary, we discussed the issue for an extended period—far too long for the relatively minor question.[10] But we persevered, and the librarian implemented the solution we determined. Unfortunately, our solution didn't work and made the situation worse.

What went wrong? I depended upon my own expertise rather than seeking direction from Christ. But we also missed an even deeper issue: *the question was not ours to solve*. The librarian herself, and perhaps her manager, should have discerned Christ's wisdom for the problem, not the elders'.

We essentially took responsibility and authority to make a decision that didn't belong to us. The consequences of our wrong decision exposed my hidden stronghold of assuming that my "professional expertise" would be sufficient to handle the problem. We centered on wisdom that did not come "down from above, but [was] earthly, natural …" The wisdom that comes from Christ, on the other hand, is "without partiality."[11]

Returning to Peter's story, when Jesus addressed him as "Satan," He revealed Peter's words as discernment from the Gates of Hades. Looking back, it's interesting that Peter practiced his new decision-making authority on the One who gave him the authority in the first place. Perhaps we all attempt that sometimes!

CAN UNBELIEVERS DISCERN GOD'S WILL?

The body of Christ often debates the question of whether non-Christians can hear the direction of the Lord. We can find answers on different levels of understanding. But I offer two stories that illustrate God's heart for reaching out to unbelievers with His loving direction. After all, sometimes more often than not, situations may require us to discern God's wisdom with a team of unbelievers.

---

10 *We missed an important red flag: when an issue takes too long to resolve, we stop and refocus on Christ. We develop this point later.*

11 *James 3:15, NASB; James 3:18*

CHAPTER FIVE KEYS OF THE KINGDOM: CHRIST-IN-THE-MIDST DISCERNMENT

On several occasions, I ministered to wives whose husbands were either not believers or not fully practicing their faith on the same level as their wives. The women struggled with tough problems that they brought to me for discernment.

After talking through the situations and suggesting to them the direction that I had discerned, I asked, "What does your husband think you should do?" In each case, the wife related that her husband had given the same or similar advice that I had given. The revelation that their unbelieving husbands could discern God's direction usually surprised them. The same would be true of husbands who have non-Christian wives.

Mary Geegh, a beloved and renowned missionary to India from 1924 to 1962, wrote a powerful little book, *God Guides*.[12] Filled with simple but profound stories of God's provision, the book is still in print and touches many lives.

With non-cluttered faith, Mary made Christ-in-the-midst discernment with non-believers a common practice. Regardless of their professed religion, whether Christian or not, when people came to her with a problem, she didn't give advice, preach, or scold, but trusted in God's personal love for them. Mary told them that Jesus was the God who speaks, and that He would show them what to do. She handed them paper and a pencil and sat with them to "listen" to Jesus' direction, with instructions to write down whatever the Lord told them.

Mary didn't divulge the impression she received until after they shared what they sensed. The discernment they wrote on the paper often confirmed her own! People sensed the Lord's direction to deal with and forgive broken relationships, confess hidden sin, or handle problems. When they obeyed, they experienced His peace, freedom, and joy. Even if not following Christ, many recognized the "real" Jesus, who cares about them enough to speak to them. They often came to trust the Lord.

---

12 Geegh, Mary, God Guides, *by* PrayAmerica.org. *Missionary Press, 2004.* www.God-Guides.com

PART ONE DISCERNMENT

What a way to practice "church" [*ecclesia*]! The questions I pose here: *What if a businessperson humbly practiced "listening prayer," even in an office of mostly non-believers? What impact would that make over time? What if congregational leaders helped people establish listening prayer beyond the four walls of the church building to where they work, live, serve, and play?*

Extending PBL in this way differs from simply passing on leadership advice or theological principles. It's modeling for others to engage in a more direct relationship with Christ. It's the *ecclesia* fully alive in the interactive presence of God.

With a renewed mindset of Christ's intention for His body, we can redraw the walls that traditionally characterize "church." Whether or not everyone in the group fully recognizes themselves as the *ecclesia*, we can call "church" to order anywhere and anytime two or more gather in submission to Christ to discern His will. As His ambassadors, we represent Christ when we meet in our homes, in the marketplace, in classrooms, hospitals, airplanes, board meetings, sidewalks, or grocery stores.

We also experience *ecclesia* in many expressions of our traditional understanding of "church." For example:

- Leadership teams discerning direction for the congregation
- Praise teams discerning how to prepare for the song service
- Small groups deciding how to care for a need in the community
- Teachers or preachers discerning what God is saying and publicly declaring that truth
- Benevolence ministers making policy decisions
- Business owners discerning how to strengthen wholesome values
- Chaplain/surgeon/nurses and family making decisions about surgery
- Youth group leadership teams planning for a weekend retreat

This is the reality of the *ecclesia* Jesus established, the everlasting government He set into motion.

CHAPTER FIVE KEYS OF THE KINGDOM: CHRIST-IN-THE-MIDST DISCERNMENT

CHALLENGE

1. *What does it look like when you are involved in an* ecclesia *discernment meeting, whether inside or outside the traditional walls of a "church" function?*
2. List areas in your sphere of leadership where you can more fully honor Christ-in-the-midst of your discernment.
3. Ask the Lord to show you what steps to take to more fully establish Christ's government in your discernment process. Take time to listen for His response. *What changes does He encourage you to make toward a lifestyle that embraces Presence-Based Discernment?*

LOOKING AHEAD

So far, we've discussed the Act of PBL, discerning what Christ is already doing and how He wants us to partner with Him in it. To fully embrace Presence-Based Discernment, we align with Christ's government by adopting *towardness*, the Attitude of PBL. In the next chapter, we explore the essence of towardness and how to cultivate this posture in our lives and leadership communities.

— PART TWO —

Towardness

THE ATTITUDE OF PRESENCE-BASED LEADERSHIP

Presence-Based Leadership
Guiding others with a posture of submission
to wisdom discerned from Christ's presence

The Art

PRESENCE
Leading from a posture of rest in and
from the circle of Trinity fellowship

The Attitude

TOWARDNESS
Cultivating a culture of prayer and honor

The Act

CHRIST-IN-THE-MIDST DISCERNMENT
Stewarding the metron of sonship within the ecclesia

©2016 TEACHING THE WORD MINISTRIES

— CHAPTER SIX —

Towardness: The Nature of the Triune Presence

A mosaic consists of thousands of little stones. Some are blue, some are green, some are yellow, some are gold. When we bring our faces close to the mosaic, we can admire the beauty of each stone. But as we step back from it, we can see that all these little stones reveal to us a beautiful picture, telling a story none of these stones can tell by itself.

That is what our life in community is about. Each of us is like a little stone, but together we reveal the face of God to the world. Nobody can say: "I make God visible." But others who see us together can say: "They make God visible." Community is where humility and glory touch. [1]

—HENRI J. M. NOUWEN

TOWARDNESS

Jared worked at his desk when an employee walked past his open doorway. He sensed a prompting to address her.

---

1 From Henri J. M. Nouwen, Bread for the Journey: A Daybook of Wisdom and Faith; May 3, "The Mosaic that shows us the Face of God." HarperCollins e-books; Reprint Edition, 2009.

PART TWO TOWARDNESS

"Sharon, how are you doing?" he asked. After hesitating, she said, "I'm good."

"Really? That took too long."

Sharon stared at the floor a moment, then said, "Well, I do have a physical thing going on."

Jared already knew the lady to be a believer, though her husband was not. "Is it okay if we pray for you?"

"Right now?"

"Yes," Jared said.

He then paged another employee whom he knew as a strong woman of faith. When she came, he asked her, "I know you're busy, but could you take ten or fifteen minutes on office time to pray with Sharon?"

"Of course!" the woman replied. She took Sharon into her own office for a time of ministry.

Later, Sharon thanked Jared and expressed how much that prayer time touched her soul and made a difference in her life.

Jared showed an attitude of respect toward all his employees, but he had a choice. He didn't have to go beyond the normal expectations of an employer. After all, he had hired Sharon to perform certain tasks for the overall progress of the company. To some, ministry belongs in church, not in the business environment. *Isn't it the responsibility of Sharon's church to minister to her personal needs? Why should I?*

But Jared had a different mindset that we call "towardness." Sharon was not just an asset to the company, but a person created in the image of God with a purpose that will have an eternal impact. Jared was part of her community as a representative of Christ. If Jared allowed the Holy Spirit to work God's grace through him in Sharon's life, he also impacted the community of Christ into eternity.

But I don't have time to do all this extra prayer! Consider this rhyme: It's not as much a matter of "time" as it is a different paradigm.

The essence of Presence-Based Leadership is less of a change of habit and more of a *transformation* to a mindset that conforms to how God originally designed human beings. "Let us make man in Our image."[2]

---

2 *Genesis 1:26*

CHAPTER SIX TOWARDNESS: THE NATURE OF THE TRIUNE PRESENCE

An image is a reflection of the original—whether from a mirror, printer, or camera. The closer to the original we move, the more accurate the image we reflect.

To walk as His image, we need to know the original—the Trinity Himself. As we move through this chapter, we explore how the triune God exists as a community of *towardness*, and how we reflect towardness as His image.

As leaders with delegated authority from the Trinity to "fill the earth and *subdue it; have dominion* over the fish of the sea…"[3], we need to understand what leadership looked like when male and female reflected a flawless image of their Creator-Leader. In other words, *how did the Trinity lead as the model for how He designed us to lead? How did God the Father, Son, and Spirit lead for all that eternity before they created us?*

The Apostle John received a glimpse of their eternal state of being, which he shared with us:

> *"In the beginning was the Word, and the Word was* **with** *God, and the Word was God. He was in the beginning* **with** *God."*[4]

In this passage, **with** is the English translation of the Greek word **pros**. *Pros* has no close English equivalent, so we settle for "with." In English, "with" is a common preposition we don't think about when we read, so we miss the full impact of the phrase "and the Word was *with* God." In English, the phrase simply means that the Word was in agreement with or accompanying God.

To the Greek reader, *pros* goes beyond proximity to be a preposition of *direction*. In fact, *pros* is most often translated as "to," or in King James, "unto." *Pros* denotes a *motion towards; forward to; because of*; pertaining to the *destination* of the relation.

If I'm *with* [*pros*] you, I'm not only near you, but I'm focused on you, *moving forward toward* you, *because of* you. My *destination* is you. We could

---

3 *Genesis 1:28, italics mine*
4 *John 1:1-2, bold mine*

translate John 1:1 as "and the Word was *unto* God...He was in the beginning *unto* God."

The understanding of *pros* as a "focused presence" strengthens when we consider both the Hebrew and Greek words translated as **presence**. In both languages—Hebrew: *panim*; and Greek: *prosopon*—the terms literally mean "face" with direction, one *facing toward* another. In fact, our John 1:1 word, *pros*, is the root of the Greek word **pros***opon*!

John D. Zizioulas, a contemporary theologian, explains the significance of the move the Cappadocian (330-395 AD) church fathers made when they first adopted the term *prosopon* [presence, face] into Trinitarian theology:

> ...*prosopon... is relational... This meant that from now on a relational term entered into ontology [study of the nature of "being"] ... "to be" and "to be in relation" become identical.*[5]

In other words, the Cappadocian fathers understood that the substance of which the Trinity consists *is* relationship. God always, eternally exists in communion. And we, as images of God, also exist as creatures of communion.

Now consider how this pertains to the phrase, "the Word was *unto* God." The Son and Father not only resided near each other, but were actively facing each other, *moving forward toward* each other. Their *destination was each other.* Throughout eternity, they share the joyful satisfaction and fruit of whole, interchanging relationship—promoting each other's purposes so that they have the same purpose.

On earth, Jesus was positioned toward His Father: "And He who sent Me is with Me. The Father has not left Me alone, for I always do those things that please Him ...My judgment is righteous, because I do not seek My own will but the will of the Father who sent me..." And the Father toward His Son: "This is My beloved Son, in whom I am well pleased. Hear Him!"[6]

Mutual towardness among the Trinity: "But when the *Helper* comes, whom *I* shall send to you from the *Father*, the *Spirit* of truth who proceeds

---

5 Zizioulas, John D., Being as Communion. *St. Vladimir's Seminary Press, 2002, pages 87-88. Bold and italics mine.*

6 *John 8:29; John 5:30; Matthew 17:5*

CHAPTER SIX TOWARDNESS: THE NATURE OF THE TRIUNE PRESENCE

from the *Father,* He will testify of *Me.*"[7] The Father, Son, and Holy Spirit find their identity in each other. John drew a beautiful picture of a relational, other-facing, outward-extending Trinity presence. No passivity or self-centeredness here!

We call this relationship among the Trinity **towardness**. This is the image in which He created us. God designed us to relate to Him and each other with the attitude of towardness. We learn to *move forward toward* the Trinity as He *moves forward toward* us, and we move *forward toward* each other.

Presence-Based Leadership brings us into the fullness of our relational substance, with mutual fulfillment in each other's presence as we fellowship in God's presence. As we find our identity in Father God and walk in the oneness of that identity, we become the joyful satisfaction and fruit of a whole, mutual, interchanging relationship, dwelling in the active presence of God and others. (Note that the attitude of towardness does wonders for marriages!)

God designed our core substance as communal. His act of creating two complementary genders and establishing the mystery of the marriage relationship where "the two shall become one,"[8] illustrates how community exists as the essence of our souls, in the image of Trinity oneness.

Whether in a marriage relationship or not, man received his masculinity from one part of God's character. Woman received her femininity from another part of God's character. God commanded male and female to rule together.[9]

When male and female lead in community together, they reflect a fuller image of God. If one ruled separately from the other, that leadership would reflect only a partial image of God. Leading together in godly communion reflects the complete image that God intended. "So we, being many, are one body in Christ, and individually members of one another."[10]

When we allow God's towardness to flow through us, we open the door for others to embrace this attitude also. Think of how the tone of

---

7 *John 15:26, italics mine*
8 *Ephesians 5:31*
9 *Genesis 1:26*
10 *Romans 12:5*

our leadership meetings would change. Instead of pressing for our own will and desires or trying to please people for our personal advancement, we actively pursue the purposes of God by assisting and promoting others' purposes toward the pleasure of God. We *move toward* the soul of each other, listening to the other's needs, encouraging each other in our identity in the Father.

Yes, it's possible! We've watched it develop in many leadership teams and boards over the years. We've witnessed the Lord's hand in what we might describe as "corporate miracles"—brilliant wisdom where little formerly existed, camaraderie emerging from heated contention, a way forward from a foundation of rubble. *No, it's not easy!* It takes sacrificial forgiveness, humility, and intentional effort to submit to the beautiful control of the Holy Spirit.

PRESENCE STRIPPED; PRESENCE RETURNED

After Adam and Eve, no human ever again lived in Eden, and the flood washed it away. We still reflect God's image, but the mirror is flawed. One day we'll see God "face to face [literally, *"prosopon pros prosopon"*], and we'll "be like Him, for we shall see Him as He is."[11] But for now, sin warps the mirror of our souls.

In Eden, the Trinity's presence clothed Adam and Eve. They walked with God in the fullness of spirit and truth,[12] nothing hidden or blocking intimacy, God-to-mankind, or person-to-person. After they sinned, "they hid themselves **from the presence** of Yahweh Elohim." With His presence stripped, "they realized they were naked."[13]

"Naked" [Hebrew word: *erom*] does not refer to physical or sexual nakedness, but to a defenseless state and abandonment without possessions or power.[14] In other words, they no longer ruled in the fullness of

---

11 *1 Corinthians 13:12; 1 John 3:2*
12 *John 4:23-24*
13 *Genesis 3:7-8*
14 *Seminary Studies, page 235 Andrews University Seminary Studies, Vol. 40, No. 2, 219-243. Copyright ©2002 Andrews University Press. THE GARDEN OF EDEN ACCOUNT: THE CHIASTIC STRUCTURE OF GENESIS 2-3 ROBERTO OURO, Villa Aurora Theological Seminary, Florence, Italy*

CHAPTER SIX TOWARDNESS: THE NATURE OF THE TRIUNE PRESENCE

God's power because they rejected the Trinity's circle of fellowship. No longer did the presence of Yahweh Elohim surround them. They were left to rule with fig leaves—in their own, defenseless state of human power—outside of the circle of Trinity fellowship.

Sin not only separated them from God, but also from each other. The consequence of sin ushered them from a place of "not ashamed" to the place of shame. From the place of full security in His presence to the place of fear.[15] Shame and fear wreak havoc in our relationships. We build emotional walls to hide our shameful parts, to keep others—not *with* us—but at a distance, for fear of the pain they may bring to our vulnerability.

The next time you see walls of strife rise to divide your leadership team—or family or church—remember that these are only the symptoms of the sickness of shame and fear. But in the towardness of His presence, "perfect love casts out fear."[16] When we chose the way of shame and fear, the Trinity did not turn His love away from us. Consider the full course of history. God created humankind as an extension of His relational substance. He opened His fellowship to include us.

US! God invited us to participate in covenant relationship with Trinity fellowship, to adopt us into the Family. The Bridegroom woos His bride. Jesus sacrificed Himself to break the boundary between us and the intimacy of Trinity Presence.

As the Son of God, Jesus represents the Trinity to His bride. As the Son of Man, Jesus represents His bride to the Trinity. He became the two-way Door in the wall between us—"the veil torn in two from top to bottom… the veil, that is, His flesh."[17] The Door stands wide open, with warm fires burning inside, inviting us back into the Presence that heals our shame, banishes our fear, and covers our nakedness.

"…that they all may be one," Jesus prayed, "as You, Father, *are* in Me, and I in You; that they also may be one in Us… I in them, and You in Me…" He didn't stop with His disciples, but invited others, "that the world may know that You have sent Me, and have loved them as You have loved Me…

---

15 Genesis 2:25; 3:7, 10
16 1 John 4:18
17 John 10:7-9; Matthew 27:51; Hebrews 10:20

For You loved Me before the foundation of the world…that **the love with which You loved Me may be in them**…"[18]

The arms of Trinity towardness—the eternal Family of Father, Son, and Spirit—opens wide to include many more children—anyone who chooses to join the circle of fellowship through the Blood (sacrifice of life) of Christ. "Behold, what manner of love the Father has bestowed on us, that we should be called children of God!"[19]

Towardness requires change and yielding to the authority of the Lord's presence in relationships and ministry. He asks us to choose the Spirit's direction, even if it hurts. Even if He hasn't yet unveiled His strategy. Even if other factors point a different way. We rest in the Trinity's supportive presence, which moves toward us as we together move toward Him.

LIKE A DANCE: *PERICHORESIS*

In 2000, Pastor Erick lounged on a chair in his backyard, contemplating God's call on his life. Though he had risen in his industry as a successful business leader who traveled the world, he sensed the Holy Spirit pressing him toward something more.

Erick had watched one of the first Sentinel videos describing the spiritual transformation of Uganda.[20] Started by a few native pastors and other Christ-followers praying for their own neighborhoods, more intercessors joined the movement. The Lord manifested His presence in many lives. Eventually, God touched the hearts of influential people within the nation's government, including Uganda's president. Through prayer, the Lord transformed the entire nation.

Erick wondered, "Why can't that happen here?" Located in a large metropolitan city in the United States, he yearned to see his street, his neighborhood, his city transformed by the power and love of Father God. He felt God's direction not only to pastor people in his church, but to pastor his neighborhood as well.

---

18 *John 17:21, 24, 26, bold mine*
19 *1 John 3:1a*
20 See: Mulinde, John, Prayer Altars: A strategy that is changing nations, *World Trumpet Missions*, 2013

CHAPTER SIX TOWARDNESS: THE NATURE OF THE TRIUNE PRESENCE

Erick's desire to extend love to others reflected the core of God's nature, an eternal invitation to include others in His family. God's love is the motive of His presence. Erick rests in His Presence as an extension of Trinity towardness. He fell into step with the Trinity dance.

Have you ever participated in or witnessed an intricately choreographed circle dance? Every gesture anticipates the interaction of the whole, each motion vital for perfect harmony. Dancers give, receive, support, and synergize each other toward a beautiful, integrated fullness. One dancer missing a beat affects the whole.

Some early church fathers[21] used the term *perichoresis* [pair-ee-KOR-eh-sis] to describe this dance-like interchange of love among the Trinity. The root word *peri* simply means "around." *Choresis* could come from the word *chorea*, which means "dance," similar to our word "choreography." Together they refer to a "round dance."

Others emphasize that the meaning of *perichoresis* reaches a deeper level. The root word *chora* refers to a word that means "place." It indicates "going around and beyond one's place" or "the great mystery by which Personas of the holy Trinity occupy the same 'space,' yet are 'near and towards' each other."[22]

To describe this mystery of *perichoresis*, over the centuries, scholars have used the word: **interpenetration**[23] (making the concept even more mysterious!). Imagine three individual beings penetrating each other's place, yet occupying a unique place, yet eternally moving toward the others' place.

Our God is three interpenetrated beings that, for eternity, have enjoyed the exhilaration of knowing and being entirely known. They always attend each other with mutual support toward fulfilling each other's harmonic purpose with such passion as to be One.

But They didn't stop there. This nature of *perichoresis*—the relational substance of God—*does not stop at all. It's forever outward reaching, seeking to expand and extend His circle. He yearns to include us in His dance.*

---

21 Gregory of Nazianzus and John of Damascus, for example.
22 Humphrey, Edith (2011) "Presumption, Preparation, Parresia, Perichoresis, and Worship," from The Great Tradition—A Great Labor: Studies in Ancient-Future Faith, *Wipf and Stock Publishers, Cascade Books, Eugene, OR.*
23 Ibid.

PART TWO TOWARDNESS

Where did Pastor Erick get his inner drive of compassion, his attitude of towardness—the appetite to pray for his city and continue praying until he saw answers? From aligning with the outward-reaching perichoresis, reflecting the forever-extending love of the Trinity *toward* the people He created. Pastor Erick's God-breathed passion also extended to develop regional teams of other pastors and intercessors with the same passion for Presence-Based prayer.

Over the years, Pastor Erick has experienced God's hand through salvations, healing of broken lives and relationships, expansion of church outreach, and partnering with governmental leaders in commitment to prayer.

"When we learned about *towardness*," Erick said, "we had to change the way we functioned as an elder team and change the structure of our staff team. We used to work in 'silos,' with different ministries responsible for different things, not communicating well, making assumptions about people and motives. We had a lot of cracks in the foundations, which opened the door for the enemy to kill, steal, and destroy.[24] But now, we're experiencing more of Christ's abundant life through a deeper level of unity and oneness. We look out for each other's well-being. There's a level of camaraderie and oneness in the elder team that flows through the rest of the staff and then through the congregation."

DESIGNED TO THRIVE IN HIS TRIUNE PRESENCE

Our PRC director, Lisa Hosler, learned how to "enter into God's rest,"[25] an ever-present peace that settles beneath even the busiest currents of work—a *posture of rest*.

When searching scripture for insight about weariness and rest, Lisa ventured onto Moses' story. Yahweh had grown so exasperated over the rebellious attitude of His people that He announced He would leave them. "I will send My Angel before you," Yahweh said to Moses, "…for I will

---

24 John 10:10
25 Hebrews 4:9-12

CHAPTER SIX TOWARDNESS: THE NATURE OF THE TRIUNE PRESENCE

not go up in your midst, lest I consume you on the way, for you are a stiff-necked people."[26]

But Moses had a relationship with the Eternal. As he honored the Lord's presence, Yahweh also honored the presence—the *face*—of Moses. "…the LORD spoke to Moses face-to-face, as a man speaks to his friend."[27]

So Moses expressed his perplexity at Yahweh's alienation. We paraphrase his dilemma: "You say to lead the people to the Promised Land, yet You won't go with us? You won't even tell me who *will* go with us. You say I've found grace in Your sight. If I've found grace, then please remember that You claim the people as Your own children!"

As a friend listens to a friend, Yahweh heard Moses and replied, "My **Presence** [*face*] will go with you, **and I will give You rest.**"[28]

Lisa Hosler had already experienced satisfying rest in her devotion times. Still, she yearned for something deeper that would penetrate every part of her daily life—how to rest *while* working. The day after Lisa recognized her weariness, she met for an orientation meeting with a new staffer, Cindy. They finished the orientation early. Lisa knew Cindy loved to pray, so she asked if they could pray together over a list of prayer items.

"To begin the prayer, I asked the Lord to show me where the weariness was coming from and to teach us how to 'rest at work,'" Lisa said. Then an image of Jesus sitting on His throne in heaven came to her mind. She prayed aloud for Christ to sit on the throne of the ministry, so when people considered the ministry, God would be preeminent.

Cindy, in turn, continued the prayer time. But instead of dwelling on the list of prayer items, she spoke with tender affection for the Lord, worshipping Him by naming His attributes: "Lord, You're our refuge, our strength…" Cindy had a level of devotion that Lisa never saw before. She continued her praise far beyond the usual introductory comments, and Lisa grew impatient, wondering when she would stop.

---

26 Exodus 33:2-3
27 Exodus 33:11. To further understand the relationship Moses enjoyed with Yahweh, we recommend the heart-transforming book by Ruth Haley Barton: Strengthening the Soul of Your Leadership: Seeking God in the Crucible of Ministry.
28 Exodus 33:12-13 (my paraphrase), verse 14, bold and italics mine

PART TWO TOWARDNESS

Then Cindy surprised Lisa by describing the scene of Jesus sitting on the throne, matching the image Lisa had already seen in her mind. As the praise continued, Lisa noticed a change in the atmosphere of the room. She felt a holy "presence" settle in, a weighty and almost tangible yet spiritual sense that the Lord inhabited that place.

They sat in the Lord's presence for some time, speechless before His royal majesty, undone by His formidable reality. Lisa realized her prayer list paled in the spiritual brightness of the moment—the needs represented were nothing for such an omnipotent God. He already saw them and met them. Worshipping Him was all that mattered, connecting with Him, honoring Him. Lisa and Cindy shared their experience with the other staffers, wondering if it marked the beginning of a spiritual refreshing for the ministry.

Before that banner morning, Lisa and her staff had spent thirty minutes at the beginning of each workday praying for the specific needs of their clients. "The daily prayer had become pretty stiff and stale by then," Lisa said. "But we kept doing it—every morning—because I thought that's what we were supposed to do. We need to be obedient and pray for these people no matter what."

But after her experience with Cindy, Lisa incorporated worship into the next staff prayer time. As they worshipped, the holy presence of the Lord surrounded the entire staff. In His presence—in the *face* of the God who sees—the prayer needs were already cared for. All questions satisfied. Perfect rest. Perfect peace. So full and gratified—"like a baby content in its mother's arms, my soul is a baby content …"[29]

As days passed, they worshipped, sang with CDs, and centered on Christ, gazing into His face. Each day the singing and waiting on His presence lasted one, two, or three hours. No one was bored or considered it a waste of time.

---

29 King David's description of his perfect peace and rest in the Lord's presence, Psalm 131:2, The Message

CHAPTER SIX TOWARDNESS: THE NATURE OF THE TRIUNE PRESENCE

"At first, having the luxury of worshipping God while we were being paid didn't sit right with me," Lisa remembered. "What would the board think? What would our donors think? I had a strong work ethic. But even though we spent so much time in worship, we were still getting our work done without stress or weariness. It was uncanny! We learned to work out of a place of God's rest."

Lisa shared their new work/worship style with the board. They, too, began opening meetings with worship and eventually experienced the same transformation of rest and productivity. For the next ten years or so, the staff continued to start each day with one hour of worship. But since then, they've settled into a "lifestyle of worship." Lisa explained, "God opened our understanding of worshipping 24/7. 'Worship and working' became woven throughout the day."

We don't suggest Lisa's story as a new "technique" for better leadership and greater productivity. If we wanted, we could develop a system called "24/7 Worship-Work," with the following steps:

1. Gather your people every morning to start the day singing to recorded worship music.
2. Keep worshipping for several hours each morning for two months.
3. Worship one hour each morning for the next ten years.
4. Allow the experience to settle into a 24/7 Worship-Work routine.

We could even develop and sell worship videos specifically for the workplace. But all of this would become "stiff-and-stale" if our motive were simply to package a procedure as a guaranteed method to get the Lord's blessing. And we would miss the point.

What is the point? God designed us to live and lead in Face-to-face, spontaneous relationship. Communion. First of all with God, and then through Him to each other. Lisa and her team learned to receive the Holy Spirit's energizing presence and wisdom for work. They learned *perichoresis*—to hear the rhythm of God's desire and commune in the flow of His meter.

PART TWO TOWARDNESS

CHALLENGE

1. One at a time, consider specific relationships you have in your sphere of influence.
   a. *What would it look like if your stance was intentionally poised toward that person's best interest?*
   b. *In what ways would the attitude of towardness change the way you relate to him or her?*
2. *How have you participated in Trinity perichoresis in your sphere of leadership? In other words, in what situation have you embraced God's dance of towardness and answered His call to reflect that in your leadership?*
3. *What practical changes can you make in your schedule to set aside time for listening prayer, to more fully participate in Trinity communion?*
4. *How might you reach out to others so you can together participate in the Trinity dance?*

LOOKING AHEAD

Coming to the Lord "empty" does *not* mean we leave our brains at the door. Our leadership is a *partnership*, not as puppets, but as sons in the Father's household. He designed us as free entities so He can work *with* us, not *instead of* us. He doesn't *over*-power but *empowers* our minds, personalities, and abilities.

In the next chapter, we discover how Father God ordains our leadership to exercise His governmental authority and responsibility as His sons. As we choose to follow the way of the Spirit, He ordains us as joint heirs with Christ, who is the Firstborn of the Father's household.[30]

---

30 *Roman 8:17; Revelation 1:5*

— CHAPTER SEVEN —

Sonship: Responsibility and Authority to Discern in Union with God

CHARACTERISTICS OF SONSHIP

Several years ago, a colleague and friend, Ben Abell,[1] sensed the Lord leading him to address the needs of the HIV pandemic in Baltimore, MD. He partnered with another minister, Pastor John Schmidt, to develop a strategy.

Plenty of people expressed interest, but in moving forward, Ben and John didn't want to waste time and energy with hit-or-miss strategies. They desired to develop an effective plan that would make the greatest use of time and talent to meet felt needs. Though now a pastor, Ben had a background in business and knew many proven methods he could have employed to develop strategy, including:

- **Expert Analysis:** contacting and working with experts in the HIV field
- **Situation Analysis:** conduct research to determine the present state of the HIV situation and how to best respond to what's currently happening
- **SWOT Analysis:** determine the Strengths, Weaknesses, Opportunities, and Threats to develop a comprehensive plan

---

[1] Ben Abell, his actual name, is founder of Hope Springs, an HIV/AIDS ministry in the Baltimore, MD area, hopesprings.org.

- **Brainstorming:** find threads between four or five of the best ideas and develop them into strategies

Ben admits they could have forged a sufficient plan using any combination of these methods. But experience taught him the best strategy: "Get a team in a room and practice Presence-Based Discernment. We say to God, 'we have no idea what to do.' We seek the Lord together and listen to His voice. Each person makes deposits of information from their own experience to add to the whole discernment, but we're there to hear God. We ask the Lord, 'What are You doing in this situation with this group of people in this moment in history?'"

Ben, John, and the team prayed and sought Christ's wisdom concerning the HIV/AIDS outreach for more than fourteen months, determined to wait until they clearly discerned God's direction before moving forward. Through the process, Christ unfolded His plan.

> We ask the Lord, "What are You doing in this situation with this group of people in this moment in history?"

He revealed vision and mission statements with pillars that involved equipping congregations and mobilizing volunteers in an empowering, highly effective process. The new organization, Hope Springs, grew to engage hundreds of people in more than 125 churches and continues to grow.

But Christ's wisdom knows no bounds! The strategy worked so well that another team of people with a passion for addressing the human trafficking issue contacted Ben to help them develop a ministry strategy.

Ben led them through the same PBL discernment process. They acknowledged Christ's authority in-their-midst as they sought and waited for God's direction in meetings and on retreat days. In time, they discerned God's plan for Araminta Freedom Initiative,[2] a ministry committed to eradicating human trafficking in the Baltimore region. It's now emerging as a national model for other cities.

---

2 See their website at aramintafreedom.org

CHAPTER SEVEN SONSHIP: RESPONSIBILITY AND AUTHORITY

It may work for some, but it feels risky for modern times. What if we pray for months and get nothing? What if we miss God? What if God doesn't answer before a deadline? What if different people claim to hear different things? It's blindly jumping off a cliff, hoping to land on something that won't break me.

Is that what Peter felt when he jumped out of the boat onto the raging water? When Jesus stood on that water with His hand stretched toward Peter and said, "Come," was His command only for Peter, or symbolically for all of us?[3]

The above questions are real, and we'll address them. Yes, it's an adventure trusting the Lord to walk on water instead of remaining on the "solid" floor of the perceived tried and true. *But what's the alternative? Missing the adventure of walking on water? Missing the growth, productivity, and life that comes from leading as a son of God? Missing His destiny for our lives?*

THE ESSENCE OF SONSHIP

Does Ben Abell have an extra special relationship with God that merited such profound answers to prayer?

The answer is: *yes.*

Yes, Ben has a special relationship with God—*and so do you!* God calls Himself our Father and calls us His *sons.*[4] In working with hundreds of leaders over the years, we've found that the more leaders understand their position as a "son of God," the more effective their leadership.

Sonship has three faces:

1. **Union:** embracing one's identity in Father God as His adopted child and joint heir with Christ

---

3 Matthew 14:23-32
4 1 John 3:1 (KJV)

PART TWO TOWARDNESS

Ben and his team sat around the Father's chair, delighting in His relationship of towardness. Face-to-face in their Father's presence, they formed an identity as valued and validated sons of Father God.[5]

2. Responsibility: submitting to His call and purpose in obedience to Christ, the Firstborn[6]

THE ESSENCE OF SONSHIP

UNION

Embracing identity in Father God as His adopted child and joint heir with Christ

(ROMANS 8:14–17)

RESPONSIBILITY

Submitted in obedience to Christ, the Firstborn, in His call and purpose

(COLOSSIANS 1:18)

AUTHORITY

Entrusted as a steward in Father God's household with anointing to establish Christ's government in the sphere He assigns

(GALATIANS 3:24–28)

©2016 TEACHING THE WORD MINISTRIES

---

5 Romans 8:15-17
6 Colossians 1:18

Christ wanted to extend the government of His household into the HIV/AIDS arena. With Ben's security firmly established as a valued son in God's house, he took the responsibility to obey the call. Instead of moving in human wisdom or pre-conceived expectations, he submitted to the supreme direction of Christ (the Firstborn of the Father's house).

3. **Authority:** entrusted as a steward in Father God's household with anointing to establish Christ's government in the sphere He assigns

After Ben accepted his commission from Christ to serve in this calling, he walked boldly in the anointing—*the empowering presence of the Holy Spirit*—to extend the government of Christ in the HIV arena.

We label these three faces—Union, Responsibility, and Authority—"The Essence of Sonship." As shown in the chart on page 94, our sonship first rests in our union with the Father. Then, out of that Presence-to-presence relationship, responsibility and authority join in alignment with Christ, the Firstborn Son and Head of the Father's household. The three faces together allow us to express our identity and purpose as sons fully.

WHY NOT "SONS AND DAUGHTERS"?

Before we move on, it's important to clarify that when we use the word *sons*, we refer to both women and men. Paul explained, "For you are **all** sons of God through faith in Christ Jesus… **there is neither male nor female**…"[7]

We stress that we celebrate both the male and female aspects of God's image. We're not diminishing the necessity of the feminine perspective in leadership. Please allow us to use the term "son" in a generic sense, just as "man" in Scripture often means "mankind" rather than "male."

Why don't we say "sons and daughters"? In this case, because we're dealing with scriptural references, we deduce the meaning of sonship

---

[7] *Galatians 3:26, 28, bold mine*

PART TWO TOWARDNESS

according to the biblical time period. In Paul's day, *sonship* had three legal characteristics:

1. Image-bearing (union)
2. Stewardship (responsibility with authority) over a portion of the father's household
3. Receiving an inheritance from the father

Both Greek and Hebrew societies generally excluded most women from these benefits of sonship. Culture didn't respect women as image-bearers of their birth parents, but pressed women to marry and meld into the identity of their husband's family. They had little, if any, stewardship authority over any part of their father's household but were considered more as possessions—a step above servants or slaves. Except for a small percentage of daughters from wealthy families, they didn't receive an inheritance. Even if they did, their husband or nearest male relative usually had authority over their bequests.

In referring to our relationship with God, when Paul used the term "sons" and clarified that there is "no male or female" in Christ, he had a reason. He desired his readers to recognize the privileges and responsibilities for both men and women as sons in the Father's household.

UNION

Embracing identity in Father God as His adopted child and joint heir with Christ (Romans 8:14-17)

To onlookers, the stranger who approached the Jordan River at first appeared as normal as anyone else who had responded with conviction to John's preaching. But curiosity rose when John the baptizer resisted the man, not because of insincerity, but because he deemed Him "too worthy" to be baptized. But the man persisted, and John yielded.

Like anyone else, Jesus felt the chill of cold water saturate and weigh down His garment. Like anyone else, Jesus needed to hold His breath when John submerged Him. And when John pulled Him up, He surely had to push away the wet hair that clung to His face so He could breathe again.

But then, something surreal charged the atmosphere. The air rustled in a way that didn't match any weather phenomenon. *Was that a voice, or a strange kind of thunder?* John heard it as a confirmation for his own mission, but more importantly, *Jesus heard it.*

"You are My beloved Son. In You I am well pleased."[8]

A few years later, on the mountain with Peter, James, and John, Jesus again heard His Father's affirmation: "This is My beloved Son, in whom I am well pleased. Listen to Him!"[9]

Teachings on these stories often concern how Father God confirmed to the witnesses that they indeed followed the true Son of God, to whom they should submit. We can also consider them in light of the precious Father-Son relationship between Jesus and His Abba.[10] In the Father's words, we find the essence of what it means to be a "son."

As fully human, Jesus experienced emotional needs—not in the sense of "being needy" or "having lack," as we do. Jesus was God and had no lack. But He simultaneously had a human soul and experienced human emotions.

God created us to find the fullest potential within an affectionate, affirming relationship with our fathers. As fully human, Jesus had a soul that thrived in healthy affirmation from His Father. The Gospels show that Jesus clung to Abba, not only as a member of the Trinity, but as a Son whose Father validated His value and purpose. As the model of a perfect Abba, Father God loved His Son with:

1. **Affirmation** that He belonged
2. **Affection** that confirmed His value
3. **Approval** that validated Him
4. **Authority** that confirmed His purpose

---

[8] Matthew 3:17; Mark 1:11; Luke 3:22
[9] Matthew 17:5; Mark 9:7; Luke 9:35 (NIV)
[10] Abba—*Hebrew term, "Daddy," intimate address to a father*

PART TWO TOWARDNESS

When someone we respect speaks sincere words to confirm our value, most of us can testify to the depth that it touches our soul. When a father speaks these words to his child, they create unshakeable pillars of secure identity as a valuable, beloved person. In the same way, the words Father God spoke touched the depth of His Son's being:

1. **"You are My"**—affirmation that Jesus belonged
2. **"Beloved Son"**—affection that valued Jesus
3. **"In You I am well pleased"**—approval, validation
4. **"Listen to Him!"**—authority that affirmed His purpose

What a beautiful picture of the Trinity's desire for relationship between father and child! We live in a broken world. None of us had perfect parents, and none of us were perfect parents. But Father God invites us into His bosom as our Abba with pure, spotless love.

Through Christ's righteousness, we stand before Father God as His beloved sons. As we allow His cleansing presence to work in us, He wholly meets our need for family, for affirmation, affection, approval, and purpose. *That* is what it means to be a son in Father God's household!

As the chart below shows, in Father's affirmation of Jesus, we find the *Union* dimension of sonship. Father to Son, Face to Face, Presence to Presence. The fullness of towardness. Complete and uncompromised

Jesus/Abba Union Dimension of Sonship

Basic Human Need	Identity Function	Father God's Expression
Prophetic Promise: "Behold! My Servant whom I uphold, My Elect One in whom My soul delights! I have put My Spirit on Him; He will bring forth justice to the Gentiles" —Isaiah 42:1		
Affirmation	Belonging	"You are My…"
Affection	Value	"Beloved…"
Approval	Validation	"I am well pleased."
Authority	Purpose	"Listen to Him!"

©2016 TEACHING THE WORD MINISTRIES

acceptance in each other's love. This is the substance and wellspring of sonship that the Trinity intended at creation. Father extends to us the open invitation to enter in.

Our union with Father God as His sons is vital for eternally effective leadership. Jesus modeled this kind of leadership by leading out of His identity as the Son of His Father. Only in this union do we find pure leadership motives. If we strive to find an identity outside of Father God, our leadership serves a self-centered purpose.

Two biblical expressions help us grasp the significance of Union as it pertains to sonship: image-bearing and inheritance.

Image-bearing

"We found that God has a lot to say about how to run a ministry," Lisa Hosler said when she described the PBL journey on which her Pregnancy Resource Center team had embarked. Their refreshed communion with the Lord transformed not only their hearts, but the entire organization. The genius of Christ's strategy and creative ideas flowed. The direction they received confirmed the biblical principles they already knew. They fulfilled their responsibility as stewards by simply imitating what they "saw" the Father do as they yielded to Him in His presence.

Jesus modeled Presence-Based Leadership: "…the Son can do nothing of Himself, but what He sees the Father do; for whatever He does, the Son also does in like manner."[11] If Jesus fully depended upon His Father's direction for His work on earth, how much more should we? This is how Jesus led: He represented His Father. This is how He designed us to lead: we represent Christ on earth.

First-century culture identified a son not only in relation to his father, but also to his father's ancestors. This explains the long "son-of" lists in Scripture. Their culture considered sons and fathers different expressions of the same seed. The identity of the father and grandfathers melded into the son's identity. They treated the son in light of this.

Sons (especially first-borns) remained in their fathers' occupations. When the father died, the son's work represented his father's work, because

---

11 John 5:19

they literally saw the son as the image of his ancestors.[12] If a man produced no son, it meant the death of the father's seed in his line.

That's why the Pharisees tried to stone Jesus when He told them He was the Son of God. They took this proclamation as evidence enough to crucify Him.[13] In assuming the identity of the Son of God, Jesus had established Himself as God.

What does "finding our identity in Father God" mean for our leadership? Let's look at what it meant for Jesus' leadership.[14] In Jesus' identity as the Son of God, He knew:

1. His purpose (given by His Father)
2. Where He came from (His roots)
3. Where He was going (His vision)

Jesus knew the purpose His Father gave Him

What was Jesus' purpose on earth? The Father had "given Him authority over all flesh, that He should give eternal life to as many as [the Father has] given Him." Throughout His ministry—being about His Father's business; overcoming temptation from Satan; cleansing His Father's house; forgiving; confronting; healing; teaching; yielding to His Father's will for crucifixion—Jesus ministered with confidence in His purpose by identifying as His Father's Son. His steadfast commitment to His Father's purpose kept Him fixed on the finish line.[15]

Father God has designed a specific purpose for each of us that we'll fully realize as we identify with Him. Recognizing that purpose will fix us in the right direction. If God is the One who instilled our purpose in us, then the only way to fully know and fulfill that purpose is through oneness with Him.

---

12 *For example: Deuteronomy 21:17; 1 Chronicles 26:29*

13 *John 10:30-39; 19:7*

14 *See Keith's book,* Healthy Leaders: Developing a Clear Sense of Identity and Direction *for a more in-depth study,* ttwm.org.

15 *John 17:2; Luke 2:49; 4:1-13; John 2:15; Mark 2:5; Luke 23:34; John 38:11; Luke 4:16-30; Matthew 11:5; 9:35; Luke 22:42; 9:53; Hebrews 12:2*

CHAPTER SEVEN SONSHIP: RESPONSIBILITY AND AUTHORITY

In Ben Abell's journey to know God, he has also become more aware of God's purpose for his life. He developed a personal *purpose statement*[16] through an intense prayerful process. Ben discerned that the Father created him to:

> *Unlock and unleash the destinies (purposes and visions) of individuals, ministries, communities, and nations.*

Ben finds his identity, then, as a reflection of the Father's capacity to *unlock* and *unleash*. He discerned his missional call to fulfill that purpose by:

1. Birthing new works.
2. Partnering with others to transition unhealthy environments/cultures into flourishing, healthy environments/cultures.

This embodies the Father's heartbeat for Ben. His responsibility to birth the Hope Springs HIV/AIDS ministry falls well within the lines of this overall purpose. Ben thrives when he functions in his purpose, and his leadership identity springs from the security of resting in God's plan.

Jesus Knew Where He Came From (His Roots)
"I came forth from the Father..."[17]

Our past—the ground in which our roots were established and formed—affects our identity. Whether we try to dismiss it as insignificant or not, our past continues to define us throughout our lives. To grow healthily, we look honestly at our experience and ask hard questions *through the eyes of the Lord*. No matter what our story, the Father has always walked with us, loving us. Questions may include:

- Where was God's place in my past experiences? How does my present response to past experiences shape me now?

---

[16] For an excellent resource for discerning your purpose, see our workbook: *Foundation Stones for Building Your Purpose. See order info on page 239.*
[17] John 16:28

- What was Christ doing in me, and how does that lead to the "big picture" of my life?
- For what do I need to repent and receive the Lord's healing and release? Who do I need to forgive?

To help discern his purpose and mission statements, Ben Abell considered his past and how that shaped and formed him to fulfill God's purpose for the rest of his life.

Jesus Knew Where He was Going (His Vision)
"I leave the world and go to the Father."[18]

A plant is more than roots. It develops from a seed all the way to fruit with more seeds. As we appreciate and understand our past—our roots—we gain insight into where we're headed and the Father's plan for our lives.

In line with the purpose and mission statements, Ben also discerned a picture, or vision, of what he would "see" as he fulfills his purpose:

> *As I Unlock and Unleash the purpose/destiny of people and organizations, thousands upon thousands of people worldwide will:*
>
> - *Begin a relationship with Christ.*
> - *Discover their God-given purpose/destiny.*
> - *Be drawn to God's heart and vision for His creation, which will catalyze transforming revival among the nations as we await Christ's return to His healthy, strong bride.*

Grasping this vision affirms Ben's identity—who God made him to be—providing clear direction for him to lead fully and well with security and confidence. The vision empowers Ben to jump out of the boat and walk on water hand-in-hand with Jesus toward his destiny. Again, Ben didn't just casually compose these statements, but spent prayerful time seeking the Lord and His word.

---

18 *Ibid.*

CHAPTER SEVEN SONSHIP: RESPONSIBILITY AND AUTHORITY

Inheritance

To understand *Inheritance*, the second expression of Union with Father God, we see Jesus as the Firstborn Son. His Father appointed Jesus *"heir* of all things… [and made Him to] sit down at the right hand of the Majesty on high… He has *by inheritance* obtained a more excellent name than [the angels]."[19]

In first-century culture, a father gave *sonship,* or *inheritance,* when he discerned the child was ready to assume stewardship of the household (usually near the age of 30 for Jewish men). Paul says, "…the heir, as long as he is a child, does not differ at all from a slave, though he is master of all, but is under guardians and stewards until the time appointed by the father." Father God confirmed *sonship* on Jesus at His baptism. "This is my beloved Son…"[20]

At this confirmation, a son received the full identity of his father. Everything the father owned belonged to the son.[21] While the father still lived, he had the greater authority, but ideally, he mentored his son to assume his inheritance increasingly.

If a father had more than one son, he divided the inheritance between them. Still, the firstborn received the "birthright" or "double-portion" because he carried the extra responsibility of caring for his parents and their household as well as his own. Jesus is the "Firstborn from the dead," and therefore "in all things He has preeminence."[22]

The nature of the term "firstborn" assumes that "second-borns" exist, and that refers to us—no longer slaves, but sons, and if sons, then heirs of God through Christ.[23]

---

19 *Hebrews 1:2*
20 *Galatians 4:1-2; Matthew 3:17*
21 *Luke 15:31*
22 *Colossians 1:18*
23 *Galatians 4:7*

Of what are we heirs? Scripture records at least four things:

1. **Grace** (I Peter 3:7)
2. **Eternal Life** (Titus 3:7; Hebrews 9:15)
3. **The Kingdom** (government of Christ, James 2:5)

In heaven, we'll fully walk in Christ's eternal government. Right now, even though journeying through a world marred by sin and death, His kingdom already resides *within* us.[24] As heirs, we have full access to His kingdom culture of "righteousness, peace, and joy in the Holy Spirit." Which leads us to the fourth part of our inheritance by which all others are contained:

4. Heirs of the Holy Spirit, the Presence [Face] of God Himself

Recall the conviction of our business leader, Jared: "There has to be a difference between the way I steward everything God has given and the way a guy runs a comparable business without Christ." What makes Christ-followers different (though not "better than") others? We find one difference, but that difference transforms the core of who we are and what we do: *We have the Holy Spirit, the presence of God Himself, living within us.*

"You are not in the flesh but in the Spirit, if the Spirit of God dwells in you. If anyone does not have the Spirit of Christ, he is not His… for as many as are led by the Spirit of God, these are sons of God."

The Holy Spirit's residence within us confirms our sonship (just like the Holy Spirit as a dove confirmed Jesus' Sonship at His baptism), sealing us "for the day of redemption."[25] The Holy Spirit is the living, breathing kingdom of God within us. He is the One who brings us into union with Father and Son. He connects us to the eternal destiny God designed for us. *If we engage in the Spirit's life within us, how could our leadership not be different?*

---

24 1 Peter 1:4; Luke 17:21; Romans 14:17
25 Romans 8:9; John 1:32; Ephesians 4:30

CHAPTER SEVEN SONSHIP: RESPONSIBILITY AND AUTHORITY

RESPONSIBILITY AND AUTHORITY

Responsibility: *Submitted in obedience to Christ, the Firstborn, in His call and purpose (Colossians 1:18)*

Authority: *Entrusted as a steward in Father God's household with anointing to establish Christ's government in the sphere He assigns*

"I will *build* My church," Jesus declared.[26]

The Greek word for *build* is *oikodomeo*. It refers to building a "house" with a sense of emboldening and edifying (as in an edifice). In other words, Jesus is building a house that He names *"ecclesia."*

Christ Himself rules preeminent as Head of the Father's household.[27] He validates His followers as fully affirmed sons. They are partners with Him in household responsibility, "for both He who sanctifies and those who are being sanctified are all one, for which reason He is not ashamed to call them brethren."[28] With a posture of attentiveness, we wait on Him as He authorizes us to discern the will of His Father's house and impart that will on earth.

As a pastor in a large urban church, Ben Abell already had numerous stewardship opportunities. His first responsibility concerned his relationships as a husband and father, and then with the people in his church and outreach in his city. Ben didn't have to accept the added responsibility of developing Hope Springs. But as a son in God's household, he heard His Father's passion for the hearts of suffering people, and Christ commissioning him to receive that responsibility.

Jesus also knew the responsibility His Father had given, and He worked that mission until He was able to tell His Father, "I have finished the work which You have given Me to do."[29] *But how could Christ's work be finished? Weren't there more demons to cast out? More hungry to feed? More lepers to cleanse? More lame to heal, weary to touch, and questions to answer?*

---

26 *Matthew 16:18, italics mine*
27 *Colossians 1:15-18*
28 *Hebrews 2:11*
29 *John 17:4b*

PART TWO TOWARDNESS

Yes, plenty more. Father God cared about all those needs and had a plan to fulfill them according to His eternal wisdom. But Jesus completed the specific mission His Father assigned to Him. As a full member of the Trinity, Jesus *could not* continue ministering to other needs at that time without separating Himself from the Trinity's community of oneness. Instead, Jesus declared, "Not my will, but Yours be done."[30]

Jesus didn't overstep the area of stewardship within His Father's will. Though the Son of God, "He learned obedience by the things which He suffered. And having been perfected, He became the author of eternal salvation to all who obey Him."[31] If Jesus had stepped outside of the Father's purpose, He would not have fulfilled His destiny. "For it was fitting for Him... in bringing many sons to glory, to make the captain of their salvation perfect through suffering."[32]

As the Father gave the Son specific responsibility, so He gives us responsibility for a specific portion of His household—a work to finish. Following Christ's example, we recognize the importance of discerning the Father's direction and what He's given us to steward. He uses every part of our lives to build and train us to fulfill that responsibility with peace, power, joy, and productivity.

On the other hand, the Lord does not require us to take responsibility outside of His destiny for our lives. If we try to steward opportunities the Lord hasn't called us to, not only will we miss our own purpose, but we may hinder the spiritual journey of others. God requires only what He calls us to do.

In the next chapter, we'll continue to explore the authority and responsibility of sonship. We conclude this chapter by touching on the difference between slaves and sons.

---

30 Luke 22:42
31 Hebrews 5:8-9
32 Hebrews 2:10

CHAPTER SEVEN SONSHIP: RESPONSIBILITY AND AUTHORITY

ORPHANS (SLAVES) OR SONS?

Much has unfolded in recent years regarding the difference between an "orphan/slave mentality" or a "son mentality" as it concerns our relationship with Father God.[33] Born as orphans in a sin-sick world, the Father accepts us as sons when we acknowledge Jesus as Master.

Though fully blood-bought children, our behavior may continue to reflect the stubborn residue of an orphan/slave nature. So Father draws us on a journey of transformation, "because you are sons, God has sent forth the Spirit of His Son into your hearts, crying out, 'Abba, Father!'" When we yield to His direction, we increasingly forget our orphan-like behaviors and grow into a sonship mindset, for "you are no longer a slave, but a son, and if a son, then an heir of God through Christ."[34]

In the chart on page 108, we list only a sample of noted differences between orphans and sons. As you review the chart, prayerfully consider where you may currently fall in the journey from slavery to sonship.

CHALLENGE

1. List the areas that God has given you to steward currently as a son in His household. *What specific responsibilities do these areas entail? In what way might you more fully join in union with the Father and the Firstborn to steward this trust?*
2. Review the list in the box on page 98 of how Father God affirmed Jesus as His Son.
   a. *In what ways has Father God affirmed you as His son?*
   b. *In what ways can you extend Father God's affirmation to those in your sphere of influence?*

---

[33] *For more information on orphan/sonship, see Jordan, James,* Sonship: A Journey into Father's Heart, www.FatherHeart.net
[34] *Galatians 4:6-7*

PART TWO TOWARDNESS

c. Review the "Orphan Mentality vs. Son Mentality" chart below. Prayerfully consider where you are in your journey toward becoming a full son of Father God. *In what areas of your life does Father God want to affirm you as a beloved son?*

Orphan Mentality vs. Son Mentality

	Orphan (Slave) Mentality	Son Mentality
View of Relationship with God	God is: Taskmaster, distant, pacifier, crutch	God is: Father with unshakeable love and truth
Self-Image	Self-rejection, feels the need to fight for position and respect	Identity rests in God's uncompromised acceptance
View of Christianity	Rules and laws to follow	Christ's love encompasses all
Demeanor	Confused, insecure, need to "prove" self	Confident, secure, no need to "prove" self
Dependence	Co-dependent on others or striving for self-reliance	Trust and depend on Christ; interdependent relationships
Service	People-pleasers or hiding self-serving motives	Joyful partnership with Christ in His kingdom
Giving Love	Loves conditionally	Loves unconditionally
Receiving Love	Demands love, skeptical of loving gestures, or feels the need to repay love	Fully receives unconditional love from others without expecting or demanding
Responsibility	Victim mentality, irresponsible, demands praise, blames others	Responsible mentality, takes full responsibility for choices, humble spirit
Reaction to Conflict	Demands others to agree with his or her viewpoint	Acknowledges truth with love and care, respects others' views

©2016 TEACHING THE WORD MINISTRIES

3. Review the list you made for the "Activity" at the end of Chapter One of the qualities of an effective leader. *How has your understanding of leadership developed?* Edit the list as appropriate.

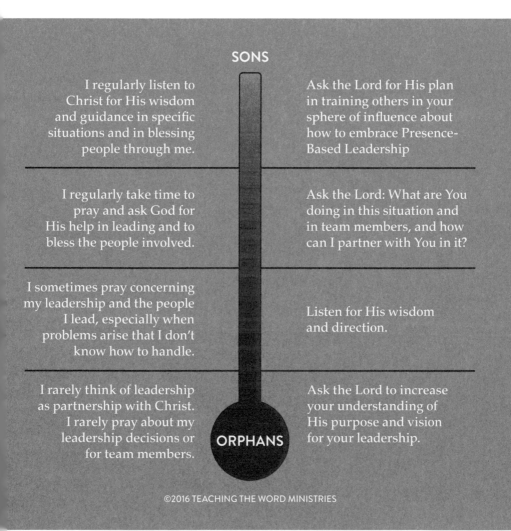

©2016 TEACHING THE WORD MINISTRIES

PART TWO TOWARDNESS

4. Take time in the Lord's presence to consider where you stand on the continuum on page 109. No matter where you rate yourself, ask the Father to draw you closer to His heart and love for you.

LOOKING AHEAD

Many leadership questions concern authority: *who has it, who's over me, and who's under me?* Part of maturing in our responsibility as sons of God concerns the respect for the boundaries of authority. How much misunderstanding and divisiveness could we avoid if we recognized that the core question in many conflicts concerns boundaries of authority and responsibility?

— CHAPTER EIGHT —

Authority to Take Responsibility in Your Metron

WHAT IS AUTHORITY?

Before the opening service of Deeper Still[1] weekend retreats, Karen Ellison[2] and her team stand in a circle, arms locked together. They engage in what has become a custom that precedes every retreat. They find that it releases the power of unity—oneness of heart together in Christ—that permeates ministry during the retreat.

As the lead facilitator, Karen begins:

"Lord God, I declare before You and my teammates that I first and fully submit myself to You. I place myself under Your authority and leadership. Next, I declare my submission to my husband's authority. He has released me and given me his blessing to serve here..." Karen continues by acknowledging the blessing from her congregation and her submission to her Board of Directors. "Thank You, Lord, that I can now fully receive Your anointing on my leadership and that Your protection and grace cover me."

Around the circle, team members in turn make similar commitments to willingly give submission with genuine trust, first of all to God, and then to their spouse, if married, and congregational covering. They further acknowledge, "I trust you, Karen, and I'm honored to serve under your

---

1 *Deeper Still, a ministry of healing to abortion-wounded hearts. See their website:* www.godeeperstill.org
2 *Karen Ellison (her actual name) is the founder and president of Deeper Still.*

authority as you follow the Lord and we together serve His purposes this weekend." In other words, they commit to preserving the unity of their team by honoring God and His structure of authority.

Karen also responds to her co-workers: "Jack, it's an honor to have you serve on this team. I trust you and thank you for your submissive heart. This team is blessed by your gift, and I release you to function fully in your purpose for this retreat."

Not just a ritual, they speak from a place of deep commitment to one another and transparency in relationship. With the attitude of *towardness*, they sense the strong presence of God and deepened love for each other. They verbally honor each other by "submitting to one another in the fear of God."[3]

In the past, confusion over authority had caused tension and confusion during retreats. This allowed the enemy to frustrate their ministry with strife and distraction and dilute their anointing to help people who desperately needed a touch from the Spirit's presence. Karen and her team have found that willing submission to authority increases the Holy Spirit's authority to touch hearts in a relevant, lasting way.

> **Willing submission to authority increases the Holy Spirit's authority to touch hearts in a relevant, lasting way.**

Since they started this practice, Karen says, "We're knit together, and we function as one unit. The Lord can move so powerfully in the leadership team. We've experienced His presence in the retreats like never before."

Now we explore the principles of how to walk in healthy authority as leaders.[4] We elaborate on authority because its use and misuse is a major factor in team function and anointing in ministry.

Understanding authority and submission can resolve or prevent misunderstandings, miscommunications, confusion, and strife. It facilitates the oneness of many parts functioning as a whole in Christ's government of peace and order.[5]

---

3 Ephesians 5:21
4 Note that in Chapter Thirteen, we explore how to honor those who are in authority over us.
5 1 Corinthians 14:40

CHAPTER EIGHT AUTHORITY TO TAKE RESPONSIBILITY IN YOUR METRON

We've found that the following principles of authority allow Presence-based discernment to flow with freedom and sincerity:

1. Exercise authority with an attitude of "submitting to one another in the fear of God."[6]
2. Clearly define and respect the lines of authority.
3. Maintain a balance between authority and responsibility. The person with the responsibility for a certain task or area should also have the authority to make decisions concerning that task or area. And the reverse: Don't give authority to people beyond their responsibility or maturity level.

To understand healthy authority, we first need to understand healthy *submission*. Sometimes we don't like that word "submit" because leaders often abuse authority. We may feel an inner wall of resistance rising to protect ourselves from perverted authority. In Scripture, however, healthy submission is willingly given, not forced.

Submission, translated from the Greek word *hupotasso*, implies "subjection of self" as opposed to a heavy-handed, coerced submission, which some may deduce from the English word.

God created us with the freedom to choose whether or not to submit. As each member embraces the voluntary attitude of submission to the appropriate authority, they open the door for the Holy Spirit to reign with freely flowing peace, harmony, and anointing.

We've found that in most cases, if the person in authority is firm in their God-given purpose and also embraces a sincere attitude of respect toward others, people generally and willingly submit to their authority organically.

In Christian circles, we often use the term "spiritual authority." What does that mean? The phrase "spiritual authority" doesn't occur anywhere in Scripture, but was constructed to express the kind of authority we find in God's government. Diverse Christian traditions, then, define the term in various ways.

---

6 *Ephesians 5:21*

PART TWO TOWARDNESS

Some describe spiritual authority as the power Christ gave His followers "over all demons and to cure diseases…to preach the kingdom of God and heal the sick."[7] To others, the term defines the authority of church elders to lead a congregation, or the authority of the church as an institution. Or to others, spiritual authority refers to a humble, authoritative presence that believers have in a seasoned relationship with God (see page 115).

What was the essence of the authority that people recognized in Jesus when they marveled because He "taught as one having authority, and not as the scribes"?[8]

The Greek word *exousia* is the most common New Testament word translated as "authority." *Exousia* gives a sense of "delegated influence," the privilege, right, or liberty to make decisions in a specific jurisdiction.

Biblical authors generally use other terms to describe an authority that "lords over" or "forcefully rules over" people.[9] But *exousia* suggests a legitimate authority that must remain submitted to the one who delegated it. As in Karen's story, she served with an authority delegated to her by those to whom she declared submission. Others on the team, then, willingly submitted to Karen's authority as they walked in the authority she delegated to them.

To understand Presence-Based Leadership, it's important to clarify how *exousia* works as we lead from the posture of listening to Christ's authority. Misusing authority causes serious problems, but at the same time, we could not accomplish much without appropriate authority.

Everything requires government. Whenever "two or three" gather, we need some sense of how the relationship works in an ordered way. As authority concerns PBL, we recognize that "there is no authority except from God, and the authorities that exist are appointed by God."[10]

The most effective use of leadership authority, then, comes from knowing God and conducting the authority He gives in the way He designs. Godly authority involves the *interaction between authority and*

---

7 Luke 9:1-2
8 Matthew 7:29; Mark 1:22, 27
9 Matthew 20:25; Mark 10:42
10 Romans 13:1

CHAPTER EIGHT AUTHORITY TO TAKE RESPONSIBILITY IN YOUR METRON

submission—stewarding responsibility with full submission to God's will in and under the authority He delegated.

The only legitimate authority on earth is what God appointed. That doesn't mean that abusive authority comes from God. Each leader has his or her choice to wield authority according to either God's design or their own selfish agenda. We discuss the ungodly use of authority a little later. For now, we focus on *exousia* as Scripture presents it.

We could assign the term "spiritual authority" to describe *exousia* as it flows from God, who is Spirit. Whether we carry delegated authority in business, church, family, or service, at the source, it all derives from a Spirit-God.

Spiritual authority flows like water from a mountain spring. At the headwaters, we call it a "spring." As it flows, it takes on different forms such as stream, river, lake, or any number of terms. But it's all sourced from the spring. We also have different kinds of authority according to position, experience, relationship, or ability. But it's all still "spiritual authority" because its headwaters flow from the source of God.

Because spiritual authority is defined in various ways, for clarity's sake as it concerns PBL, we instead use the term "submitted authority." By this we mean willing submission to the authority appointed by God:

> **Submitted Authority:** *the degree to which we align with the measure of truth that the Father entrusts to us to discern and enact Christ's will within our spheres of responsibility.* [11]

The definition has a lot of substance, each part vital to understanding effective authority. We dissect it into four parts:

1. Aligned with the measure of truth
2. Entrusted by the Father
3. To discern and enact Christ's will
4. Within our spheres of responsibility

---

11 Matthew 20:25-26

PART TWO TOWARDNESS

Standing in submitted authority releases the full spiritual support of Christ's anointing and wisdom into a situation. As in Karen's example, when we submit to the authority Christ has established, we place ourselves within the boundaries of Christ's presence. This releases an authority that transcends position or title to establish the rule of Christ's government in our spheres of responsibility.

We now explore the four parts of Submitted Authority.

SUBMITTED AUTHORITY #1: ALIGNED WITH THE MEASURE OF TRUTH

Submitted authority and truth are integral to one another:

> *True authority is founded on Truth.*
> *If it's true, it ultimately has authority.*
> *If it's false, it ultimately does not have authority.*

In answering the religious rulers when they questioned Jesus's authority to speak for God, Jesus proclaimed, "He who sent Me is *true*...I speak to the world those things which I heard from Him."[12] Jesus proved His authority by claiming the truth in His relationship with the Father. It didn't matter what His enemies did or said. Truth emerged as the ultimate authority.

Because Jesus embodies Truth as His own essence, He commands "*all* authority in Heaven and earth... authority over all flesh..."[13] Taking Jesus' example, when we work according to the direction that comes from Trinity Presence, we work in His Truth—submitted authority supported by God. This pertains to those in leadership positions and to those who live by and speak truth in their spheres of influence.

---

12 *John 8:26, italics mine*
13 *John 14:6; Matthew 28:18; John 17:2*

CHAPTER EIGHT AUTHORITY TO TAKE RESPONSIBILITY IN YOUR METRON

We've all seen "authority" that is *not* true. Two types:

1. **Usurping**—unlawfully seizing authority through control or manipulation. Because usurped authority involves people making decisions that are not theirs to make, it is false, and therefore not kingdom authority.
2. **Dominating**—exercising power over someone or imposing one's will on another.

"You know that the rulers of the Gentiles lord it over them," Jesus said, "and those who are great exercise authority **over** them. *But it will not be so among you!* Whoever desires to become great must become a servant…"[14]

Christ's governmental authority has the attitude of servant-hood—first of all to God, and then to those in our spheres of influence. Others have thoroughly explored the understanding of servant leadership, so here we simply clarify that *servant leadership is a reflection of Trinity towardness.*[15]

Even when leaders stand in legitimate positions of authority, if they choose to assert their own control rather than submit to God's will, they fall outside of the boundaries of God's rule and miss the power and wisdom of submitted authority. Leaders who stand secure in godly authority do not demand submission. Yes, they confidently deal with issues that concern their sphere of responsibility, but they recognize that if it's healthy submission, it's willingly given, not demanded.

Godly leaders don't grasp for authority, boast of their authority, or defend their authority. They confidently and humbly carry out their delegated responsibilities with towardness for those in their spheres of influence. If someone resists their authority, they fully process the matter with the person(s) involved, seeking Christ's wisdom with a heart for restoration. They take the right course of action to protect team oneness, but they do so with a heart of mercy for the individual.[16]

---

14 *Matthew 20:25-26, bold and italics mine*
15 *Blanchard, Ken; Hodges, Phil,* The Servant Leader, *2003, Thomas Nelson. Also: Leman, Pentak,* The Way of the Shepherd: Seven Secrets to Managing Productive People *(2004), Zondervan.*
16 *See "Speaking Truth in Love" on page 182.*

How Do We Know What is True?

How do we know what is "true" to align ourselves with the authority that resides in Truth? The Father gave us three ways to know Truth during our stint on earth:

1. **Jesus Christ:** the embodiment of TRUTH[17]
2. **The Holy Spirit:** leads us to Christ who is TRUTH[18]
3. **The Scriptures:** inspired by the Holy Spirit to point us to Christ who is TRUTH[19]

In other words, Jesus reveals Himself to us as Truth through the direct revelation of the Spirit of Truth and the Spirit's inspiration of Scriptural truth.

Scriptural Truth and Spirit Interpretation

What do you do when Barry insists, "We *can't* do that because Scripture says…" but Marcie counters, "But we *can* do it because Scripture says…"? They both claim scriptural authority. Understanding the dynamics of scriptural authority and interpretation can help us handle the truths of scripture with wisdom and a humble attitude.

---

17 *John 1:1-4; 5:38-40; 14:6; 2 Corinthians 1:18-20*
18 *John 14:17; 15:26; 16:13; 20:22*
19 *Psalm 119:160; John 5:39; 2 Timothy 3:15-17; 2 Peter 1:20-21*

CHAPTER EIGHT AUTHORITY TO TAKE RESPONSIBILITY IN YOUR METRON

Scripture points to Christ, who is TRUTH, and has authority in our decisions by outlining boundaries for Christian character and behavior. But we also can have conflicts, or gray areas, in issues such as:

- How much grace to give a delinquent employee
- How to approach evangelism in the workplace
- How to honor women in leadership
- How to vote in a political election
- How to conduct artistic expressions in church services
- How to approach church membership

What we may not realize is that a core cause of the division often doesn't spring from Scripture itself, but from our different approaches to *interpreting* Scripture.

The influence that our culture and experiences have on our interpretation of Scripture are deeply engrained, so passions can intensify. In working with Christian leaders from a variety of traditions, we've come to understand that we can move toward the oneness of Christ when, instead of polarizing our perspectives as *differences*, we see them as *complementary truths* balanced with Christ's wisdom as the fulcrum.

Scripture has authority as it points to Christ, who embodies Truth. "You search the Scriptures, for in them you think you have eternal life; and these are they which testify of Me."[20] In other words, Jesus exposed the religious leaders for resting their hope on their interpretation of Scripture. They missed the point—the Truth that Scripture illuminates is Christ Himself, not a doctrine or teaching. In our effort to stand on the written *words* of God, we may miss the Word of God Himself.[21]

---

20 John 5:39
21 John 1:1

PART TWO TOWARDNESS

COMPLEMENTARY, OR *BALANCED* TRUTH

In his book, *Paradigm Shift in the Church*,[22] Christian Schwarz labels this overall understanding of "complementary truths" as "bipolar ecclesiology." We describe our own version of the pattern here as it pertains to interpreting Scripture, but recommend Schwarz's book for all Christian leaders.

As shown in the chart below, one pole or perspective of an issue is usually "dynamic." It's the side that concerns change, growth, movement, or spontaneity. The "static" side concerns tradition, stability, structure, or ritual. To find Christ's wisdom, we recognize the truth of both perspectives and how they complement each other in the balance of healthy tension.

To apply this model to our topic of interpreting Scripture, we recognize two perspectives. Those who lean toward the "illumination" perspective tend to interpret Scripture through the direct guidance of the Holy Spirit. They listen for the Spirit's voice and direction to reveal what a passage

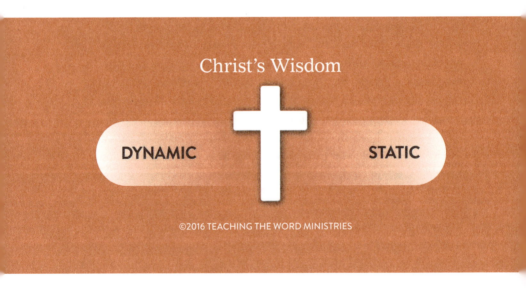

---

22 Schwarz, Christian A., Paradigm Shift in the Church, *ChurchSmart Resources, Carol Stream, IL, 1999.*

means. Believers on this side may include those influenced by the charismatic or Pentecostal movements.

With the "logical deduction" perspective, we have those who believe that because the Holy Spirit inspired Scripture, it already contains everything we need to hear from God, so truth is logically deduced from Scripture. If Scripture doesn't say or show it, then it's not permitted. People who tend toward this pole may be influenced by Reformed or Fundamentalist churches.

Because this graph is a continuum, other styles of interpreting Scripture fall in between the two perspectives. Other methods include:

- If Scripture doesn't forbid it, then we can permit it, as long as it keeps with the unity of the congregation (Evangelical/Traditional perspective)
- Scripture presents allegories to compare with our present situations (Liberal perspective)

If we move too far on either side of the continuum, we fall into error. As shown in the illustration on page 122, too far left means Scripture has no or little authority. This can include *spiritualism* or interpretations centered on something other than Christ, such as Eastern religions or scientific theory. Too far right means *institutionalism*, with doctrine fixed by the logical and/or experiential deduction of the institutionalized church. This allows no openness for spontaneous illumination from the Holy Spirit for specific ways that Scripture applies to people's lives, such as we see in the Pharisees.

No matter what perspective we use to interpret Scripture, it's important to understand that *Scripture itself does not directly teach any of these* **methods** *of interpretation*. (The only exception would be the principle of having "two or three witnesses" to determine a truth.[23])

The Bible says we should study so we can "rightly divide" scriptural truth,[24] but it never gives us a method for rightly dividing. In other words,

---

23 *Matthew 18:16*
24 *2 Timothy 2:15*

PART TWO TOWARDNESS

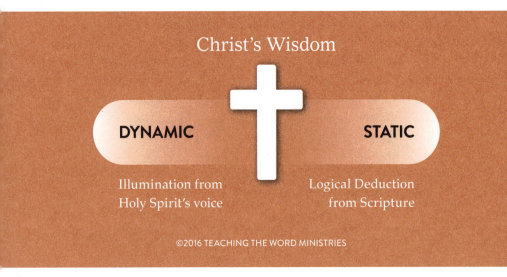

the Bible doesn't prefer one hermeneutical method over another. Scripture claims itself as "given by inspiration of God, and profitable for doctrine, reproof, correction and instruction in righteousness." It declares that the "entirety of His word is truth;" that Jesus came to fulfill it; and that the Holy Spirit inspired it. It says that "no prophecy of Scripture is of any private interpretation."[25] *But how do we know whether our favorite interpretation is a "private" one or one that rightly divides truth?*

Scripture also tells us that the Son of Man Himself was "led by the Spirit." That it's the Spirit who gave life to the words of Jesus. That the Spirit of Truth will guide us into all truth. That "everyone who is born of the Spirit" will move mysteriously like the wind. That those who are sons of God are "led by the Spirit of God." That being led by the Spirit, we're "not under the law." That "the letter kills, but the Spirit gives life."[26] *But how do we know that the impression we sense is actually the Spirit of God?*

The Gospels describe Jesus using both methods of *logical deduction* (Mark 12:35-37) and *Spirit illumination* (Matthew 19:8-9). Paul likewise

---

25 2 Timothy 3:16-17; Psalm 119:160; Matthew 5:17; 2 Peter 1:20-21
26 Matthew 4:1; Luke 4:1; John 6:63; 16:13; 3:8; Romans 8:14; Galatians 5:18; 2 Corinthians 3:6

CHAPTER EIGHT AUTHORITY TO TAKE RESPONSIBILITY IN YOUR METRON

interpreted Scripture in a logical way (I Timothy 5:17-18) and with illumination/allegory or revelatory insight (Galatians 4:22-28).

In PBL discernment, we find wisdom in the center of the two perspectives, where Christ dwells. Christ's wisdom is found in His presence, in the balance where logical deduction and Spirit-inspiration work together.

The Hebraic mindset of "wisdom" embodies that of *interdependent truth*—viewing an issue from many perspectives to know more fully what the core is about. Without moving to the extremes, the two poles of an issue are not opposites, but complementary in Christ.

Like two sides of the same statue, they are two perspectives of the same truth. When Bella looks at the front of a statue, she sees something very different than Steve, who looks at the back, yet the two are seeing the same statue. If they share their views, they'll both have a more complete understanding of the entire statue.

> **As we diligently and carefully study Scripture within the *ecclesia*, we submit to the leading of the Holy Spirit to guide us into the Truth of Christ in each situation.**

As we diligently and carefully study Scripture within the *ecclesia*, we submit to the leading of the Holy Spirit to guide us into the Truth of Christ for each situation. "God has revealed them to us through His Spirit. For the Spirit searches all things, yes, the deep things of God… no one knows the things of God except the Spirit of God. Now we have received, not the spirit of the world, but the Spirit who is from God, that we might know the things that have been freely given to us by God."[27]

Here's a revelatory insight: *None of us knows everything.* "…we know in part and we prophesy in part…for now we see in a mirror, dimly…"[28] In our discernment, instead of speaking with a dogmatic attitude that says, "I'm right, and you're wrong because Scripture says so," we recognize our input as one perspective of truth found in the person of Christ—one side of the statue. We welcome the input of others to help us develop a fuller perspective.

---

27 *1 Corinthians 2:10-12*
28 *1 Corinthians 13:9, 12*

PART TWO TOWARDNESS

As we look to trust and obey Christ, the embodiment of Truth, to reveal His truth in our discernment, our spiritual authority increases. We will discuss how to practically apply such discernment to our leadership teams in Part Four.

SUBMITTED AUTHORITY #2: ENTRUSTED BY THE FATHER

When Jared expanded his business by buying a company in another state, he desired to re-hire as many of the current employees as possible. He discerned to employ everyone except one man, whom I'll call "Len." Len's behavior indicated that his core values were not compatible with those of Jared's company. Jared, then, could not entrust Len with authority to work in the company, and so let him go.

In time, Jared sensed the Spirit leading him to invite Len to breakfast. Len accepted the invitation and wanted to discuss why Jared hadn't hired him. Jared laid out the company's core values, including the standard of honoring God. Len acknowledged the discrepancy between those values and his own. He didn't want to change enough to honor the company standards.

In the meantime, Jared was aware that Len's teenage son worked for the business in another town and had a less-than-desirable attitude toward work. But when a good friend of Len's son was killed in an alcohol-related car accident, some of the Christian men in the company intentionally reached out to help the young man cope with the tragedy. Jared even transferred him to his own location. The men simply loved him in a fatherly way and modeled for him a better lifestyle than what he currently lived. Over the year, Len's son showed remarkable progress in work attitude and ethic.

The story came full circle when recently Jared's company ran a help-wanted ad for a job position. Who would apply but Len, who said he'd never forgotten the breakfast conversation! He'd come to realize the difference that godly leadership made, not only in the company, but also in his son's life. Len had since taken steps to deal with his unhealthy attitudes.

Jared hired Len, entrusting authority to him. Now, as Len is fully immersed in the environment of Presence-Based Leadership, he has in

CHAPTER EIGHT AUTHORITY TO TAKE RESPONSIBILITY IN YOUR METRON

turn incorporated those principles into the agenda of a local community board on which he serves. Jared honored the trust the Father had given him in his sphere of authority and delegated that trust to Len, only as it pleased Father God.

Apply this to your own life by asking the Father: *What specific authority have You entrusted to me in Your government, and how can I honor that trust?* With Christ as our model, we dwell in the Father's Presence, hearing His will in our lives and leadership, receiving and exercising only and all of the authority He entrusts to us.

SUBMITTED AUTHORITY #3: DISCERN AND ENACT CHRIST'S WILL

In Chapters Four and Five, we explored the act of PBL as "Christ-in-the-midst discernment." As "two or three" who gather as the *ecclesia*, we hear Christ's wisdom from heaven and align as His partners to implement His will on earth. As long as we remain submitted to Christ's truth, we'll be serving within the full authority of God.

For example, police officers wear a badge while on duty to indicate that the government has delegated to them the authority to enforce the law. As long as they stay within the boundaries of the law, they have the government's authority supporting them. Legitimate authority won't support them, however, if they try to enforce their own will outside of the law. If they dishonor the law, they're no longer within the authority of the badge, whether they wear it or not.

I know a man who once drove on a freeway taking his wife and another couple to dinner. As he passed an exit, a police officer pulled off the exit in front of him and cut him off. He had to brake to avoid hitting the police car.

I can imagine him smiling as he said, "Watch this." He flashed his lights at the police officer. Sure enough, the officer pulled off the road, and my friend pulled in behind him. He rolled down his window as the policeman walked over to him.

"Can I help you?" The officer asked.

With respectful confidence, my friend said, "Do you know you just cut me off? It could have caused an accident."

The officer said, "Yes, sir. You're right. That was a violation of the law. I apologize."

My friend said, "Thank you," smiled, and rolled up his window. The officer returned to his car, and the two drove on down the highway.

My friend obviously had solid security in his own identity. Not everyone has the courage to do that. He also knew how governmental authority worked. The officer had authority only as he remained within the boundaries of the law. Because he moved outside of those boundaries, my friend had the full authority of the law to pull him over. In the same way, when we submit to and remain under the authority of the Father, we will have the full authority of Christ's will in heaven empowering us.

SUBMITTED AUTHORITY #4: SPHERES OF AUTHORITY–*METRON*

As Karen Ellison's story illustrates, we can avoid problems that occur on leadership teams by clarifying the boundaries of authority and areas of responsibility. Sometimes leadership teams spend too much time debating confusing situations that would otherwise be simple matters if they had identified boundaries.

For clarity and convenience, from now on, when we refer to our "sphere or measure of influence," we use the Greek word *metron*. *Metron* conveys this definition or, in our case, "the measure or portion of authority." For example, a farmer has a certain amount of land. He has the authority to decide what crops to plant in the fields within the measure of his acreage. That's his *metron*. He doesn't have authority to decide what his neighbors plant in their fields because that's not his metron.

CHAPTER EIGHT AUTHORITY TO TAKE RESPONSIBILITY IN YOUR METRON

The Apostle Paul used the word *metron* to explain the measure of his authority in the Corinthian church. I quote Paul's passage here, inserting the word *metron* where it appears in the Greek text.[29] Though not an easy read, it merits the focus to glean the meaning of metron:

> *For we dare not class ourselves or compare ourselves with those who commend themselves. But they, metron-ing [measuring] themselves by themselves, and comparing themselves among themselves, are not wise. We, however, will not boast beyond metron, but within the metron of the sphere [boundaries] which God appointed us—a metron which especially includes you. For we are not overextending ourselves (as though our authority did not extend to you), for it was to you that we came with the gospel of Christ; not boasting of things beyond metron, that is, in other men's labors, but having hope, that as your faith is increased, we shall be greatly enlarged by you in our sphere [boundaries], to preach the gospel in the regions beyond you, and not to boast in another man's sphere [boundaries] of accomplishment.*[30]

Paul understood that he had a measure of authority and responsibility that covered the Corinthian church. This church was within Paul's metron because Paul submitted to the authority and difficult responsibility God had given him to father the church spiritually. God has also measured to each of us a metron of authority and responsibility. Authority is the power to carry out our responsibility within our *metron*.

We're not to "think of ourselves more highly than we ought, because God has given everyone "the *measure* [*metron*] of faith." We're to stay within our own measure because "we have many members… but all the members do not have the same function…"[31] Christ delegates to us the authority to follow His call within our own metron, but not outside those boundaries.

---

29 *In the Greek text, the word* metron *occurs in its various grammatical forms and tenses. For simplicity's sake, I write "metron" wherever the Greek base word occurs.*
30 *2 Corinthians 10:12-16*
31 *Romans 12:3-4*

PART TWO TOWARDNESS

Father God gave Jesus Christ the metron of "all authority in heaven and earth" so that "at the name of Jesus every knee shall bow... and every tongue confess that Jesus Christ is Lord."[32]

Why did Jesus receive this authority?

Consider the time when James and John boldly asked Jesus if they could sit beside Him on His throne.[33] How did Jesus respond? "Are you able to drink the cup that I drink, and be baptized with the same baptism that I am...?"

Here Jesus revealed how He received His own authority. He obeyed the responsibility His Father had given Him to suffer (drink the cup) and submit to the delegated authority of Spirit-fire baptism.[34] Jesus indicated that James and John would, indeed, walk the path of obedience through suffering and fire baptism, and so would receive authority, though not necessarily in the way they desired right then. Anyone who has walked in godly leadership for even a short period will agree that accepting the mantle of authority is literally accepting the responsibility of obedience through suffering.

Jesus gave us the precedent for accepting positions of authority: in submission to His Father's will, Jesus received the weighty responsibility to win back the authority humankind had handed to Satan. Through His sacrifice, Jesus enabled people to take up the authority once again to fulfill their purpose within their metrons. Christ's submission to the responsibility of sacrificial suffering gave Him the legal authority overall.[35]

As Jesus did when He accepted delegated authority, we also have responsibility to sacrificially empower the people within our metron to fulfill their purposes within the organization and in their lives. That's the essence and joy[36] of godly leadership. Of course, we need to walk out a healthy balance of what that sacrifice entails for our own situations, a concept we continue to explore in the remainder of this book.

---

32 *Matthew 28:18; Philippians 2:10-11*
33 *See Mark 10:35-40*
34 *Matthew 3:11*
35 *Hebrews 5:8-9*
36 *Hebrews 12:2*

CHAPTER EIGHT AUTHORITY TO TAKE RESPONSIBILITY IN YOUR METRON

THE BALANCE OF AUTHORITY AND RESPONSIBILITY

Simply put, we delegate the measure of authority that correlates with the responsibility. If we assign responsibility without also delegating and honoring the authority that's equal to it, we undermine rather than empower leadership. Likewise, assigning (or assuming) authority that exceeds the responsibility, we have unbalanced, heavy-handed leadership.

"I urge you, brethren," Paul wrote the Corinthians, "you know the household of Stephanas… that they have devoted themselves to the ministry of the saints—that you also **submit** to such, and to everyone who works and labors with us."[37]

For example, you're a leader in a congregation, and you give someone responsibility as an usher. You arrive at a service that is especially crowded, and people are waiting for the usher to seat

> The level of authority we delegate should fit the level of responsibility that person carries.

them. You need to respond to the usher's authority and wait to be seated, rather than push ahead and seat yourself, even though you're the one who delegated the authority. When you make a decision that concerns a metron of someone within your own metron, honor the authority that equals the person's responsibility by collaborating with him or her as appropriate.

A leader we know once asked a volunteer to research a certain product to determine which would best suit the organization's needs. The volunteer already had a full schedule. Still, because of his interest and knowledge of the product, he made time to invest in the project. But the leader failed to think of his request as "delegating responsibility with the authority to make a decision." He casually mentioned the project to another volunteer and also asked that person to research the best product.

So, unknown to each other, the two volunteers gave time and energy to the project because they assumed the weight of the decision was their own. The results? One volunteer settled on a product vastly different than the other's choice. The leader quickly chose one. Naturally, the other volunteer

---

37 1 Corinthians 16:15-16, bold mine

felt disrespected and that he had wasted a lot of time. Seeds of mistrust against the leader were planted in him.

This illustrates the effect of unclear balance of responsibility and authority—not to mention the disregard toward the volunteers. The leader could have better managed the situation by prayerfully selecting the volunteer(s), praying together to discern the best way to conduct the product research and how the decision would finally be made. Even though the leader had the short-term results he wanted, the offset balance between responsibility and authority resulted in an unwanted breach of trust in his leadership.

Christ calls us as leaders to extend the peace and truth of His Father's household by commissioning us to govern metrons of submitted authority and responsibility. Leading with Christ in-our-midst, we discern the Lord's will and accept responsibility to obey as He anoints us with His delegated authority.

CHALLENGE

1. Thoughtfully consider the following concepts, and answer the questions below:
    - Spiritual authority
    - Submission
    - Submitted or delegated authority
    - Responsibility balanced with authority
    a. *How is the Lord working in your understanding of authority, submission, and responsibility or confirming what you already know?*
    b. *Describe how you deal with boundaries of authority in your metron. How might the Lord be directing you to address these issues in your metron further?*
    c. *In what way might the Lord be confirming, adjusting, illuminating your understanding of authority and submission?*
    d. *Have you felt any "walls" or "defenses" rising as you grapple with the information in this chapter? Discuss your thoughts with others to work through the issues.*

— CHAPTER NINE —

Authority and Responsibility as Kings and Priests

COMMISSIONED TO SERVE AS KINGS AND PRIESTS

Jared and several other leaders in his industry were concerned about a legislative situation that affected their businesses in a major way. They handled the issue delicately, because any action would impact several different layers within the industry. They knew of a specific state representative who could have a strong influence on the matter, but he was hard to reach, and no one could connect with him—until God moved.

Jared was invited to a gathering that celebrated the passage of an unrelated industry bill. Without connivance on Jared's part, he found himself standing side-by-side in line with the state representative that he had wanted to contact. Jared struck up a conversation with him about the matter of concern. From this conversation, Jared was invited to meet with the representative. Jared subsequently remained in contact. He and others continued to pray over the issue, listening for God's wisdom and solution.

In the process of working with the representative, the Spirit impressed Jared to contact his "arch" business competitor. Though their marketing adamantly rivaled each other in day-to-day operations, because the issue concerned both, Jared asked his opponent to join him in meeting with the representative. Since then, Jared has contacted additional competitors to join the conversation. Together they've spent many hours grappling through the issue for the good of the whole industry.

As Jared remains Christ-centered in this situation, the Lord uses Him to influence the government with a spiritual authority submitted to Christ. Through Jared's obedience, Christ builds His kingdom government within the industry. Note that Jared didn't push his own scheme with arrogance or manipulation. As he waited on God and walked in obedience, he grew as a person who wielded submitted authority, even among politicians.

Kings

As illustrated in Jared's story, Christ commissions His followers to establish His government—His *metron*—on earth. In this sense, we walk as kings under the authority of the King of kings.[1] As we hear and obey His will, Christ delegates to us kingly authority for the responsibilities within our metron. Because that metron concerns people, whether over, under, or beside us, we embark on this journey as honorable kings who embrace towardness as the attitude of authority. Neither under false humility nor by usurping authority, we're simply responsible for the authority Christ delegates.

Priests

Christ also commissions us to serve as priests. Jesus is the one and only High Priest, and we're priests under His authority. He "has made us kings and priests to His God and Father…"[2] As *kings*, we have delegated authority to make decisions that establish Christ's government in our metrons. As *priests*, we have delegated authority in two respects:

1. To represent people to God
2. To represent God to people

---

1 *Revelation 1:6*
2 *Hebrews 9:11; Revelation 1:6*

CHAPTER NINE AUTHORITY AND RESPONSIBILITY AS KINGS AND PRIESTS

Hebrew priests represented people to God by interceding for them. For example, by bringing the blood offered on behalf of their sins before God's presence at the Mercy Seat and declaring God's forgiveness. They represented God to people by declaring to them the words that God spoke. For example, when the priest Eli declared God's word to Hannah that He would grant her petition,[3] or when Ezra reestablished the reading of the scriptures.[4]

In the PBL sense, we're not referring to the office of priest as in some Christian traditions. Instead, in a spiritual sense, we use priest to describe the role of all believers. "You are a chosen generation, a royal priesthood..."[5] Our motive in representing God to people and people to God is to draw others into relationship with Jesus, so they go directly to Him to confess and receive forgiveness for sins and develop their own interactive relationships with Him.

Through Jesus' sacrifice, we have access to the circle of Trinity fellowship. As one with Christ, we stand in His righteousness to extend Trinity fellowship to others and bring them into that circle. To walk in PBL, we accept this assignment in our everyday leadership. We represent God by showing Christ's character and extending His love. In another sense, we can affirm people in their repentance by agreeing with Jesus' declaration that, indeed, "your sins are forgiven."[6]

---

[3] *Leviticus 16:16; I Samuel 1:17*
[4] *Nehemiah 8*
[5] *1 Peter 2:5*
[6] *Luke 5:22-24; Mark 2:9-10*

PART TWO TOWARDNESS

As represented in the illustration above, we can accomplish both directions of priesthood—representing God to people and people to God—in listening prayer (or intercessory prayer).

As the Holy Spirit impresses us to pray for others, especially those in our metrons, we represent them and their needs to God. We intercede for them, not by praying our own will or strategies (which would be a form of control or manipulation) but by listening for what the Spirit is praying and agreeing with Him, "because the Spirit intercedes for the saints in accordance with God's will."[7] In our intercession, as we hear the will of God in heaven, then we represent Him on earth by agreeing with Him and declaring His will in prayer or proclamation.[8]

---

7   Romans 8:26-27. For an in-depth understanding of listening prayer, order Keith's audio: Prayer: Intimacy to Victory, *from our website (see page 8).*

8   *For deeper insight on intercessory prayer, order Keith's audio,* Prophetic Intercession, *from our website (see page 8).*

Representing our God by declaring His word is not to be taken lightly, because we're relating to souls who are precious in His sight. We recognize our own limitations to perfectly hear the Shepherd's voice and remain accountable to the *ecclesia*.

FORGIVING AND RETAINING SIN

In His discourse with the disciples after His resurrection, Jesus said something interesting that theologians have attempted to explain for centuries:

If you forgive the sins of any, they are forgiven them.
If you retain the sins of any, they are retained.[9]

But who can forgive sins but God alone? Formerly in Jewish tradition, only God had the authority to forgive sins. But Jesus extended that authority (another radical act) to the sons of God—to you and me—to use in our daily discernment.

What does this authority mean for us? "Forgiveness" is easy to understand. If we forgive, we're forgiven.[10] Forgiveness is part of our *priestly* responsibility in God's kingdom. We represent God to others, extending His forgiveness that breaks the power of sin in their lives. Recall that the keys of "binding and loosing" have to do with forgiveness—*to loose* means *to forgive*.

What does "retain" mean? Some may deduce that retain means "refuse to forgive," but this is an incorrect assumption. In Greek, "retain" is a military term, *krateo*, which literally means to "seize, obtain, or take." When a conquering army brought the enemy's territory under their power, they "retained" authority by removing the former government and establishing their own in its place. They "seized" the government and culture of the defeated leaders to "keep" or retain their own in its place. When Jesus gave His disciples permission to retain sin, He gave them *kingly* authorization

---

9 John 20:22-23
10 Mark 2:7; Luke 5:21-24; Mark 11:25

PART TWO TOWARDNESS

to remove the power of the control, or root, behind the sin, and to establish the government of Christ in its place.[11]

At one time, I worked with a church leadership team whose congregants often commented that they yearned for "deeper" teaching. This perplexed the pastoral team because they knew the teaching was scripturally in-depth and relevant to real life. When we took time to seek the Lord's wisdom concerning the matter, He helped us recognize a long-term division between two sets of leaders: those who had the motivational gift of teaching, and those with the gift of administration.[12]

Instead of using their gifts to complement each other, they chose to defend their own passions and positions, causing disunity in the relationship. We recognized that this division had carried down through several generations of leaders in this church. God showed us that the congregants sensed the spiritual tension even though they didn't directly pinpoint it. The root of their heart cry was for unity among the leaders, rather than for deeper teaching.

With the sin of strife no longer hidden, we took the responsibility and authority that Christ delegated to retain the sin spiritually. First, we corporately repented for the strife. We declared that the root of this division be removed from power in the congregation. Leaders repented for their own involvement in the sin and established a new way of supporting each other in oneness. After that, the congregation expressed a new appreciation for the quality of teaching.

Retaining sin means a change of order. By declaring and obeying the truth of Christ, we remove the sinful patterns and mindsets to establish Christ's rule. Retaining sin means a change in government, habit, process, and/or culture. Christ delegates priestly and kingly authority to us to extend His forgiveness and retain the spiritual "government" of situations to align them with Christ's government.

---

[11] *Keith explains "retain" in detail in* Binding and Loosing: Keys of the Kingdom of God. *Order from our website (see page 8 for information).*
[12] *Romans 12:6-8*

CHAPTER NINE AUTHORITY AND RESPONSIBILITY AS KINGS AND PRIESTS

At a pastoral counseling session, Pastor Erick listened to a woman share about her challenging experiences at a former church. As she spoke, Erick realized he didn't know from his own experience how to help her toward healing, but he kept his ears tuned to the Holy Spirit.

At some point, the Spirit impressed him with a mental image of a "cloud" over her whole family. The issue of her family had not previously surfaced during the conversation, so Erick explored with the woman how certain negative mindsets—"ways of thinking and reacting" (scripture calls them "strongholds"[13]) pass down through the generations by parents modeling them to their children.

His word deeply touched the woman's soul. She took notes and couldn't write fast enough. The hidden mindset of unhealthy family patterns was exposed. This new light of truth brought godly transformation into her life. The picture Erick sensed was not only God's truth for the moment, but through the Holy Spirit's guidance, Erick was training the woman to develop a presence-based lifestyle. By aligning with the direction of the Holy Spirit, Erick "retained" the sinful stronghold, established God's government in its place, and trained the woman to do the same.

KINGDOM MINDSET

Early on, our PRC director, Lisa, assumed all of the speaking engagements for the ministry's abstinence program. She spoke well and inspired students toward sexual integrity. It made sense for Lisa to serve in that way, having written and developed the abstinence program. But through the process of learning to rest in the Lord, she sensed God calling others to share in speaking. She asked another employee to take on the role of abstinence education. As Lisa listened to her speak, the woman delighted the student assembly. With her acting background, she engaged them in a wonderful way.

---

13 *2 Corinthians 10:4-5*

PART TWO TOWARDNESS

Resting in the Lord, Lisa felt His peace and grace in the situation, with no jealousy or desire to limit this woman's opportunity to validate her own career. The Lord had provided an open door for the new speaker and much needed time for Lisa. Leading from the perspective of a kingdom mindset, Lisa saw the bigger picture and realized, "It's not about me. It's about the Lord and building His kingdom."

Developing a kingdom mindset embeds us in the reality of "eternal time"—that place where "He has put *eternity into the hearts of men...*"[14] Instead of wearing blinders that keep us focused on our own problems, pleasures, or interests, in the Trinity's presence, the blinders come off. He unfolds His eternal plan in an eternal community and our place in it.

This perishable earthly realm prepares us for our eternal reign with Christ as kings and priests.[15] What we do and say, how we live and breathe, is not just "unto us," but ripples with connections to each other, to our culture, to God, and throughout eternity. The truth that stuns us into reverent awe of our holy God remains: He intentionally strategized for our partnership with Him in His eternal plan.

Sometimes we so desire success in our leadership, and yes, with the motive to please Him and serve others, but we strive to succeed in our own ideas and leave Christ behind. We do and do and study and study and pray and pray and serve and serve to build His government. Still, we forget to report to the Head, the Master, the King of this kingdom.

We don't have the wisdom to lead in a way that produces eternal fruit. We need His wisdom. Focusing our inner attention on Christ, seeking to understand things from His perspective, waiting on His wisdom, through listening prayer, we begin to view everything in a different light. Our patience grows. Mundane tasks are full of life because we see the eternal value, the bigger picture, how every detail helps build Christ's community. Those mundane tasks are not so mundane after all!

---

14 *Ecclesiastes 3:11, italics mine*
15 *Revelation 1:6; 5:10*

CHAPTER NINE AUTHORITY AND RESPONSIBILITY AS KINGS AND PRIESTS

In His presence is fullness of joy![16] This is not just a line of poetry written to combat a sour mood, but a solid truth. By touching His presence, we touch joy, patience, peace, wisdom, righteousness, and strength, and extend that into our metrons. Taking time to wait on God, in His word and Presence, brings deep inner peace. A sense of eternal purpose and security. A place where we know, deep down, "that all things [*really do*] work together for good to those who love God, to those who are the called according to *His* purpose." "…the government will be upon His shoulder … of the increase of *His* government and peace *there will be* no end."[17]

CHALLENGE

1. *In what situations in your own life has God called you to act as a king? A priest?*
2. *In what capacity have you established Christ's government in your sphere of authority?*
3. *What was the result of representing people to God or God to people in your own life?*

LOOKING AHEAD

In the first part of this book, we explored the *Act* of PBL, discerning wisdom from Christ, who is present in our midst. In Part Two, we learned to embrace the *Attitude* of towardness, cultivating a culture of honor toward the Trinity and each other as His sons with responsibility and authority in His household. We now move to Part Three, where we explore the *Art* of Presence-Based Leadership, the essence of *Presence*: leading from a posture of rest in and from the circle of Trinity fellowship.

---

16 Psalm 16:11
17 Romans 8:28; Isaiah 9:6-7

— PART THREE —

Presence

THE ART OF PRESENCE-BASED LEADERSHIP

Presence-Based Leadership
Guiding others with a posture of submission
to wisdom discerned from Christ's presence

The Art

PRESENCE
Leading from a posture of rest in and
from the circle of Trinity fellowship

The Attitude

TOWARDNESS
Cultivating a culture of prayer and honor

The Act

CHRIST-IN-THE-MIDST DISCERNMENT
Stewarding the metron of sonship within the ecclesia

©2016 TEACHING THE WORD MINISTRIES

— CHAPTER TEN —

Our Presence Transformed by Christ's Presence

OUR PRESENCE

At a local church conference, the late Dallas Willard[1] told a story from his years as the Director of the School of Philosophy at USC Los Angeles. A doctoral student selected a Christianity-based thesis for his dissertation. The student's non-Christian supervisor refused to approve a thesis based on a Christian Worldview. The student appealed to Dallas for help and set up a meeting with himself, Dallas, and the supervisor.

During the meeting, Dallas remained in an attitude of listening prayer and spoke almost no words. The supervisor talked on and on about why he would not approve the thesis. Then, something interesting happened. During his speech, the supervisor actually talked himself into accepting the thesis without Dallas needing to persuade him.

Because Dallas submitted his will to Christ, he opened the door for the presence of Christ to have authority in the meeting. Dallas' presence became one with Christ's presence. Simply by submitting to the Spirit's presence, Dallas brought the authority of Christ's government into the situation.

---

1 Dallas Willard authored several books, including The Spirit of the Disciplines; Renovation of the Heart; and The Divine Conspiracy.

PART THREE PRESENCE

WHAT IS PRESENCE?

In his book, *Invisible Imprint*,[2] Richard Dobbins defines "presence" as: *the invisible impact we feel when we're around certain people, places, or things, whether positive or negative.*

God wired us for spiritual connection. Trinity *towardness* happens within *community*. We can't escape the fact that our presence spiritually affects others. God created us for interdependence. Though sin hinders that, the deeper we commune with and in Trinity Presence, the closer our connections to each other conform to His original design.

As we explore *Presence*, we begin by evaluating our current "presence." Take a moment to rate yourself on the following scales honestly. Your answers help reveal your "presence."

What does someone feel when I walk into the room or when they spend time with me?

1 MORE RESISTANT	MORE ATTRACTED
2 MORE FRUSTRATED	MORE AT PEACE
3 MORE DEFENSIVE	MORE ENCOURAGED

©2016 TEACHING THE WORD MINISTRIES

---

2 Dobbins, Richard D. *Invisible Imprint: What Others Feel When in Your Presence. Deep River Books, 2002.*

CHAPTER TEN OUR PRESENCE TRANSFORMED BY CHRIST'S PRESENCE

How is "presence" formed? Richard Dobbins explains that throughout our lives, we make choices in response to stimuli or circumstances. The two ways we choose concern *reactive* or *active* choices. Many things happen to us that we can't control, but as adults, we can control our response. Our accumulative choices over time shape our character and our overall presence.

Reactive choices happen when we *automatically react* to circumstances without checking ourselves. **Active choices** occur when we *willfully decide* how to respond.[3] If our habitual reactions are anxious, controlling, or angry, we develop a presence that *negatively* affects those around us. If our choices are more peaceful, liberating, or loving, we develop a presence that *positively* affects those around us.

Often our past circumstances—especially the family environment in which we were raised—affect whether our *reactive choices* are positive or negative. Emotional pain that we haven't yet dealt with often festers beneath the surface of our behavior. Whether we like it or not, "out of the abundance of the heart, the mouth speaks."[4]

We can take responsibility for our choices by understanding how our reactions may be shaped by heart-wounds and deal with those wounds as appropriate. As we allow the Lord to resurface, cleanse, and heal emotional pain, then, instead of reacting to circumstances in an uncontrolled way, we can train ourselves to respond with Christ's attitude.

We react according to what degree our souls embrace one of three different viewpoints:

1. Satan's perspective (revenge, deception, destruction)
2. Self-centered perspective (self-pity, self-protection, control, manipulation, blaming, justifying)
3. Christ's perspective (peace, mercy, truth, joy, humility, forgiveness, meekness, self-control)

---

3 Dobbins, Richard D., Ibid.
4 Matthew 12:34

PART THREE PRESENCE

The viewpoint we regularly embrace affects our overall presence. We aim to adopt Christ's perspective. If we prayerfully discern the reality of our responses, whether Satan, self, or Christ, we can take steps toward healing that further transforms our presence into that of Christ's.

TRANSFORMING OUR PRESENCE INTO CHRIST'S PRESENCE

Jared describes the evening he returned home from work, overwhelmed with impossible financial difficulties that resulted from the tumultuous economy.

"I thought I was drowning," he said. "I would normally get a cup of coffee, go out to eat, or watch TV. But this time, I tilted back in my chair and said, "Lord, I'm a dry vessel. I have nothing; I can do nothing. Fill me with Your wisdom and faith."

Jared quoted Scriptures that rose to his mind: "be anxious for nothing… in everything give thanks…" He sang songs to encourage his faith. He meditated on things that are "true, just, pure and of good report… building himself up on most holy faith, praying in the Holy Spirit."[5]

"In two hours, I was in a different place," Jared said. By embracing God's eternal presence, his perspective significantly changed. The difficulties still existed, but no longer reigned as overwhelming. As he invested time in the Lord's presence, submitted to kingdom perspective, Christ's presence became Jared's presence. He found wisdom to confidently handle the situation with faith in the Lord's purpose and provision.

Trinity Presence transforms us from the inside out if we choose to dwell there. Scripture is filled with stories of people who were somehow changed in the presence of God. For example, after Moses encountered Yahweh at the burning bush, he returned home a changed man—no longer just a herder of sheep, but the ruler of an emerging nation.

At first, Moses approached the Lord with fear, and like Adam, tried to hide from God's presence. But Yahweh drew him close. He transformed the shy shepherd into a world-class ambassador, the bearer of a

---

5   Philippians 4:6; 1 Thessalonians 5:18; Philippians 4:8; Jude 1:20

CHAPTER TEN OUR PRESENCE TRANSFORMED BY CHRIST'S PRESENCE

miracle-producing staff, the man to whom Yahweh spoke "face to face, as a man speaks to his friend."[6]

Likewise, the Lord's presence transformed Saul into the Apostle Paul; from a persecutor to one being persecuted for Christ's sake, from a man who built his identity on intellect, heritage, and accomplishment, to a man who counted it all as dung to identify with Christ.[7]

At first, these examples may seem radical—different than what ordinary people like us would experience. "But we all with unveiled face, beholding as in a mirror the glory of the Lord, are being transformed into the same image from glory to glory, just as by the Spirit of the Lord."[8] An encounter with Trinity Presence leaves us transformed. We walk as friends of God.[9] As leaders, we must allow the Holy Spirit to transform our presence, so our active choices bring His peace, life, truth, love, and faith into the lives of people.

When we publicly confirm someone's calling to leadership through "laying on of hands,"[10] it's more than just ritual or routine. If we intentionally yield to the Lord's presence in the moment, He brings transformation. Scripture records the precedent that concerns leading and making decisions from and in God's presence:

1. **General leadership:** Moses would not lead the people without the presence of the Lord. He said to Yahweh, "If Your presence does not go with us, do not bring us up from here" (Exodus 33:15).
2. **Succession:** Moses *transferred leadership* to his successor, Joshua, in the presence of the Lord at the Tent of Meeting (Deuteronomy 31:14-23).
3. **Strength and Encouragement:** Joshua received courage as an emerging leader. The promise that the Lord's presence would be with him enabled him to assume more responsibility (Joshua 1:5, 9, 17).

---

6   Exodus 3:6; 33:11
7   Acts 9:1-25; Philippians 3:8
8   2 Corinthians 3:18
9   John 15:15
10 1 Timothy 4:14; 2 Timothy 1:6

4. **Discernment:** Joshua discerned God's plan for how to distribute the land to the tribes of Israel as they settled the Promised Land (Joshua 18:1, 8; 19:51).
5. **Confirmation:** God confirmed leadership responsibility by drawing individuals into His presence (Jeremiah 30:21).
   a. **Wholeness:** *Approaching God brings wholeness.*
   b. **Affirmation:** *God's presence distinguishes the leader from the people.*
   c. **Anointing:** *The Spirit's anointing is the power and presence of God.*
   d. **Transformation:** *God's presence changes leaders.*
6. **Validation:** God validates genuine leadership authority in the face of rebellion or when leadership is undermined (Numbers 16:5).

As you read scripture in your own study, continue to take note of how biblical leaders interact with the presence of God and how it affects their leadership.

I had ministered for many years out of a motivational gift of teaching, and I enjoyed the process of study and research. I arranged and presented truth in a highly structured manner of outlines and word studies. But by 1980, I experienced a growing sense of dryness and lack of fulfillment. Sharing the results of my study no longer sparked life. I desired something more.

During this period, several people had responded to my problem-solving insights by affirming in me a prophetic motivation. Because I identified with being a teacher, however, I didn't connect with their affirmation. Later, when leaders of my congregation invited me to present a workshop session, I prepared an outline as usual. But I wasn't satisfied with my preparation. As the morning progressed with various activities for the leaders, my desperation increased. I yearned for the capacity to teach in a life-giving way.

My presentation was scheduled immediately after lunch. During the lunch break, I sat with a good friend who had a gift for encouragement. He expressed excitement about what I would have to share. But inside, I felt empty with very little to give. My friend wasn't aware of this inner anguish.

Fifteen minutes before the workshop, I retreated outside and walked up the driveway toward a private home in a wooded area. I prayed and cried out to God for something fresh. I felt that with all integrity, it wouldn't be right to teach from this state of dryness.

As I came to the edge of the woods, to avoid stepping onto the homeowner's property, I knelt on the macadam, lifted my hands and prayed, "Lord unless you give me something to say, I have nothing to say." I purposed in my heart that I would tell the group that I have nothing to say and then sit down so I wouldn't waste their time.

When I took that posture in prayer, I sensed a spiritual "weightiness" come down on me and rest on my shoulders. I believe this would be similar to the presence of God as described in Scripture, a *weighty* anointing.[11] I encountered God and sensed that He imparted something to me.

At one o'clock, I returned to the meeting room for my presentation. After someone introduced me, I went to the podium with my prepared notes. As I began to speak, I sensed a new authority in my voice, a fresh passion, what I would describe as a life-giving river of truth flowing spontaneously from my heart and mind.

In effect, I had received a prophetic anointing from the Lord. I no longer passively followed my prepared notes, but the notes became markers along the highway of truth. As I spoke, I was in tune with how the hearers were receiving the words. I sensed the Lord's wisdom and insight to speak in a way that they could receive truth from the Holy Spirit directly into their souls.

When I sat down, I realized I was a different kind of teacher than when I had entered the room that morning. As more teaching opportunities followed, it became clear that the prophetic anointing had integrated with the teaching anointing. Others began to recognize me as a prophetic teacher. The encounter with the presence of the Lord changed me and my presence.

THE HOLY SPIRIT WITHIN US

The Spirit's presence in us is not just a doctrine, but a reality, and the difference is genuine. God has revealed His secrets "to us through His Spirit…we

---

11 Numbers 14:5; 16:22; 20:6; 1 Kings 18:39; 2 Corinthians 4:17; Revelation 7:11

have received…the Spirit who is from God, that we might know the things that have been freely given to us by God…not which man's wisdom teaches, but which the Holy Spirit teaches."[12]

The Spirit is the presence of God, the anointing, working in and through us. *How can we recognize His work?* Consider how He manifests Himself in your life and leadership team with the following exercise:

Identify a way the Holy Spirit has manifested Himself to you through one or more of these characteristics:

- He leads (Romans 8:14; Galatians 5:18)
- He fills (Acts 2:4, 17-18; 6:3; 7:55; 10:38)
- He brings revelation of God (John 14:17)
- He speaks (Acts 10:19; 11:28; 13:2; 21:11)
- He testifies of Christ (John 15:26; Acts 5:32; Hebrews 10:5)
- He speaks what He hears Christ speaking (John 16:13)
- He helps us, teaches us (John 14:16, 26)

In what ways has the Holy Spirit shaped your character or spiritual growth through the following attributes?

- He cleanses and justifies (Romans 15:16; I Corinthians 6:11; II Thessalonians 2:13; I Peter 1:2)
- He gives life, regenerates and renews (John 6:63; Romans 8:2; II Corinthians 3:6; Titus 3:5)
- He gives fruit (Galatians 5:22; Ephesians 5:9)

In what ways have the following attributes of the Holy Spirit impacted your leadership?

- He manifests Himself in us through gifts (I Corinthians 12:4-11)
- He is the mind of Christ in us (Romans 8:27; I Corinthians 2:14-16)

---

12 1 Corinthians 2:9-16

- He bears witness of the right direction (Romans 9:1; I Corinthians 2:10-16)
- He brings fellowship and unity (Ephesians 4:3-4; Philippians 2:1-2)
- He gives liberty (II Corinthians 3:17)
- He gives joy (I Thessalonians 1:6)

Which of the following ways has the Holy Spirit ministered through your leadership as you have reflected His presence and government into the lives of others?

- He pours out God's love (Romans 5:5; 15:30)
- He intercedes through us (Romans 8:26-27)
- He empowers (Acts 1:8)
- He leads into truth and wisdom (John 14:17; 16:13; Acts 6:3, 10; I John 5:6)
- He calls (Acts 20:28)
- He sends (Acts 13:4)
- He strengthens (Ephesians 3:16)

As we submit to the Spirit's presence, the above attributes will appear in our lives. The temple of God's Spirit no longer exists as a physical building, but as the flesh-and-blood bodies of all who follow Christ.[13] He reveals Himself in the world through our bodies as His temple on earth.

Our world changes when we walk as priests who minister His presence and government. Through us, the Spirit speaks what Christ speaks. Through us, He empowers others, bears fruit, gives wisdom and direction. We fulfill our responsibility as sons of Father God only as we join with the Spirit's ministry through us.

---

13 *1 Corinthians 6:19*

PART THREE PRESENCE

CHALLENGE

Schedule a block of time for prayerful reflection. Re-read through the list of the Holy Spirit's characteristics. Highlight two or three items that stand out as significant in your life. Listen for the Lord's perspective on your heart condition as you ask the following questions:

1. *Lord, show me which of these characteristics You currently display in my life and leadership.*
2. *In what situations do You desire to further reveal that characteristic in me?*
3. *In what leadership situations might I be blocking Your life and direction?*
4. *What are You speaking to me right now? (For example, is He bringing Scripture to mind? Nudging toward action? Surrounding with His peace?)*

LOOKING AHEAD

We've explored the concept of "presence," both His and ours. Now we'll more specifically explore the journey of learning to "know the voice of the Shepherd."[14]

---

14 *John 10:3, 14, 27*

— CHAPTER ELEVEN —

Hearing the Shepherd

THE SHEPHERD'S VOICE FILTERED THROUGH OUR HEARTS

Lisa Hosler's pregnancy resource ministry swelled beyond the building's capacity to house it. Her staff and intercessors prayed for God's answer. When a building across the street came up for sale, they believed God was opening a door. During their next prayer meeting, Lisa shared with the intercessors the plan to house the center on one side of the street and headquarters on the other.

After an intercessor read scriptures about asking God for His will, Lisa sensed so strongly God's heart in the matter that she put her faith out on a limb: "I sense God is saying, 'Ask Me for the building,'" she announced to the others. "He says, 'I want to give you the building, but you need to ask for it.'"

"The intercessors agreed, so we petitioned God," Lisa said. "As we prayed, we pictured the building filled with people."

Despite God's seeming confirmation, one final aspect needed to come into alignment. To accommodate the needs of their ministry, they would need to enlarge the new building, and that required zoning approval. They attended the zoning meeting that afternoon after the prayer session.

"We were so surprised and disappointed when the zoning didn't go in our favor," Lisa recalled. "I asked God, 'Why?' I thought so strongly this was our building. How could zoning deny it? Had I missed God?"

Then, within a week, another building—the one directly beside the first—also went up for sale at a reasonable price. God had answered their prayers after all. Now, instead of only one building, He provided funds to purchase both. They would have the space to meet their needs without spending extra money on a build-out. The week of disorientation allowed the team to learn to trust God even in the face of disappointment, and the Spirit affirmed that Lisa and the prayer team had heard the Shepherd's voice.

It's a lifelong journey, learning to hear the voice of God. It's by "reason of use," having our "senses exercised to discern both good and evil."[1] But this journey is necessary because "it is not for man to direct his own steps…"[2] Even King Solomon knew his limitations and desired above all to hear God's wisdom with an "understanding heart to judge [God's] people, that [he] may discern between good and evil."[3]

What does hearing God entail? To answer that, we can start with people who we know heard God: the writers and compilers of Scripture. Through the pen of humans, we encounter the inspiration of the Holy Spirit—recording history, speaking wisdom, coordinating poetry, and prose.

The Spirit wove bits and pieces of text from more than forty different contributors over several millennia into an integrated story of God's purpose for humankind. Human language was turned into a pathway that leads to an eternal God whom we can't contain in human language—a humanly impossible feat managed by the Spirit's divine brilliance.

Scripture introduces us to God, but we learn to know God personally through the Spirit's inspiration of His word in our souls. For example, even before he met the Apostle Paul, Apollos knew the Scriptures well and taught the repentance message of John the baptizer. Priscilla and Aquila then taught him about the Messiah whom John had foretold. That opened Apollos' understanding more fully to the true meaning of Scripture, so that "he greatly helped those who had believed through grace; for he vigorously refuted the Jews publicly, showing from Scriptures that Jesus is the Christ."[4]

When Apollos was out of town, Paul himself finally met some of Apollos' disciples. He asked, "Did you receive the Holy Spirit when

---

1 *Hebrews 5:14*
2 *Jeremiah 10:23*
3 *1 Kings 3:9*
4 *Acts 18:28*

you believed?" Or, as Eugene Peterson puts it, "Did you take God into your mind only, or did you also embrace him with your heart? Did He get inside of you?"

The disciples answered, "We've never heard of that—a Holy Spirit? God within us?"[5] They had only received the baptism of John, the baptism of "water unto repentance."[6]

Paul introduced them to the baptism of the Holy Spirit and fire, the baptism in the name of the Lord Jesus,[7] the baptism into the body of Christ.[8] Now their knowledge of Scripture was infused by the interactive, personal inspiration of God the Spirit.

Through the Holy Spirit, we hear and know God. How does that work in our human vessels of physical flesh? Using the model of the writers of Scripture, we see that the Holy Spirit inspired each of their texts, despite unique voices, various personalities, and diverse cultures that differed markedly from each other.

God spoke the same message through each writer—to worship Jesus Messiah, the Lord of All.[9] But the writers expressed the message in different ways, for different audiences, with different purposes, circumstances, and perspectives. For example, if we read the four Gospels, on the surface, they may seem to disagree on minor points.[10] But we can settle the discrepancies when we consider the unique purpose, perspective, personality, and culture of each writer.

> **In our leadership teams, though each member may hear the same direction from God, they may express it in different ways.**

As we recognize the work of the Spirit in the writers' lives, we also realize that the Holy Spirit continues to inspire and speak to Christ-followers today. First-century men and women heard the Shepherd's voice and used

---

5   Acts 19:2, *The Message*
6   Matthew 3:11
7   Acts 1:5; 19:5
8   1 Corinthians 12:13
9   John 5:39
10 See, for example, the discrepancies in the Genealogies of Joseph (Matthew 1:2-17; Luke 3:23-38) and the discrepancies for the date of the Last Supper (Matthew 26:17; John 19:14).

His wisdom to solve problems. Jesus continues to give wisdom "from above"[11] to solve problems through the Holy Spirit.

He speaks the same message to all—to know and follow Christ as partners with Him in eternity. But we each hear uniquely, according to our individual design and function in the *ecclesia*. Practically speaking, in our leadership teams, though each member may hear the same direction from God, they may express it in different ways.

ISSUES OF LIFE THAT SPRING FROM THE HEART[12]

Our consciousness—our individual identity—lives at our core. We label this as "heart" in the diagram on page 155. In our hearts, we experience the Spirit-to-spirit communion as "deep calls unto deep." It's the place where God sends "the Spirit of His Son into our hearts, crying out 'Abba, Father!'"[13]

Surrounding the heart, we have the content and expression of our souls—the "issues that spring from our hearts."[14] Heart expressions include abilities, passions, personality, spiritual gifts, Biblical understanding, relationship with God, et al. These affect the life that flows from our heart and shape our environment according to how we think, react, and behave.

The soul issues around the heart filter how we hear the Shepherd's voice, so each of us uniquely contributes to the texture of beauty and creativity in Christ's body. Because of sin, however, our filters can be shaped in a negative way that hinders or warps God's voice.

The "feeling" that we developed in our childhood—how we learned to perceive our world—filters God's voice The walls we build to protect our emotional wounds can block or twist what Christ speaks and may cause us to "deceive ourselves"[15] in discerning His will.

---

11 *James 3:17*
12 *Proverbs 4:23*
13 *Psalm 42:7; Galatians 4:6*
14 *Proverbs 4:23*
15 *James 1:22*

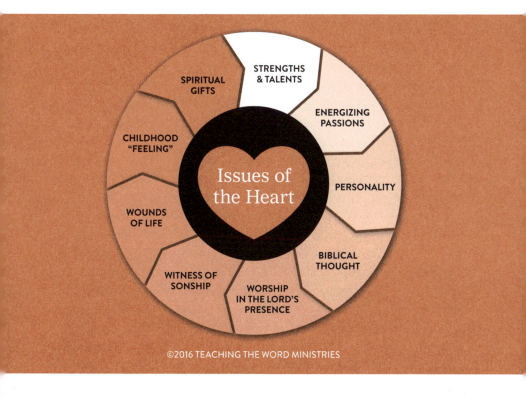

But God uses even the negative issues for His purpose, to reveal the things from our old nature that hinder our participation in godly fellowship. Or to show us how empty we are outside of His fellowship. God can use any part of our soul, positive or negative, for His purposes.[16]

For example, when King David prayed concerning His persecutor, "Let his children be fatherless, and his wife a widow," was he any less inspired by the Spirit than when he prayed, "He makes me to lie down in green pastures; He leads me beside still waters"?[17]

The Spirit was speaking a message of the Lord's protection both times, but David expressed it in different ways according to His specific circumstance, environment, prejudice, and passion.

---

16 Romans 8:28
17 Psalm 109:9; 23:3

PART THREE PRESENCE

Why do we study the cultural and historical context of biblical authors? Because their environments affected their choice of words, which helps illuminate the meaning of the text. God used people with limitations as vehicles for His inspired word.

I was part of a church elder team meeting where one member expressed passionate concern about the direction of a congregational leader whose behavior was arguably not aligned with Scripture, and, according to this elder, would negatively affect the church. The elder bluntly announced that if we didn't follow his recommendations, he would resign.

As the weight of his statement settled, we sat in silence. We could have allowed those words to control us and submitted to their stolen authority over us. We could have catered to his wishes or tried to negotiate, appease, scold, or talk him out of his demand. If our motives were to do whatever was necessary to keep the leadership team intact or to keep ourselves from an embarrassing situation, we would have reacted in human wisdom, either trying to control or appease. No one spoke.

We were meeting in an elder's living room, and I thought it humorous that during the "loud silence," the owner's cat padded through the center of our group with his tail curled like a big question mark. Then I heard the Holy Spirit's prompting to gently speak what proved to be His wisdom. "It's okay for you to voice your perspective, and if you feel the Lord leading you to resign, then you must resign. But to use that as a threat to leverage the outcome should not be the basis for team discernment."

We needed to discern our direction from the Lord's prompting, not give control to one member's manipulation. The elder had a heart for God, saw his error, and repented, which then freed us to discern God's will. The wisdom came from waiting on the inner prompting of the Lord and responding according to His direction.

In this case, each of us sensed the Spirit's leading, but how we expressed it differed as it filtered through our individual hearts. The elder who reacted out of the passion of the moment may have had insecurities stemming from unresolved emotional wounds. Or he may have been accustomed to leadership from a different model. He didn't at first trust God to work through the discernment of the group. Whatever the cause, it impacted how he handled the Spirit's leading.

CHAPTER ELEVEN HEARING THE SHEPHERD

If the content of our heart affects how we hear the Shepherd's voice, then we recognize the importance of our responsibility to "keep your heart with all diligence, for out of it spring the issues of life."[18]

The chart below illustrates the relationship between spiritual maturity and sensitivity to the Shepherd's voice. Spiritual maturity concerns *our habitual surrender to Christ and His attitude as the Spirit prompts or convicts us to respond*. The more we exercise obedience, the closer we move toward Him, and the more we hear His voice.

This concept—that our hearts filter God's voice—reiterates the importance of Christ's directive for "two or three" witnesses to confirm His wisdom. When we recognize our limitations to hearing God, we intentionally seek the input and confirmation of the *ecclesia*.

Rather than a dogmatic, "this is what God says," we adopt an attitude that offers our *perspective* of the Shepherd's direction—one part of many parts. As we recognize and respond to Christ within others, we'll more

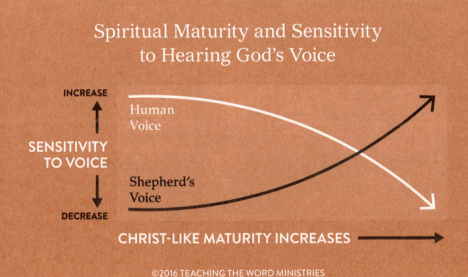

---

18 Proverbs 4:23

clearly discern the Spirit's voice. Instead of reacting to how their message is filtered, we respond to the source of the message, which is Christ in them.[19] This is not "majority rule," but discerning Christ's rule.

The chart below summarizes how the condition of our heart affects group discernment in two aspects:

1. **Life in:** Heart shapes how we hear God
2. **Life out**: Heart shapes how we influence others with what we hear

In the environment of the Trinity's presence, the in-out flow of God's life works in rhythm for wise group discernment. With mutual honor, we share the life of Christ filtered through our souls, and we receive the life of Christ as expressed through the hearts of others.

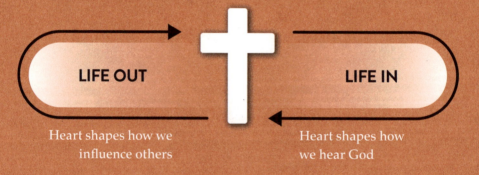

---

19 *In Chapter Thirteen, we will more thoroughly explore building a discernment culture of honor.*

HEARING CHRIST-IN-THE-MIDST OF COMMUNITY

Paul wrote to the Corinthians, "*We* have the mind of Christ."[20] It's interesting that Paul used the plural pronoun "we," rather than "*I* have the mind of Christ," or "*each of us* has the mind of Christ," or "*you* have the mind of Christ." But the plural "we." All of us together, as His body, share His mind. Christ is the Head (Mind) of an integrated body.

In this sense, **our capacity to connect with God (His mind) corresponds to our capacity to connect with others.** We must comprehend this community-oriented sensitivity to hearing God.

If Christ speaks "in the midst," then we need a community of at least "two or three" to provide a "midst" where He can speak.[21] Wisdom is found in plurality, whether from Scripture, from directly hearing the Shepherd's voice, or as God speaks through circumstances.

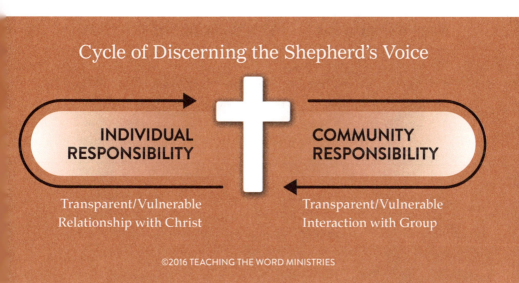

---

20 *1 Corinthians 2:16, italics mine*
21 *Matthew 18:20*

Paul said, "see then that you walk circumspectly, not as fools, but as wise."[22] In other words, prudent, careful to consider all perspectives and consequences. To do that, we need other people. We understand God's will through community interaction, not in isolation.

As the basis for community discernment, however, we need to develop our individual sensitivity to the Shepherd's voice. Again, we have two poles that feed each other:

1. Our community responsibility to discern (interact) within the transparent, vulnerable **community** of Christ's body
2. Our **individual** responsibility to develop a transparent, vulnerable relationship with Christ

VULNERABILITY AND TRANSPARENCY

Vital for both levels of sensitivity, we introduce here the key concepts of *vulnerability* and *transparency*:

1. **Vulnerability:** the extent to which I allow others to engage and share their perspective of what is true about me; allowing God and others to know me and address what is known
2. **Transparency:** the extent to which I share with God and with others what is true about myself

In other words, our "vulnerability" allows others to help us deal with the issues that we "transparently" share with them. The key to freedom in vulnerability is the security of being a valued member in that relationship, first with God and then with others. It's a cycle, as the following graphic illustrates.

Our vulnerability with God leads to an increased sense of being valued and validated. With that security, we're more able to trust others with our vulnerability. From a place of safety in God's affirmation, it no longer

---

22 *Ephesians 5:15*

CHAPTER ELEVEN HEARING THE SHEPHERD

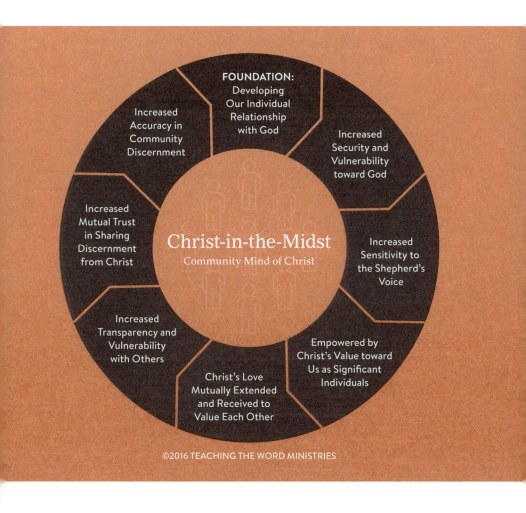

matters what others think about us. We can be vulnerable because we don't fear their judgment.

"There is no fear in love; but perfect love casts out fear."[23]

In PBL, we seek to develop a transparent community deeply seated in Christ's affirmation, with the exchange of His truth and life: Presence-to-presence-to-presence-to-Presence. This interaction is vital for team discernment.

---

23 1 John 4:18

In transparency, we gladly offer wisdom to others, and in vulnerability, we receive their feedback according to the discernment Christ builds in our group. (Find more on building discernment in the next chapter.) Collectively growing in this exchange of life, our group will develop increased sensitivity to the Shepherd's voice.

Sometimes in group discernment settings, I sense that certain members of the group have insecurity issues where they feel the need to force their opinions to be heard. In those cases, I take measures to validate them as valued members of the group. I may express genuine appreciation for something they've said or done. I repeat back what they say to affirm that we've heard them and they no longer need to push their opinions. I may give direction for how their perspectives can fit with the discernment at hand. These measures often help them feel more secure so they can participate in more productive ways.

With Christ-in-the-midst, interpenetrated with Father and Spirit, His fellowship flows through us—like rivers of living water—to each other. In this circle of Trinity fellowship, we have the mind of Christ, mutually testing and enlarging our understanding. We "become complete...of one mind..." with the "God of love and peace."

We seek to know the mind of God, just as first-century believers discerned the Holy Spirit's direction to "separate to Me Barnabas and Saul..." In Spirit-led consensus, we recognize that Jesus is Lord over all decisions. We yield to His wisdom and join together in the same mind and judgment, "like-minded, of one accord."[24]

HEARING GOD IS A LIFESTYLE

Presence-Based Leadership only arises from a Presence-Based *Lifestyle*. Recently, we partnered with a leadership team who prayerfully considered the essentials of *Presence-Based Living*, which we discerned as a model of the lifestyle our Creator originally designed for us. The more we walk

---

24 *John 7:38; 2 Corinthians 13:11; Acts 13:2; I Corinthians 1:10; Philippians 2:2*

The Essence of Presence-Based Living in and from the Presence of the Lord

Moment by moment...

Worship: Intentionally honoring God's worthiness to actively engage in His presence (PSALM 100: 1–5)

Intimacy: Confident vulnerability and transparency rooted in our identity as sons of Father God (ROMANS 8:14)

Quietness: Satisfied in God's intimate care (PSALM 131:2)

Humility: Abandoned to God's perspective, attitude, and mercy toward others (PHILIPPIANS 2:3–5)

Attentiveness: Anticipating God's desire and being available to serve Him (ROMANS 12:1; PHILIPPIANS 2:22)

Responsiveness: Yoked and yielded to God's every move and call (JOHN 8:28–29)

Reflection: Seeking God's counsel and definition for relationships and tasks (GENESIS 1:31; II CORINTHIANS 10:18)

Wisdom: Embracing God's purpose in confidence with the qualities of mind of Christ (COLOSSIANS 2:3; PHILIPPIANS 2:5; JAMES 3:17)

©2016 TEACHING THE WORD MINISTRIES

in His Presence, the closer to God's intention we become. We summarize the elements of Presence-Based living in the chart above.

In the next chapters, we explore how these dynamics can practically work with others in a leadership team. For now, let's consider how we can mature at hearing God's voice in our individual hearts. For effective group discernment, members each develop a Presence-Based *lifestyle* that "presses toward the goal for the prize of the upward call of God in Christ Jesus... as many as are mature have this mind."[25]

A lot of people claim to hear God say a lot of things. *How do we know if they're genuinely hearing the Shepherd's direction? How do we*

---

25 Philippians 3:14-15

know if we're hearing His voice, not the voice of our own intellect or the noise of our hearts' filters?

Sometimes people specify what God's voice "sounds" like. For example, some explain that a voice from our intellect feels like it comes from our brain, while God's voice feels like it comes from our bosom. Or God's voice comes spontaneously, while our intellectual voice comes through a line of reasoned thought. Or God's voice sounds clear, while Satan's voice sounds raspy.

While such advice may help as guidelines, any of these observations may or may not be true in different situations. Many people could easily manufacture an inner voice that sounds to them like God's voice. On the other hand, God may indeed speak through a line of reasoned thought. Scripture doesn't teach any of those methods for hearing the "still small voice"[26] of God. It just assumes that we hear Him.

We recognize that we have no easy method for hearing God's voice, whether it be through visions, scripture, circumstances, or a whisper in our hearts. We discern His voice through "practicing His presence," as Brother Lawrence would say, and again, "by reason of use," having our "senses exercised to discern both good and evil."

Scripture tells us to recognize "the wisdom that is from above" as "first pure, then peaceable, gentle, willing to yield, full of mercy and good fruits, without partiality and without hypocrisy."[27] God designed us—expects us—to make judgments according to His voice as His *ecclesia*.[28]

We have another bipolar framework for hearing God. On one side, Christ does the work. Using circumstances, experiences, relationships, and revelation, He draws each of us to break down our heart-walls of fear and shame to reach our deepest soul. We trust Him as Master of the process. On the other side, we also do work to adopt the following scriptural practices into a Presence-Based Lifestyle:

---

26 *1 Kings 19:12*

27 *Hebrews 5:14; James 3:17*

28 For hearing God as a community, read Ruth Haley Barton's Pursuing God's Will Together. *For the individual journey, see Dallas Willard's* Hearing God: Developing a Conversational Relationship with God. *For scriptural principles and practice, see Deborah Wiley's* Ears to Hear.

1. Worship
2. Praise and Thanksgiving
3. Listening Prayer
4. Obedience
5. Study of Scripture
6. Guarding the Heart
7. Transparent Fellowship with Other Believers

Worship

Taking time for intimate devotion to God is the central nerve of every believer's life. Paul indicates, in so many words, that our identity as worshippers—people who glorify God—is what makes us human rather than beast.[29] The Father seeks those who worship in Spirit and truth.

Worship is no longer attributed to a building, but our bodies now serve as the temple of worship—the dwelling place of the Holy Spirit. Our offering is no longer the blood of an animal, but the living sacrifice of our bodies, "holy and pleasing to God—this is your spiritual act of worship."[30] Developing a life of worship—moment-by-moment yielding to the Trinity's presence—involves all of the spiritual practices listed above and embodies the Art of Presence-Based Leadership.

Praise and Thanksgiving

We release the authority of Christ's government into our lives as we remain in an attitude of thanksgiving because the Lord is "enthroned in the praises" of His people. Praise is "the fruit of our lips, giving thanks to His name," the public expression of thanksgiving and passion for our Lord, "speaking to one another in psalms and hymns and spiritual songs, singing and making melody in your heart to the Lord, giving thanks always for all things…"[31]

Thanksgiving raises our hearts away from anxious thoughts to allow the "peace of God, which surpasses all understanding, to guard our hearts

---

[29] *Romans 1:20-24*
[30] *John 4:23-24; 1 Corinthians 6:19; Romans 12:1 (NIV)*
[31] *Psalm 22:3; Hebrews 13:15; Ephesians 5:19-21*

and minds through Christ Jesus."[32] Praise reverts our self-oriented focus to God, laying us to rest in His worthiness, casting our care upon Him.[33]

We train ourselves to adopt the attitude of praise through practice. When tempted to complain about the weather (or anything else), instead, we thank God for the blessings that come from rain or snow. A woman we know sets the alarm on her phone for various times during the day to remind herself to thank God for how His hand is moving in her life at that moment.

Thank God for blessings that come from relationships with people who are difficult to love. Praise Him for the wisdom He gives. Thank Christ for the difficult circumstances that strengthen our walk with Him. Yes, the author of Hebrews described praise as a "sacrifice" for good reason! But sacrifice brings us closer to identifying with Christ in the fullness of His "righteousness, peace and joy in the Holy Spirit."[34]

Listening Prayer[35]

Listening Prayer is related to our understanding of *ecclesia* discernment. Recall from Chapter Four that Presence-Based discernment doesn't depend on human intellect alone, but on hearing Christ's wisdom and declaring His will. So it is with prayer. As we open our souls to God, we realize that only He has the resources and wisdom to answer our requests in the way that's eternally best. We don't even "know what we should pray for as we ought, but the Spirit Himself makes intercession for us with groanings that cannot be uttered."[36]

To know how to pray, we *listen* to the Holy Spirit's heart. We discern His wisdom in how He desires to pray. Jesus with His Spirit is the Intercessor.[37] When we pray, we don't pray our own will or agenda. We listen for what He prays and align our prayer with His. We respond as Christ responds.

---

32 *Philippians 4:7*
33 *1 Peter 5:7*
34 *Hebrews 13:15; Romans 14:17*
35 *Also read* The Praying Life *by Paul Miller, 2009, Navpress*
36 *Romans 8:26*
37 *Isaiah 53:12; John Chapter 17; Romans 8:34*

God desires that we approach "boldly the throne of grace to obtain mercy and grace to help in time of need."[38] Christ gave His life so He could commune with us in the intimate fellowship of the Holy Spirit as we share our heart with Him in prayer. The Father already "knows the things we have need of before we ask Him."[39] But still, He desires our honest conversation—the joys and sorrows, peace, pains, and requests of our heart.

Again, developing an every-day listening stance in His presence is a journey, but an adventurous one! God doesn't always reveal everything. Sometimes, He leads us into fasting or sabbatical. Sometimes, He shows us nothing, and all we can do is wait. The Hebrew term for "wait" often means: *to bind (perhaps by twisting), to expect patiently.*

Imagine an ivy vine twisting up a tree trunk, rooting into it, drawing nourishment from it, conforming to its shape, becoming one with it. If we apply this attitude of waiting to our own leadership, rather than striving to control by relying on human resources, we quiet ourselves before our Lord. We bind with Him, drawing from Him His nourishment. We grow into Christ's form, His will, and His way, waiting expectantly for Him to reveal His attitude and plan.

Obedience

Like Christ, our "food is to *do* the will of the Father."[40] With genuine surrender and communion, obedience to the Shepherd's voice will flow as naturally as eating a meal when we're hungry. As we obey, we partake in the dynamic life of God's government, in a love-partnership with Christ.

Eternal fruit and favor increase. When we prove "faithful over a few things," He will make us ruler over many things.[41] Obedience to the Father's cycle of "pruning-and-increase"[42] brings greater influence, spiritual authority, and fruit into our lives. If we "hear" only, without obedience, we deceive ourselves, "having a form of godliness, but denying its power."[43]

---

38 *Hebrews 4:16*
39 *Matthew 6:8*
40 *John 4:34*
41 *Matthew 25:21*
42 *John 15:2*
43 *James 1:22; 2 Timothy 3:5*

PART THREE PRESENCE

Study of Scripture

We confirm all of our discernment with scripture. Through His word, the Holy Spirit inspires wisdom, "doctrine, reproof, correction, and for instruction in righteousness, that the man of God may be complete, thoroughly equipped for every good work."

As we study, we increasingly recognize the character of the Trinity. His desires, His decisions, perspective, loves, hates, and values. If we're diligent in studying and "rightly divide the word of truth," we'll increasingly recognize the counterfeit, the "profane and idle babblings" that increase ungodliness. With minds renewed in God's word, we can prove the "good and acceptable and perfect will of God."[44]

The Holy Spirit inspired the writing of Scripture for millennia. He continues to use His sword today, "piercing to the division of our soul and spirit, joints and marrow, discerning the thoughts and intents of our hearts." The "entrance of [His] words gives light and understanding to the simple," so we gain "more understanding than all our teachers."[45]

Chew on nuggets of the word. At the same time, read through the entire Bible repeatedly, allowing the truth and revelation of His character to soak into our being. As the Spirit's inspiration through His word saturates our souls, we move beyond simple "knowledge" of God to become like Him, with His wisdom and His compassion. His Presence becomes our presence.

Guarding the Heart

God created us in His beautiful image with holy passion and desires. But our fall into sin marred that image. He has placed many good things in our hearts, but sin deforms our passions and desires and can hinder the clarity of the Shepherd's voice. How can we differentiate between our desires and the Lord's when "the heart *is* deceitful above all *things*, and desperately wicked"? Harsh words from Jeremiah. If our hearts deceive us, what can we do? There is hope: "*I* the Lord, search the heart, *I* test the mind…"[46]

Our compassionate, true God cannot be deceived. Our open heart is safe in His hands. Jesus desires to intimately know us and heal our pain and

---

44 *2 Timothy 3:16-17; 2:15-16; Romans 12:2*
45 *Hebrews 4:12; Psalm 119:99, 130*
46 *Jeremiah 17:9, italics mine*

sinful nature more than we do, proving His love by giving His all on the cross for us.

He heals and re-forms our souls, "faithful and just to forgive us our sins and cleanse us from all unrighteousness." With zeal, He re-establishes "the kingdom of God within you," where "the increase of His government and peace there will be no end… the zeal of the Lord of hosts will perform this."[47]

As we engage in listening prayer, we practice "guarding-your-heart" by hearing the Spirit's leading in the following ways:

1. Being alert to unhealthy behaviors or egos that may arise within and consider them as "red flags"—something is wrong, and I need to surrender that area to Christ. Red flags may include:
    a. *Bitter anger or contentious spirit/critical spirit*
    b. *Defensiveness*
    c. *Deceitfulness*
    d. *Resentment or offensiveness*
    e. *Unforgiveness, revenge, or holding grudges*
    f. *Possessiveness, control, demanding others to conform*
    g. *Impatience*
    h. *Jealousy*
2. Confessing sin to God and receiving His cleansing.
3. Asking the Lord: *what is the root cause of this behavior?* Causes could include:
    a. *Wounds from the past*
    b. *Shame and/or fear*
    c. *Childhood feelings, experiences, and/or conditioning*
    d. *Unmet need for significance and/or security*
4. Taking steps to deal with the root causes, which may include:
    a. *Confess sin to God and others*
    b. *Forgive those who have sinned against us*

---

47 1 John 1:9; Luke 17:21; Isaiah 9:7

5. Replacing unhealthy mindsets with truth from God's word.[48] (For example, memorize or display scripture to proclaim during times of pressure or temptation.)
6. Replacing unhealthy behavior with godly behavior. (For example, in place of watching soul-harming movies, seek God for His alternative, such as: developing new habits of scripture meditation, prayer, and worship; spending more time with family; taking a course; learning a new hobby; etc.)
7. Sharing your journey of transformation with others, to develop vulnerability and transparency.
8. Receiving counsel and/or prayer ministry as the Lord leads.

Transparent Fellowship with Other Believers

We already addressed the understanding of transparent fellowship and will deal with more practicalities for creating such a culture in later chapters. God established the family unit as the first and foremost incubator for safe, transparent community. In this broken world, however, most of us experienced only a small reflection of Trinity family relationship. But no matter how we were raised, Father God opens wide the door to His circle of fellowship where we experience a safe vulnerability and extend that to others in our spheres of influence.

CHALLENGE

1. Reflection is a powerful tool to help train us to apply godly principles. Use the chart on page 155 to consider the "issues that spring from your heart" in these reflections:
   a. *First, recall an incident when you needed wisdom. Did you hear and follow Christ's direction, react in your own way, or somewhere in between?*

---

48 Romans 12:2

CHAPTER ELEVEN HEARING THE SHEPHERD

    b. *Consider one or more "issues of your heart" that may have filtered your response, whether positively or negatively.*
    c. *What insight might you glean from this understanding? What impressions do you receive from the Holy Spirit regarding the issues that spring from your heart?*
    d. *What attitudes or behaviors can you adopt to "guard your heart with all diligence"?*
2. Consider the following behaviors. Share about situations when you expressed those behaviors and/or how the Spirit may be leading you to express them more fully.
    a. *Showing transparency in leadership: sharing honestly with others about what is true in your heart.*
    b. *Showing vulnerability: allowing someone else to give you feedback concerning what is true in your heart.*
    c. *Influencing others with towardness in a divisive situation.*
    d. *Taking time in listening prayer to discern Christ's wisdom in a situation.*
3. Prayerfully review the "Essence of Presence-Based Living" chart on page 163 with a partner or group.[49] *Where do you see Presence-Based Living characteristics in your own life? In the life of your partner or group?*
4. Prayerfully consider how Christ is leading you to grow in the following areas. *How will your life need to change to follow the Spirit's direction?*
    a. *Worship*
    b. *Praise and Thanksgiving*
    c. *Listening Prayer*
    d. *Obedience*
    e. *Study of Scripture*
    f. *Guarding the Heart*
    g. *Transparent Fellowship with other Believers*

---

49 Use passcode "PBL" for access to printable versions of the charts in this book for use within your team. See page 8 for information.

— PART FOUR —

Community Discernment in Practice

It's one thing to learn theory or theology. It's another to actually practice it. We've found it's easy to read (and/or write) an entire book about PBL and intellectually grasp the principles. But when real-life circumstances arise, we can slip back into autopilot and start making decisions in status-quo mode, without realizing we're missing Christ's Presence in our midst. Theory comes off the pages into real life when we take time to reflect on our actual situations and intentionally seek the Shepherd to direct our responses to them.

As you read, remember that reflection is a powerful discipline for leadership growth. Be sure to keep your leadership situations in mind and how these principles might practically apply to your specific community and situation. Also remember that PBL is based on Presence, not only God's presence, but being present in transparent fellowship with each other. Discussing these issues with a peer or a mentor helps give us a broader and clearer view of Christ's mind.

Integration of Presence-Based Leadership Principles

MINISTRIES:
Equipping
Pastor, Teacher, Prophet, Apostle, Evangelist, King, Priest, Servant, Governor

CHURCH: Equipping
AUTHORITY: Governance
ONENESS: Towardness
IDENTITY: Sonship
PRESENCE: Presence-Based Leadership
CHRIST: The Wisdom of God

©2016 TEACHING THE WORD MINISTRIES

— CHAPTER TWELVE —

Building Discernment in *Ecclesia*

COMMUNITY DISCERNMENT

In Chapter Six, we narrated how Lisa Hosler and her PRC team experienced God's transforming presence in worship. Guided by the Holy Spirit, engaging in worship as an activity shifted to embracing *worship as a lifestyle*. For ten years, the Lord trained them in the reality of His moment-by-moment fellowship. God deepened the bond between worship and service. Presenting their "bodies as a living sacrifice, holy acceptable to God…"[1] emerged as a lifestyle. Worship, discerning prayer, and community building became the culture of their ministry, not just a program or an 'extra' activity.

"Before God changed me, my style of leadership was like a lone ranger. I holed up with the Lord until I could figure out what to do, and then I would share it with the board and staff." It's not that Lisa was heavy-handed. She led as an exhorter who thought her job as director was to discern the best way forward and then influence people to follow.

"But God changed my heart," Lisa explained. "I came to realize we need to lead together, as a community—like the Trinity. I have only one set of ears, one set of strengths, one way of hearing Him. I need to be in a community of others who have complementary strengths. When the whole team is involved in strategy and decision-making, we get a better perspective, and I'm not carrying the full weight."

---

1 *Romans 12:1*

CHAPTER TWELVE BUILDING DISCERNMENT IN ECCLESIA

Lisa didn't have to "force" her new community-inclusive leadership style on herself or her team. The Lord had cultivated everyone's heart through the deep experience of worship. The new process came organically, as if the practice had always existed and they just needed to dance with it. Lisa and her team simply conformed to the Trinity community they had experienced when spending time in God's presence.

Unity or Oneness?

In describing Presence-Based discernment culture, we like to make the distinction between "oneness" and "unity." PBL discernment cultivates a oneness that goes beyond unity.

Paul urges us to "endeavor to keep the *unity* of the Spirit in the bond of peace."[2] "Unity" implies an unvaried or uniform character among a group. Concord, harmony, agreement, or the absence of division. On this level, Christian unity means that we strive to maintain an attitude of love and working together, even if we disagree.

A leader of a retail company, for example, strives to maintain unity among the workers. In a healthy situation, the leader works with the employees to keep everyone "on the same page," or moving toward the same goal. But inevitably, not all the workers will agree with the policy set by the leaders.

In the interest of maintaining company unity (and keeping their jobs), they compromise or "agree to disagree." In the spirit of unity, all the parts intentionally work together to function satisfactorily.

In an unhealthy situation, while workers may appear unified, underneath the surface (e.g., in the break room), animosity simmers, with low morale and/or manipulative resistance against unity.

"Oneness," on the other hand, moves to a higher level, and implies the "sameness of *identity*." When Jesus prayed, "that they all may be one, as You, Father are in Me, and I in You; that they also may be one in Us…"[3] He wasn't referring to a state of mind where we all follow the same rules or act in the same way. He referred to our *identity* as sons in the family

---

[2] Ephesians 4:3, italics mine
[3] John 17:21

PART FOUR COMMUNITY DISCERNMENT IN PRACTICE

of Father God. Oneness affirms and celebrates our harmonic diversity. Though each individual is unique, we together bear the same identity.

In the work environment, we move beyond unity to the level of "oneness" as each employee identifies with the company's mission—when they take ownership by embracing the purpose of the business. It no longer matters who gets credit for doing what as long as it advances the purpose. Everyone's contributions work seamlessly together with synergy. Areas of disagreement become springboards for creativity that improve systems and progress. Oneness doesn't repress individual uniqueness, but instead provides freedom for individuals to grow in their unique capacities by identifying with the vision as a significant part of the team.

While we don't want to conjure up a plastic form of "unity" by wearing a mask of agreement that keeps issues of strife hidden, we also acknowledge that unity is something Christ-followers need to work toward. Living in this fallen world, we won't yet enter into full oneness in identification with Father God. We'll remain in the state of "endeavoring to keep the unity of the Spirit in the bond of peace,"[4] of negotiating and navigating unity. But as we cultivate a lifestyle of PBL, we move closer to oneness in the Trinity and each other.

"Oneness" and "towardness" describe the same thing—the image that God designed us to reflect. We grow in oneness only as we stand together in Trinity Presence and allow His towardness to flow through us, even in situations of tension and conflict. We find oneness in connection with God, in whose presence He gathers "together in one all things in Christ…"[5]

A Presence-Based discernment group centers on Christ and His vision, His *Truth*, rather than trying to spin issues in clever ways to convince people to join a bandwagon. "We should no longer be children, tossed to and fro and carried about with every wind of doctrine, by the trickery of men, in the cunning craftiness of deceitful plotting." In transparent community, we "speak the truth in love," so that we "may grow up in all things into Him who is the head—Christ."[6]

---

4 *Ephesians 4:3*
5 *Ephesians 1:10*
6 *Ephesians 4:14-15*

CHAPTER TWELVE BUILDING DISCERNMENT IN ECCLESIA

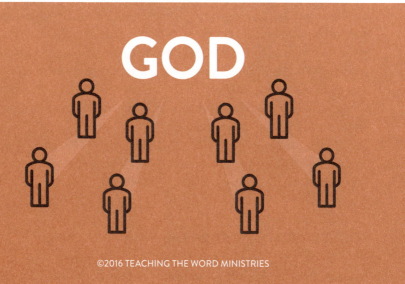

We illustrate this dynamic in the diagram above. As each member draws closer to God, we naturally move closer to each other. Also notice that moving away from God pushes us further away from each other.

COMMUNITY BUILDING

At Lisa Hosler's Pregnancy Resource Center, they schedule community-building exercises[7] into their board meeting agenda. Not just an "extra appendage," the activities build on already existing fellowship. At each session, they re-establish the mutual trust and respect that infiltrate the meeting.

---

7 Use the passcode "PBL" to access community-building ideas and activities from Lisa on our website. See page 8 for access information.

"For instance," Lisa explains, "whoever leads may lay out a question such as: *In what area of your life do you see God working?* Or, *where have you found most delight in the Lord this week?* Or, *what was the greatest challenge?* We openly share and savor our relationship as brothers and sisters in a real, in-the-moment way."

Such exercises help free everyone to share and increase respect for each other's capacity to hear the Lord.

"We're more apt to speak honestly," Lisa says, "rather than gloss over conflicting issues or remain quietly irritated about it. We care about each other like family. It creates a deeper level of trust."

ECCLESIA WITH CHRIST-IN-THE-MIDST REPRISED

Lisa describes the posture of her leadership teams during discernment: "Each one receives a puzzle piece of what God is saying. When anyone receives an idea, we place it in the center of the table where Christ is. When we put the pieces together, we find God's solution. It's far better than brainstorming. We call it 'Spirit-storming.' Instead of bearing the weight of responsibility to come up with a solution, the weight is on God. We trust Him to guide us. Back when we depended on manmade programs or philosophies, though we meant well, we fell short of the fruitfulness that God desired for our ministry."

The leadership experiences we describe in this book are simple, present-day expressions of the church Jesus established more than two millennia ago. His radical idea never changed. Christ continues to make the keys of the kingdom available to His decision-makers wherever they gather to honor His presence in their midst.

"If two of you agree on earth concerning anything that they ask, it will be done for them by My Father in heaven," Jesus explained. "For where two or three are gathered together in My name, I am there in the midst of them."[8]

---

8 *Matthew 18:19-20*

Let's unpack Jesus' proclamation:

- **Two or three:** Jesus acknowledged the biblical standard that requires two or three witnesses to confirm something as true and applies that standard to discernment gatherings. Note again that we discern Christ's will in community, not in isolation.[9]
- **Gathered together:** Jesus reiterates the community culture of His kingdom, together in the Trinity attitude of towardness.
- **In My name:** We don't gather "outside" of His name, but "in" Christ's name. We gather under the umbrella of His authority and the government that His name represents. We remain safe under His authority as we align with His direction and purpose.
- **There I am:** The *ecclesia* maintains an awareness that the Eternal, Self-Existent, Omniscient One presides.
- **In the midst:** We recognize that Christ *actively* orchestrates the involvement of those gathered to discern.
- **It will be done for them by My Father in heaven:** When we discern the wisdom of Christ and declare that direction on earth, *it will be done!*

The picture on page 180 illustrates the structure of Christ-in-the-midst discernment. Each participant yields to Christ, who reigns in the center. Christ reveals His wisdom like a many-faceted diamond, showing a part of the whole to each member.

In other words, He gives each of us a "key" (or a puzzle piece). With the posture of towardness, we share our perspectives, and Christ builds the discernment. This structure provides a powerful way for the group to rid itself of any self-oriented motives and clear the way to hear the Shepherd's voice. It's simple, but it requires hearts genuinely humble before God.

For example, at one point, Lisa's PRC had five different locations in Lancaster County, PA. They were gaining resources and momentum to open a sixth. She and her team worked for a year with other ministries to find a good location. In the meantime, however, Lisa learned that God was moving across the nation to open inner-city locations in large metropolitan

---

[9] *Deuteronomy 17:6; 1 Timothy 5:19*

PART FOUR COMMUNITY DISCERNMENT IN PRACTICE

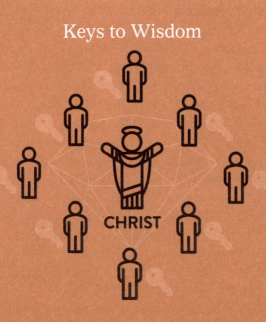

cities. But many PRCs avoid setting up such locations because those areas lack resources. Lisa also learned that her board chairman had privately prayed about partnering with centers in Philadelphia.

"We were already a year into blazing the trail for the next location in Lancaster, and ready to send out 10,000 newsletters to announce it! So the chairman and I decided not to share the idea with the rest of the board. If God wanted us to move into Philadelphia, it would have to be by His initiative."

At the next board meeting, they discussed their progress on the new center in Lancaster until one member felt the Lord prompting him to ask, "Are we sure this is what we want to do—open another center here when the need is so much greater in Philadelphia?" Then another board member shared that he'd been wondering the same thing.

Lisa wasn't expecting this response, but at the same time, she wasn't surprised. The chair of the board confirmed that he'd been praying about Philadelphia for over a year. Together, they agreed that Christ was leading them into Philadelphia. Lisa sat in awe of the Lord's guidance. With humbled hearts, they apologized to the staff for the energy and time they'd committed in the past year. By faith, they threw away the 10,000 newsletters to embrace God's direction for Philadelphia.

"There are several elements present," Lisa explained when asked how her team discerned the Lord's direction. "There's a combination of an atmosphere of worship and honoring God, corporate prayer, feedback from others, confirmation of Scripture—always the foundation of Scripture—and circumstances confirming the way of Christ's peace. It's a different paradigm—allowing things to unfold at God's pace. If we rush ahead, we fall into error with wasted time and resources."

CONSOLATION AND DESOLATION

Saint Ignatius of Loyola (1491-1556) used the terms *consolation* and *desolation* to describe a way of recognizing God's direction—a way to determine "yes" or "no" answers from God:

> Consolation: *God's "yes," or a sense of peace from God*
> Desolation: *God's "no," or a caution; a lack of peace*

In discerning direction, Ignatius recommended that we first use conventional decision-making methods to find the best course of action. Then we present that course before God to ask Him whether or not it's His will. If we sense a feeling of peace from God, it means consolation, or "yes." If we sense a lack of peace, it means desolation, or "no." [10]

---

10 Also see Silf, Margaret, Inner Compass: An Invitation to Ignatian Spirituality, *1999, Loyola Press, Chicago, Illinois;* and Morris, Danny; Dr. Olsen, Charles, Discerning God's Will Together, *1997, Upper Room Books.*

PART FOUR COMMUNITY DISCERNMENT IN PRACTICE

Though we use the terms *consolation* and *desolation* in PBL, we understand them in a more engaged sense. Rather than waiting until the last step in our discernment to present a question to God, we recognize Christ's active participation, speaking to us, orchestrating our discernment from beginning to end. From the time we discern the core question and move through any research, reports, cognition, discussion, or prayer, we remain alert to Christ's peace (consolation) or caution (desolation).

Christ is the Prince of Peace, who reigns in His kingdom of peace with the fruit of peace that "surpasses all understanding... Of the increase of His government and peace there will be no end."[11] If we move in alignment with Christ, we're moving in His peace.

Consolation, then, describes the sense of peace we find within the Spirit's presence. In desolation, we sense a "check," or a lack of peace, or a caution concerning a certain direction. The more we practice His presence, the more we become accustomed to His peace, and the more we're able to recognize when a sense of desolation disrupts that peace. When anyone on our team senses desolation, we continue to prayerfully process until Christ leads us into the way of peace and oneness.

Note that the way of peace does not necessarily mean the "easy" way. God's peace may (and often will!) lead us into difficult waters. After all, it was Jesus who sent His disciples across the lake, fully knowing that a storm was brewing.[12] In this sense, "peace" does not refer to circumstances, but to an inner sense of moving in the righteous direction.

SPEAKING TRUTH IN LOVE

Sometimes the concept of "oneness in community" looks better in theory than in practice. Moving group dynamics from where they are now into a Presence-Based model may appear a long, bumpy road. Developing the practical capacity to deal with conflict or difficult behavior patterns will

---

11 *Galatians 5:22; Philippians 4:7; Isaiah 9:6-7*
12 *Matthew 14:22*

CHAPTER TWELVE BUILDING DISCERNMENT IN ECCLESIA

help in that process. Several good resources[13] cover the practicalities of conflict management, so we won't dwell on it here. Whether written by a Christ-follower or not, at the core of many techniques, we find the biblical principle of "speaking truth in love."[14]

"Truth and love" or, in PBL terms, "Christ's wisdom and towardness," flow from the essence of Christ's character. PBL revolves around this truth-love balance and facilitates the process of working through conflicts in a life-giving way.

In a culture of mutual respect, people feel secure enough to share without fear of rejection or judgment. This is the "love" part of the balance. Seeking and submitting to Christ's wisdom (rather than our own agendas) marks the "truth" part of the balance.

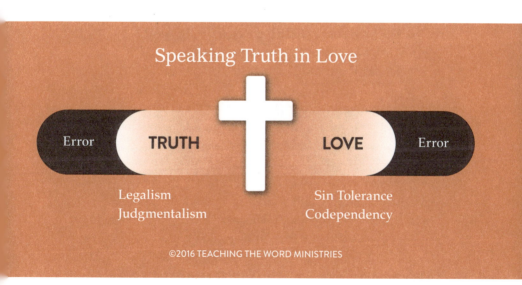

---

13 Patterson; Grenny; McMillan; Switzler, Crucial Conversations: Tools for Talking When Stakes are High. McGraw-Hill Education, 2011; Augsburger, David, Caring Enough to Confront: How to Understand and Express Your Deepest Feelings Toward Others. Revell, 2009.
14 Ephesians 4:15, 25

Love: *making a safe place for the vulnerable and transparent exchange of Christ's empowering life and truth*
Truth: *transparent sharing of the truth of one's perspective*

We can't separate truth and love. Truth without love is not truth; love without truth is not love. Scripture often expresses truth and mercy together as characteristics of God. In Christ, "mercy [love] and truth have met together."[15] Jesus poured out *love* by fulfilling the *truth* of God's justice on the cross. To understand the truth-love dynamic, we again use a two-pole scale, with Christ as the fulcrum, and error in the extremes on either side:

When working out issues of conflict, consider the following:

1. **Take time for listening prayer.**
    a. Pray for each person what you hear Christ praying.
    b. Pray that each one (including yourself) would yield to Christ's love and truth more deeply and fully.
    c. Pray for peace to prevail over strife.

2. **Align your motive with Christ's desire** for the situation. Love always seeks the way of the fullest possible restoration and oneness, never revenge or unforgiveness.

3. **Seek the *truth* of the situation** by recognizing the root of the conflict and any misunderstanding, miscommunication, or need for more information. To discern the truth, listen carefully to all sides involved and to the Spirit's guidance.

4. **Speak your perspective of truth with towardness,** in a way that shows respect for the view and feelings of others and seeks the best for them.

---

15 Genesis 24:27; Psalms 25:10; 61:7; 85:10; 89:14; Proverbs 16:6; 20:28; 1 John 3:8

5. **In confrontation, speak "I" rather than "you,"** owning, and not blaming the other person for your reaction. For example, instead of saying, "You hurt me," say, "I felt hurt." Or, instead of "You make me mad when you do that," say, "When that happens, I feel angry."

6. **Take full responsibility for your conceptions, actions, or reactions.**

7. **Confront the *behavior* of others, not the *motive* of others.** Because you can't know the full story of what's in other people's hearts, you can't assume to know their motives. Let the confrontation speak the "truth" of how you observed the behavior and your response to it. Then allow the other people to share their perspective.

8. **Allow the other person to share** the truth of what they feel, giving them the freedom to choose their own reactions and responses without trying to control them.

9. **Seek a resolution** and freely give any necessary repentance or forgiveness.

10. **Trust Christ.** As we seek and express truth, He stands among us, speaking His wisdom and restoration.

11. **Consider word choice.** Often, how another person receives the truth we speak is a simple matter of word choice:
    a. Instead of "I disagree," say, "I understand your point of view. How would that work with [*another perspective*]?"
    b. Instead of "That's the wrong way," say, "How can we work this out together?"
    c. Instead of "That will never work," say, "We could also consider…"

Sometimes restoration is postponed or not possible if someone resists either love or truth. Sometimes we need to make hard decisions. But as we cultivate an environment of towardness that nurtures humble hearts of truth, we build a secure place to process conflict with healthy tension that moves us forward into God's purpose.

Use this list of questions to help you work through conflict in a specific situation. Prayerfully reflect with the Holy Spirit for His truth and wisdom:

1. **What is the "truth" in the situation?**
   a. What is the core question or issue?
   b. Are there any possible misunderstandings or miscommunications?
   c. Is there any possible control or manipulation where you or someone else needs to submit control to Christ?
   d. Is God convicting you to repent of any unhealthy attitudes, words, judgments, or actions that perpetuate the conflict? Do you need to ask forgiveness?
   e. Is the Holy Spirit impressing you to forgive the other person for any genuine offense against you?

2. **How can I respond to the truth with love?**
   a. What is God's perspective and will for the other person(s)? For yourself? For the relationship?
   b. What is Christ's wisdom for speaking the truth in such a way that you affirm the God-given value of the other person(s)?
   c. What is Christ's wisdom for speaking truth in such a way that will help affirm and strengthen your relationship with the other person?

CHAPTER TWELVE BUILDING DISCERNMENT IN ECCLESIA

CHALLENGE

1. Use the chart on page 188 to prayerfully consider where your team may fall in the process of moving from disunity to oneness. Mark the points that most fully describe your group.
2. Ask the Holy Spirit to show you His direction for moving the group onward in the journey toward oneness in Christ together. *In what practical way is Christ leading your group to partner with Him in this work?*
3. Review the characteristics you listed to describe godly leadership for the Challenge in Chapter Two. Change, alter, or add to the list according to how your understanding of leadership may have developed.

LOOKING AHEAD

In the final chapters, we flesh out PBL principles for developing Presence-Based culture in our leadership circles. We realize the power of PBL where it counts—in the trenches of a discernment meeting. We learn to move our team into the attitude of towardness through a culture of prayer and honor, then culminate with Christ-in-the-midst discernment in action.

PART FOUR COMMUNITY DISCERNMENT IN PRACTICE

Characteristics of Team Cohesiveness

Disunity	Unity	Oneness
Members don't share input that's different than leader's	Members rally around a common cause	Members participate because Christ called them there
People demand their own opinions	Members' abilities fulfill a role or function	Gifts and abilities "make room" for the person as the Spirit orchestrates each one's function
Manipulation and control are present at the meeting or behind the scenes	Mutual respect	Members take "ownership" of the vision and identity
Misunderstanding, miscommunication is the rule	Agree to disagree	Towardness with God and each other behind the scenes
Seeking self-advancement without concern for team or cause	Misunderstanding, miscommunication resolved with respect	Members share truth in confidence that God values them
Lack of fulfillment	Members sometimes compromise their own perspectives in the interest of unity	Solve problems by submitting complementary perspectives to Christ's authority and wisdom
Dissatisfaction and lack of morale behind the scenes	Unity of the cause isolates people with vision or abilities that don't fit the need of the group	Consensus found by discerning Christ's wisdom, rather than compromise
	As long as the cause advances, members show satisfaction even behind the scenes	Fulfillment in identity with Father God

©2016 TEACHING THE WORD MINISTRIES

* Use the passcode "PBL" on our website to access a printable version of the *Characteristics of Team Cohesiveness* chart. Info on page 8.

— CHAPTER THIRTEEN —

Cultivating a Culture of Prayer and Honor

PRESENCE-BASED LEADERSHIP *CULTURE OF PRAYER*

"During any business day," Jared said, "we try to remain sensitive to the Holy Spirit and respond to impressions to pray. Any one of us can ask a co-worker to take a moment to pray for something. For instance, if we're going to send out an important set of documents, we'll pray over them that they communicate and accomplish their purpose. We pray not only for company issues, but we show God's love for people by praying for their personal needs.

"One of our customers had a very distraught neighbor. His young niece had cancerous tumors on both eyes, diagnosed at 18 months old. By the time I heard about this, any treatments the doctors tried were not working. Her parents had to decide whether to let the doctors remove her eyes or try to continue treating the cancer. We started praying for her."

Jared bought a yellow singing-duck toy for the girl and anointed it with oil and prayers for healing. She loved the duck and took it everywhere she went. And through many prayers, God healed her. Now, the girl is cancer-free. One eye is legally blind, but the other is corrected at 20/20. God literally raised her up from the point of death to living a healthy life. She is a teen active in sports.

PART FOUR COMMUNITY DISCERNMENT IN PRACTICE

Prayer is part of the culture in Jared's business. "We have voluntary prayer meetings at work every Tuesday, but on any given day, we stop many times and pray. I keep a record of the prayers that God has answered—He has done remarkable things!"

Developing a prayer culture in our metrons is the umbilical cord that keeps the organization connected to the life-giving nourishment of Trinity fellowship and wisdom. It starts with the leaders.

We've witnessed, over and over, that when the leadership nurtures prayer "without ceasing,"[1] "praying always with all prayer and supplication in the Spirit, being watchful to this end with all perseverance and supplication for all the saints."[2]—especially in board or leadership meetings—they influence managers and staff, who, in turn, influence coworkers in their own metrons.

Like a light spreading in the darkness, a leader's living, breathing fellowship with God naturally extends to the rest of his or her metron and beyond.

To understand what a prayer culture looks like in meetings, I like Charles Olsen's description of what one *doesn't* look like:

> *I often hear the term "book-end prayers" used to refer to the routine way in which prayer can be scheduled and offered at the beginning and close of a church board meeting. It traditionally separates the spiritual aspects of the meeting from the "business at hand."*[3]

We continue to value efficiency, effectiveness, reasoned judgment, and reports and recommendations. But rather than treating prayer as an appendage, we *maintain a continuous posture of prayer and reliance upon the wisdom of Christ*. Such a posture of prayer is vital to following the practical aspects of a Presence-Based meeting (as we'll explore in the next chapter).

---

1   1 Thessalonians 5:17
2   Ephesians 6:18
3   Olsen, Charles M., Transforming Church Boards into Communities of Spiritual Leaders, The Alban Institute. 1995.

INTENTIONALLY CULTIVATING A *CULTURE OF PRAYER*

1. Establish a team of intercessors to pray before, during, and after the meetings.

Sometimes we may underestimate the need for appointing people to pray for us, whether we serve in business, service, or church. As leaders, we work in a vulnerable position. God gifted people to serve through prayer, so we can connect with them to provide spiritual covering and protection.

We may wish to organize different tiers of prayer partners: those who pray for general items, and those we trust with more sensitive requests. We can occasionally include the intercessors for part of the meeting. For example, asking one to lead the time of devotion. Regularly keep in contact with the intercessors, and always report to them the results of their prayers.

2. Redefine the Purpose of a Leadership Meeting.

As members of God's kingdom, through His mercy, we offer Him our work—our "bodies as a living sacrifice, holy, acceptable to God, which is [our] reasonable service,"[4] or "spiritual act of worship."[5] We embrace our service on leadership teams as worshipful work.

3. Allow Prayer to Permeate.

Frame the Agenda with Prayer:
    a. Open with prayer that focuses hearts on Christ-in-the-midst.
    b. Include a time of devotion and worship to engage with Christ, Presence-to-presence-to-Presence.
    c. Close with prayer to:
        – Praise God for what He has done in the meeting
        – Dedicate all to trust in Christ, His will and timing
        – Release control to Christ
        – "Cast all your care upon Him, for He Cares for you."[6]
        – Rest matters in God's hands for peace, not anxiety.

---

4 *Romans 12:1*
5 *Romans 12:1 (NIV)*
6 *1 Peter 5:7*

4. Glean for Prayer.[7]

All members should feel free to suggest prayer or praise whenever they sense the Spirit prompting for either a few moments or a more extended time. To intentionally train ourselves in the attitude of "prayer without ceasing," we can assign people to take turns watching throughout the meeting for opportunities to pray, such as:
   a. Thanksgiving for God's hand at work
   b. Prayer for people in the leadership metron
   c. Requests for God's provision or protection

5. Offer Prayers of Confession.

Confession is a good starting place that leads to developing corporate spirituality in an era of individualism.[8] Each member should keep alert to Spirit promptings to confess errors of action or attitude. Sometimes Christ may call the leadership to confess corporately.

6. Take "Time out" for Prayer.

After a period of debate over an issue on which people seem divided, egos can take over. Take several minutes or several days "time out" for refocusing and prayer. Anytime unhealthy words or frustrations arise, consider them "red flags" to take a prayer break. During the break, members consider questions such as the following:
   a. What characteristic of Christ needs to be manifested?
   b. What is Christ's attitude and wisdom in this situation?
   c. Am I closing myself off from necessary information?
   d. Do I need to forgive or ask forgiveness?
   e. How does the Scripture shed light on us in this situation?
   f. Am I operating in a need-to-win or save-face mode?
   g. Am I embracing the attitude of a servant-leader?

---

7 Olsen, Charles M., Ibid., Philippians 4:6
8 Ibid.

7. Draw upon Model Prayers in Scripture.
Use examples from Scripture during the devotion time or any other appropriate time. Read a biblical prayer aloud. Members may then meditate on the words and share insight or impressions they receive from the Holy Spirit.
   a. Psalms (for example, Psalm 27; 40:1-16; 71:1-6)
   b. The Lord's Prayer (Matthew 6:9-13)
   c. Jesus' prayer in John 17
   d. Paul's prayers (for example, Ephesians 1:15-23; Philippians 1:3-6; Colossians 1:9-12)

8. Other possible opportunities to pray:
   a. Pray for new board members, staff members, or volunteers as they begin or retire from their service. Physically surround them as a group, lay hands on them and speak blessings over them as the Spirit leads. "Stir up the gift of God which is in you through the laying on of my hands..."[9]
   b. Invite intercessors to attend an appropriate part of the meeting to pray with the team for a specified issue.
   c. For particularly important issues, invite intercessors to pray somewhere on-site throughout the meeting, whether in the same room or a different place.
   d. Invite other leaders within the organization to the meeting for a time of prayer support, especially if they face difficult issues or decisions.

As we mature in our attitude of towardness, a prayer culture will organically grow. But towardness has two dimensions, horizontal to each other as well as vertical to God. We develop a culture of *prayer* by "loving the Lord our God with all our heart, soul, mind and strength." Then we move on to "loving our neighbors as ourselves"[10] by fostering a culture of *honor*.

---

[9] 2 Timothy 1:6
[10] Mark 12: 30-31

PART FOUR COMMUNITY DISCERNMENT IN PRACTICE

PRESENCE-BASED LEADERSHIP *CULTURE OF HONOR*

As we've seen, our friend Lisa Hosler served well as director for her PRC. For a long season, Lisa also served as staff shepherd.

"I had positional authority as staff shepherd, and I carried out my responsibilities satisfactorily. But at some point, I noticed another woman who organically ministered to staff members. She carried discipleship and mentoring gifts that naturally drew people to her. She had more of a pastoring anointing than I did."

Lisa's co-worker didn't at first have "positional authority." Instead, with a humble heart, she carried authority in a spiritual/relational sense, based on the gifts God designed within her. She in no way vied for Lisa's position. She simply flowed in her personality and calling. Lisa honored her for sharing her gift.

"I saw what a good job she did with pastoring members of the staff," Lisa said. "We prayerfully talked it through and decided that she should carry the position of staff shepherd. Now she wears the mantle. She plans staff meetings and serves in the up-front role. I take a large portion of the staff meeting only once or twice a year, but most of the time, she leads."

Lisa simply walked in the "culture of honor" that permeated her organization. In deciding to lay down her position of authority as staff shepherd humbly, she honored her co-worker's relational authority.

"It's not always easy to release and let go," Lisa admits, "because I care about each aspect of the ministry. But God gives me grace."

"Honor all people. Love the brotherhood. Fear God. Honor the king."[11] Clean, clear instructions from Peter. Giving honor to someone means that we recognize their value, contribution, or authority. Godly honor does not flatter according to self-serving motives.

---

11 1 Peter 2:17

CHAPTER THIRTEEN CULTIVATING A CULTURE OF PRAYER AND HONOR

Flattery misses the pure joy and freedom that comes from the Trinity's culture of honor. Godly honor comes from the posture of towardness that we embody in the circle of Trinity presence. We give someone honor as an extension of the honor Christ has already given them.

For example, Lisa didn't lightly honor just anyone with the position of staff shepherd, but the one that God had called and prepared. At the same time, we owe the blessing of honor to *all* people, simply based on their value as persons who bear God's image. We honor everyone with respect for their God-given value. Honor, then, means *to validate and affirm the identity and authority that Christ has assigned and is fulfilling in someone.*

We'll cover several types of appropriate honor, but the simplest way to show honor is to *listen*. As appropriate, when someone gives input, speak back to them what you hear them saying. Give feedback rather than glossing over someone's contribution. Ask questions to help them clarify. When you disagree, rather than confronting directly, use the "yes…and" approach, or make open-ended statements, such as:

- "*Yes*, I hear what you're saying, *and* we could consider…"
- "How do you think that would work if…"
- "That's another option [yes]. Let's consider what the Lord is speaking [and]…"

Recall a time when a leader treated your contribution with this kind of honor. *What happened to your attitude? Did you feel more confident and empowered? How did it impact your level of "taking ownership" in the purpose and identity of the group?* Developing a culture of honor empowers the group to let go of fears and ego, to take ownership and mutual responsibility. It's the fuel that brings oneness of heart.

PART FOUR COMMUNITY DISCERNMENT IN PRACTICE

SCRIPTURAL WAYS TO HONOR FOUR TYPES OF AUTHORITY

In Chapter Eight, we explored the biblical concept of how to *wield* godly authority. Here we discuss the other side of authority: how we *honor* those with authority. We extend "honor to whom honor is due."[12]

In our study, we've found four types of godly authority:

1. Positional Authority
2. Authority of Competence
3. Spiritual Authority
4. Authority of Relationship

Positional Authority: Honor through Submission and Respect

We honor those in positions of authority by willingly submitting to them in their metron of responsibility. Both Peter and Paul imply that giving honor to those in positions of governmental authority is ultimately honoring God. The authority rulers have is foundationally from God. "Submit yourselves to every ordinance of man *for the Lord's sake*," Peter writes, "whether to the king as supreme, or to governors…For this is *the will of God*…"[13] Paul reiterates, "Be subject to the governing authorities. *For there is no authority except from God*."[14]

The attitude of honoring God helps us "be submissive to [our] masters with all fear, not only to the good and gentle, but also to the harsh."[15] Even though it's sometimes difficult to honor rulers who mistreat us, we keep our eyes on Christ, honoring Him by honoring the position of authority, forgiving and releasing the hurt to Jesus.

God does lead people to remove themselves from under abusive authority (as Paul sometimes hid from or avoided governmental persecution). Still, we should adopt an overall attitude of respect and honor.

---

12 *Romans 13:7*
13 *1 Peter 2:13-15a, italics mine*
14 *Romans 13:1, italics mine*
15 *1 Peter 2:18*

A culture of respect applies not only when the authority figure is in our presence, but also when that person is absent from the conversation. "Whoever resists the authority resists the ordinance of God, and *those who resist will bring judgment on themselves.*"[16]

We've often noticed that when an attitude of dishonoring or complaining about authority shapes the culture of an organization, it will create the same disrespect aimed toward that organization. A group with a culture of dishonor toward governmental officials or policies, such as building codes, will often have to deal with disrespectful attitudes from their own clients, or from those in authority over them.

How do we respond when others display attitudes of dishonor? We can express thanksgiving and praise to God for what He's doing. Through the attitude of thanksgiving, we establish Christ's government in the situation, because the Lord is "enthroned on the praises" of His people.[17]

If we expect our organization to adopt a culture of honor, we need to model that attitude ourselves. We serve in our positions of authority with attitudes truthfully honoring the godly values of those over or under us in our metrons.

Authority of Competence: Honor through Deference

Someone with the authority of competence may not necessarily also serve in an official position of authority. These people have a talent, expertise, gifting, or skill in a particular area on a higher level than others on the team. Lisa's co-worker illustrated this with her shepherding gift. We honor these people by deferring to them, as Lisa did.

"Let nothing be done through selfish ambition or conceit, but in lowliness of mind let each esteem others better than himself."[18] As Christ reveals His wisdom, we defer to the one with the greater understanding of the issue at hand.

---

16 Romans 13:2, *italics mine*
17 Psalm 22:3, NRSV
18 Philippians 2:3

PART FOUR COMMUNITY DISCERNMENT IN PRACTICE

We may advise leaders to surround themselves with people who have gifts and abilities that differ from or exceed their own. For this strategy to work, leaders need to develop a humble heart of deference that can objectively recognize the wisdom that Christ reveals through a skilled expert.

Other examples of those who may carry the Authority of Competence include a younger team member who can relate to the younger generation more genuinely; someone with more expertise in technology; someone with more world-travel experience, etc.

Spiritual Authority: Honor through Submission

Over the years, I've experienced the joy of hearing many people honor Teaching the Word Ministries (TTWM) for our integrity and truth in ministry. From the very beginning, I committed my leadership to the "paperclip principle." Even if I use a paperclip from the ministry for convenience of carrying something that belongs to me to my house, I will return the paperclip so I in no way take something from the ministry.

I realize people have different ways of perceiving such matters, but I felt the need to establish this discipline in my own leadership. If I remain faithful, even with something as small as a paperclip, then I position myself to remain faithful in larger issues,[19] and to create that same respect for the organization.

The paperclip principle is one way I honor the authority of the ministry. That sets a spiritual precedent of integrity that leads to spiritual authority evident in the oversight of TTWM.

Consider these two scriptural precedents:

> "…those who resist [authority] will bring judgment on themselves."[20]
> And,
> "…whatever a man sows, that shall he also reap."[21]

---

19 *Luke 16:10*
20 *Romans 13:2*
21 *Galatians 6:7*

CHAPTER THIRTEEN CULTIVATING A CULTURE OF PRAYER AND HONOR

While others may not have conscious awareness of my paperclip standard, they honor the organic authority they perceive. It's an authority that is "felt," even though TTWM has no positional authority over our clients. They often describe a sense of safety and trust for what we suggest and speak into their lives.

We can develop this characteristic of spiritual authority, whether as an organization or in our personal lives, through a lifestyle of *submitted authority*.[22] We consistently yield to and align with the Trinity's heart and direction by submitting to those with delegated authority over us.

Have you ever known people who, when they walk into a room, carry with them a sense of authority? They are usually older persons—but not necessarily—and may or may not have an official position of authority. Without even knowing them, others seem to respect and trust them naturally. People feel safe in their presence because of the living towardness they project.

I immediately think of several intercessors who fit this description. They may or may not have ever held a powerful leadership position, but in the spirit realm, they've faced many giants and overcame through faith and power in Christ. From the exercise of faith and obedience, they grew in strong spiritual authority that comes from dwelling in the Presence of the Source of all authority.

We honor those who have developed spiritual authority by "submitting ourselves to our elders. Yes, all of you be submissive to one another, and be clothed with humility, for 'God resists the proud, but gives grace to the humble.'"[23]

Authority of Relationships: Honor by Preferring

A long-time friend of mine, and pastor of a local church, invited me to conduct an evaluation for his congregation. The church members and other leaders had shown resistance and loss of confidence toward his leadership, and he sought the Lord for direction.

---

22 Recall the definition of submitted authority *from Chapter Eight:* the degree to which we are aligned with the measure of truth that the Father entrusts to us to discern and enact Christ's will within our spheres of responsibility.

23 1 Peter 5:5

My friend and I had served together in organizational settings for approximately fifteen years at one time or another in leadership and team teaching. He had come to my aid and comfort once when a counselee physically attacked me. I was glad to serve him with a congregational review.

As I compiled the results of the evaluation, it became clear that an unhealthy pattern in my friend's leadership was central to the problem, as well as some other leadership issues that were out of order. The pattern was so strong that it merited a recommendation for my friend to relinquish his leadership.

He received this news with difficulty. But after realizing the rationale of the review, and knowing my heart of towardness for him, he resigned. As his life unfolded, he came to embrace the recommendation as "wisdom from above."[24]

After we completed the process of resignation and transfer of leadership, my friend disclosed to me that he initially agreed with my recommendation only because of our friendship. If it had been anyone else, he would not have believed its validity. In this instance, I had sufficient *relational authority* that led him to trust God's wisdom and direction for his life.

We develop relational authority in friendships (as well as marriage relationships) of strong trust and respect, where we experience exchange of the life of Christ. When such a friend (or spouse) speaks the truth from the stance of towardness, with "kind affection… and brotherly love," we "in honor give preference"[25] to her or his relational authority. Leaders who develop this kind of relationship with team members will reap relational authority.

---

24 James 3:17
25 Romans 12:10

CHAPTER THIRTEEN CULTIVATING A CULTURE OF PRAYER AND HONOR

CHALLENGE

1. Review the suggestions for ways to create a culture of prayer on pages 191 to 193. Consider these questions:
   a. *Which practice(s) are already a part of your leadership community?*
   b. *Choose one or two items from the list where you sense a challenge to make that particular practice of prayer a part of your community discernment. What is the Lord's direction for incorporating that?*
2. Name the type(s) of authority in which members of your team may function. *In what ways can you intentionally honor them as they contribute to the team in their authority? What can you do to empower them to mature in their function of that authority?*

LOOKING AHEAD

Everything up to this point lays the foundation for understanding, developing, and walking in PBL, as you witnessed in Chapter One. Now we build a structure of practical application that will stand secure on the foundation of Presence, Towardness, and Christ-in-the-midst discernment.

— CHAPTER FOURTEEN —

Practical Elements of a Discernment Meeting

When we gather in His name (not in our own name),
We surrender to His presence (not our own agenda),
We seek His face (not our own reputation),
We hear His voice (not the voice of a stranger),
We discern His wisdom (not our own strategy),
We pray and declare His will (with no political compromise),
We follow His direction (with no ulterior motive).

WHERE THEORY BECOMES PRACTICE

Jared hung up the phone, disappointed. He had anticipated hiring a man who seemed perfect for a company position, and the process was progressing smoothly. But the man just informed Jared that he couldn't take the position after all.

What happened? Why didn't God work it out? Jared thought hiring this man was an answer from God. The process had already taken too long. Now he'd have to start over again to find another person.

CHAPTER FOURTEEN PRACTICAL ELEMENTS OF A DISCERNMENT MEETING

Within a few minutes, however, Jared received a call from another man that he'd talked with a few weeks earlier. The man had previously managed multiple outlets and already had numerous contacts in the region, so Jared already thought him a good fit for the company. Jared thanked God for providing an answer so quickly.

During the interview, Jared laid out the company's core values of PBL. The man had no problem with the values, so Jared hired him. He wanted to accompany his new employee to work the next morning to introduce him to the people he'd be leading, but Jared woke up sick. He asked the man to wait a day or two until Jared was well enough to go with him. But the man ignored his request and went in anyway.

According to another manager's report, on the first day, the new boss violated almost all of the company's Core Values and showed a lack of respect for co-workers. He didn't prove a good fit for the team, after all.

Jared then realized that he'd decided to hire the man quickly and without prayerful discernment. Because everything seemed to fall smoothly in place, Jared had assumed that God's hand was in it.

> **God designed my mind to fully come alive in His presence**

"Rather than seek Christ's wisdom, I allowed my emotions and need to dictate my decision," Jared said. "But I learned through that."

The model of PBL discernment shifts from an attitude that says, "God gave me intelligence, and He wants me to use it," to "God designed my mind to fully come alive in His presence, functioning in partnership with Christ toward an eternal purpose."

It sounds good in theory, *but will it work in my everyday situations?* We now address that question by exploring the Act of PBL, where theory becomes practice—in a discernment meeting. While we specifically refer to a board meeting, anyone can practice these principles in any kind of a discernment effort. And as we covered in Chapter Five, even if not everyone in the meeting follows Christ, believers can adopt the PBL mindset in their own hearts.

PART FOUR COMMUNITY DISCERNMENT IN PRACTICE

Agenda (Flow) for PBL Discernment

1. Preparation
2. Ministry
   a. Prayer, Worship
   b. Equipping
3. Review of Agenda
4. Reporting
5. Discernment
6. Serendipity
7. Assignment Review
8. Next Meeting
9. Reflections
   a. Appreciation
   b. Observation
   c. Clarification
   d. Resolution
   e. Improvement
10. Dedication of Rest

©2016 TEACHING THE WORD MINISTRIES

In PBL discernment, the agenda takes on a less rigid purpose. Like the banks of a river, an agenda provides the framework for discernment, which flows as a continual attentiveness to the Spirit's direction. Instead of using the term "agenda," some leaders prefer to use the term "flow."

Over the years in our consultation with leadership teams, we've adopted a board agenda—or flow—that you see outlined in the chart at the left. It works well with the PBL model. Though you may already use some of these items, we briefly describe each as they work according to PBL principles. We also elaborate specifically on the practicalities of preparation and discernment.

TEMPLATE FOR PRESENCE-BASED DISCERNMENT

You may adapt this agenda to your own situation while keeping in mind that the items of "Preparation," "Ministry" (Worship and Equipping), and "Reflections" are vital to cultivating PBL. Embrace this mindset throughout the meeting:

Our commission is to carry the government of Christ into our metron by discerning and aligning with His will in the oneness of Trinity towardness.

CHAPTER FOURTEEN PRACTICAL ELEMENTS OF A DISCERNMENT MEETING

1. Preparation

For efficient, effective meetings, we discern and post the agenda (flow) in plenty of time that allows members to prepare for the meeting adequately. In PBL, we move beyond that to spiritual preparation, which is vital for an atmosphere of Presence and Towardness. Find a wealth of insight and suggestions from Pastor Erick for spiritual preparation in the next section (starting on page 209).

2. Ministry

   a. **Prayer and Worship.**[1] Not only does this devotional time help our team practice and increase sensitivity to the Spirit, it's also vital for ourselves to center on Christ's presence. We recommit to an attitude of towardness that continues throughout the meeting.

   It's not a matter of "inviting Jesus to come." He's already present in the hearts of His followers. It's a matter of honoring the Firstborn's commitment to lead in the way that will produce eternal fruit.

   The chair or another member prepares an activity that will help us acknowledge, worship, and commit to Christ, who presides "in the midst" of the gathering. This may include worship music, but it doesn't have to. Members can take turns leading so each can express their unique perspective of worship.

   I appreciate it when leaders present a worship experience with inspired creativity and deeply meaningful times of devotion. During this time, we also pray for certain aspects of the organization or the meeting as the Holy Spirit impresses us. Also keep in mind the "Culture of Prayer" principle. At any time during the meeting, any member may express praise for what the Lord's doing in the moment.

   b. **Equipping.**[2] Including time for equipping supports leadership development and community building. The chair, or someone to whom he/she delegates, prayerfully prepares a learning experience.

---

1 Use the passcode "PBL" on our website to access ideas for Prayer and Worship *activities*. See page 8 for information.
2 Use passcode "PBL" on our website for Equipping *activities*. See page 8.

This may include activities such as topical studies on leadership or a review of God's purpose/vision for the organization.

We could use this time to explore and apply PBL principles, especially if we're in the process of introducing the concept, drawing from any section of this book for training topics.

Equipping is vital for oneness and towardness. As appropriate, leaders can use the following questions to help the group evaluate its spiritual posture and align with Christ and His character:
- *Do we prefer one another with an attitude of towardness?* (Philippians 2:3-4)
- *Are we sincerely honoring and accepting truth?* (I Peter 1:22)
- *Are we positioned to find Christ's wisdom by attending to the Spirit?* (Ephesians 2:14)
- *Do we fear the Lord above reputation? Is aligning with Christ's wisdom paramount?* (Proverbs 1:7; Ecclesiastes 12:13)

3. Review of Agenda

Already a common practice in board meetings, members prayerfully review the agenda and/or expected outcomes to ask questions, make suggestions, additions, changes, or deletions. Once affirmed by the whole, no further changes are permitted during the meeting. Prayerful attention to this item helps members focus on priorities and eliminates detours (See Serendipity below).

4. Reporting

This section includes all information that does not require discernment, such as minutes, financial reports, and committee reports. Remember to maintain an attitude that gives thanks to Christ for all things[3] and petitions Christ for any concerns. "If we know that He hears us… we know that we have the petitions that we have asked of Him."[4]

---

[3] *1 Thessalonians 5:18*
[4] *1 John 5:15*

CHAPTER FOURTEEN PRACTICAL ELEMENTS OF A DISCERNMENT MEETING

5. Discernment
As illustrated in Chapter One's Board Story, when learning to apply PBL principles, we sometimes set an empty chair at the head or in the center of the group. This reminds us of the reality of Christ's presence in our midst and our place of submission to Christ and each other. We'll detail practical means of discernment in the next section (page 213).

6. Serendipity
Members briefly relate any items brought to mind during the meeting that were not on the agenda. If items require further discernment, they may be added to the agenda for the next meeting, or plans are made for when and where to attend to them. This is not the time to re-open previously discussed items.

7. Assignment Review
Confirm that all members know and understand their assignments or responsibilities that accumulated during the meeting. Ask: *What specific action steps have we discerned for walking in obedience to Christ's wisdom?*

8. Next Meeting
Determine the date (if not already set) and any information or preparation necessary for the next meeting.

9. Reflections
Consider the function and fruitfulness of the session. The discipline of reflecting together on the "meeting as a meeting" adds a deeper dimension to your board's collaboration. We've found this discipline a powerful way to:

  a. Engage the group in sharing the responsibility of managing meetings well.
  b. Help build a culture that values each participant.
  c. Resolve any tensions or misunderstandings in their own context. *Are our relationships clear? If not, what understandings, forgiveness, or healing is needed?*

PART FOUR COMMUNITY DISCERNMENT IN PRACTICE

Just before the conclusion, reserve a few minutes for members to reflect and share on one or more of the themes below. Maintain the boundary that this is *not* a time to introduce or re-discuss an agenda item. Note that we can also apply this reflection time to other types of gatherings, such as Bible studies or discussions. People may share any of the following:

a. **Appreciation:** Affirm an individual or group for a characteristic or contribution.

   For example, Aung, I appreciate the way you helped us to be sensitive to children today.

b. **Observation:** Identify what is noteworthy about the nature of the meeting or trends among meetings over time.

   For example, when everyone is present, our meetings are more energized and balanced.

c. **Clarification:** Constructively edit remarks made during the meeting either as a correction of oneself or to assure clarity of intention.

   For example, as I stated my thoughts, I realize I was harsh and rigid in my opinion. I'd like to restate my position that I believe it's best to take decisive, prompt action.

d. **Resolution:** Clarify relationships, especially if someone perceives she/he has offended another or desires to clear conscience over a remark made.

   For example, Leila, I apologize for cutting you off before you were finished speaking. Will you forgive me for that?

e. **Improvement:** Suggest ways to increase the effectiveness of meetings concerning focus, efficiency, outcomes, or growth of participants.

For example, I'd like to receive written reports three days before our meeting so I can better prepare my responses.

f. **Dedication and Rest:** See the discussion "Allow Prayer to Permeate" in the previous chapter on page 191. Most of all, carefully consider each line according to how we're responding to issues:

*Trust in the Lord with all your heart
and lean not on your own understanding;
In all your ways acknowledge [submit to] Him,
and he will make your paths straight.*
—PROVERBS 3:5-6

MEETING PREPARATION

Any professional painter knows that to maintain high quality, most of their time and sweat goes into preparing the surface before applying paint. We do need a good quality paint, of course, but the finished product can only be as good as the quality of the surface under the paint.

The same principle applies to leadership discernment. "The preparation is actually more important than the process," Ruth Haley Barton writes in her book, *Pursuing God's Will Together*.[5]

While the examples below may specifically concern the chair or leader of a meeting, each participant can develop a discipline of preparation in a similar manner. Prepare not only for meeting tasks, but for our hearts to receive and give what Christ-in-the-midst speaks.

---

5 Barton, Ruth Haley. *Pursuing God's Will Together: A Discernment Practice for Leadership Groups.* IVP Books, 2012.

PART FOUR COMMUNITY DISCERNMENT IN PRACTICE

Consider this example of practices for preparation from Pastor Erick. He shares how he prepares for leadership meetings and trains other ministry leaders to do the same:

1. Re-order my calendar.
I look at my week, month, or quarter and rearrange my calendar to make room for the necessary presence-based time to hear the Lord. *This practice changed everything for me.*

2. Absolute surrender.
I realize that, in light of my awesome God of infinite wisdom, I don't have a clue how I'm to facilitate or lead in each leadership moment. I recognize my complete dependence on the Lord and His wisdom. I submit any preconceived opinions to the process of discerning Christ's wisdom.

3. Hindrances.
I ask the Lord to reveal any self-serving motives or anything in my heart that might hinder me from clearly hearing His voice. I confess and repent to Christ, dealing with anything He reveals so His Spirit and voice can flow through me to others.

4. Connecting and Staying Connected.
I regularly participate in listening prayer, worship, and reading scripture to help soften the soil of my heart to receive. *This takes time.* It's not a ritual, but a devotion to deepen relationship with the Trinity.

5. Posture of Humility.
I posture myself in a spirit of humility. I ask the Lord, "What do you want for this gathering? What do you see? How should the meeting flow? What message do You have for this group?" *Then wait.* I don't move ahead until I hear Christ's direction.

CHAPTER FOURTEEN PRACTICAL ELEMENTS OF A DISCERNMENT MEETING

6. **Questions to Ask the Holy Spirit while Waiting.**

I can't rely on past experiences for this moment. Everything now is different than past leadership moments, just as the Lord gave different instructions to Joshua for each battle.

   a. What do Your people need right now, spiritually, emotionally, physically?
   b. What else is going on in each of their lives and hearts for which I can pray?
   c. How do You want me to create an environment for these leaders to flourish, experience ownership, and oneness? Because You inhabit the praises of Your people,[6] how might I usher them into Your presence through worship, prayer, word, or fasting, preparing their hearts to hear from You?
   d. As I sit in Your presence with open hands and ears, what direction, challenge, encouragement, or healing do You have for us during this gathering?
   e. Where do You want us to go in this gathering?
   f. As I reflect on the agenda and the core questions for discernment, are You giving any further clarification?

7. **Intercessors.**

I have relationships with trusted intercessors who pray for this gathering. I give them a copy of the flow (I prefer not to use the term "agenda") so they can pray before and during the meeting. Afterward, I inform them of how the gathering went. They're also free to share with me anything they sense the Spirit might be speaking.

---

6 *Psalm 22:3, KJV*

8. Preparation for Physical and Spiritual Environment.
I arrive early to the meeting room to prepare the spiritual environment through worship, prayer, and reading Scripture out loud.

9. Ongoing Sensitivity to the Holy Spirit.
During the meeting time, I try to remain sensitive to the Holy Spirit, constantly reminding myself and the group to ask Him, *what are You doing? Where are You taking us?* I listen for His direction for any adjustments to the flow, what He might be doing in a specific person or situation. I remain flexible to lead the group according to what I sense the Spirit speaking.

10. Connecting to the Group's Vision.
I regularly remind the team about our purpose, vision, and PBL model. I try to keep our focus connected to God's divine destiny for our group—why we're doing what we're doing.

11. Immersion Days.
We ensure that our team members have regular times of immersion (spending at least a day or more away) to practice Presence-Based discernment. They, in turn, can mentor their teams with Christ-in-the-midst leadership.

To summarize, meeting preparation is more than a list of disciplines to perform before each meeting. It's developing a posture that remains sensitive to the Lord's voice at *all* times, not only during leadership meetings. Erick shares this insight from Henry Nouwen:[7]

> *Living a spiritually mature life requires listening to God's voice within and among us. The great news of God's revelation is not simply that "I Am," but also that God is actively present in the moments of our lives at all times and places. Our God is a God who cares, heals, guides, directs, challenges, confronts, corrects. To discern means first of all to listen to God, to pay attention to God's active presence, and to obey.*

---

7 Nouwen, Henri J. M. (1932-96), with Michael J. Christensen and Rebecca J. Laird. *Discernment: Reading the Signs of Daily Life.* Harper One, 2013.

CHAPTER FOURTEEN PRACTICAL ELEMENTS OF A DISCERNMENT MEETING

LEADERSHIP DISCERNMENT

At one point, Pastor Erick asked me to facilitate an elder retreat to begin discerning, among other things, how to respond to the congregants' questions about the building funds. The members of Pastor Erick's church had raised a significant amount of money toward a new facility, but in the meantime, the church had lost a large number of people in a conflict. Now, the donations were sitting in a bank account, and people wanted to know what was going to happen to the money. The leadership team didn't have a clear vision of how to proceed.

They wrestled with questions of how this happened. They knew their response would greatly affect the people's attitude toward the leadership team and the church as a whole. They needed the wisdom to care for the people in a way that would foster oneness and fresh vision, steering away from disillusionment or distrust.

Erick and the other leaders spent several hours praying over the issue. One elder who had done the financial research drew an overall picture of where the situation stood. Together they asked the Lord, "What's the next step?"

All of the leaders testified of the weighty, almost tangible peace that settled on them as they intentionally took the stance of listening in the Lord's presence. They knew God saw them, valued them, and affirmed their purpose as a church. They chose to rest in His peace, to "be anxious for nothing," but "by prayer and supplication, with thanksgiving," kept their requests before the Lord.[8]

Though specific answers didn't fully emerge at that meeting, in the months to come, God unfolded His plan for working with and developing oneness in the congregation. As they continued seeking Him, step-by-step, the Lord gave the wisdom for relating to the members and sorting out the vision and details. By their Presence-Based stance, Erick and his team established the government of Christ in their situation.

---

8   Philippians 4:6

PART FOUR COMMUNITY DISCERNMENT IN PRACTICE

The weight of our leadership responsibility rests on the fact that we have the delegated stewardship to make decisions that serve and affect people who are made in God's image. People trust leaders to:

1. Discern and initiate direction that will enhance growth and productivity
2. Manage their finances wisely
3. Set the tone for a work environment that empowers them to flourish in towardness and fulfill the organization's purpose as well as their own

How can mere humans dare embrace such responsibility without ultimate failure? We can't. It's not our work anyway. It belongs to the Firstborn. The only way to responsibly steward His work is to submit our leadership to Christ as the Head and eternal King, to lead in and from Presence-to-presence-to-Presence Trinity fellowship.

HOW TO RECOGNIZE WISDOM FROM CHRIST

"Who is wise and understanding among you?" James asks in his epistle to fellow believers. His answer reiterates that wise and understanding leaders show "by good conduct that his works are done in the *meekness of wisdom*."[9]

What is "the meekness of wisdom"?

James first explains what this wisdom is *not*. It does not come from hearts of "bitter envy, self-seeking, boasting and lying against the truth." Ungodly "wisdom" is either "earthly, sensual, or even demonic... Where envy and self-seeking exist, confusion and every evil thing are there."[10] And so, if confusion

> **If confusion characterizes our discernment meetings, it's a red flag that, in some way, we're missing God's wisdom.**

---

9 *James 3:13, italics mine*
10 *James 3:14-16*

CHAPTER FOURTEEN PRACTICAL ELEMENTS OF A DISCERNMENT MEETING

characterizes our discernment meetings, it's a red flag that in some way we're missing God's wisdom.

The term "meekness" does not mean false humility (another form of pride) that devalues what God does in our lives. *Meekness* is "strength under control." Picture a muscular, tough, large man who's tenderly holding a tiny newborn infant that almost fits into the palm of his hand. The man has enough power to harm the child, but he masters that power to cradle the baby with gentleness instead.

Jesus displayed this meekness when He stood before those who came to arrest Him, "a great multitude with swords and clubs, from the chief priests and elders." Recall that Peter drew his sword and cut off a man's ear. Jesus healed the ear (great power displayed with meekness) and corrected him by saying, "Do you think that I cannot now pray to My Father, and He will provide Me with more than twelve legions of angels?"[11]

Jesus literally had the power of angelic armies of heaven at His command, who could destroy not only the crowd but the entire planet. He didn't use His superior strength to coerce the adversary. In meekness, He chose the way of trust and submission to His Father's will.

James' use of the term "meekness of wisdom" refers to our embracing Christ's attitude of "love and truth." Though we may have the position, authority, or knowledge to enforce a personal agenda, instead, with hearts of love, we recognize Christ gives each one only a part of His wisdom. We keep the strength of our capacity of truth under the Spirit's control. We submit our wisdom to Christ and each other. *What does God's wisdom look like?* James says that the wisdom from above is:

- pure
- peaceable, gentle
- willing to yield to reason
- full of mercy

---

11 *Matthew 26:53*

- full of good fruits
- without partiality
- without hypocrisy[12]

James ends this passage by stressing the posture and power of peace. "…the fruit of righteousness is sown in peace by those who make peace."[13] The "peace of God which surpasses all understanding"[14] is the manifestation of the Prince of Peace in our midst. When we discern and declare Christ's will for the moment, this peace is the substance of what "will guard your hearts and minds through Christ Jesus."[15] In Pastor Erick's story above, his team felt this peace (consolation) deeply.

On the other hand, if any one person in the group does not sense the Spirit's peace concerning a certain decision (desolation), this indicates the need to process the discernment further. Seek the cause of the unrest and hear Christ's wisdom.

PRACTICAL PRINCIPLES FOR BOARD OR TEAM DISCERNMENT IN PRESENCE-BASED CULTURE

Keeping in mind the spiritual peace we know when we align with the Presence of Christ, we also outline other practices and indicators for recognizing the Spirit's wisdom. The chair or leader of the team takes responsibility to facilitate and train the other members in the following practices.

---

12 James 3:17
13 James 3:18
14 Philippians 4:7
15 Ibid.

Attitudinal Principles

1. Each person acknowledges Christ as the Head.
While the meeting chair and other members have their functions or roles, we defer to Christ-in-our-midst as the authority in the meeting. We seek and share the perspective that we sense He is speaking.

Why spend time debating our own opinions when we can discern the solution from our omniscient God? In this life, we'll never fully rise above all of the human nature that remains in our souls, but we trust that Christ is strong enough to lead us into His wisdom.

2. Each member adopts the attitude of Towardness.
Nurture towardness until it characterizes the culture of the team. Cultivate the attitude of "submitting to one another in the fear of God,"[16] "being like-minded, having the same love, being of one accord, of one mind. Let nothing be done through selfish ambition or conceit, but in lowliness of mind let each esteem others better than himself. Let each of you look out not only for his own interests, but also for the interests of others."[17]

3. Maintain a posture of listening to the Spirit while submitting input to Christ in the center.
Remind the group by asking the question, "What is the Lord saying?" Include each member in sharing input as appropriate.

4. Remain aware of Metron.
In each issue for discernment, recognize where the authority and responsibility lie in implementing a decision. Honor those with the appropriate authority in each issue and the boundaries relevant to board, advisor, staff, and other participants.

---

16 *Ephesians 5:21*
17 *Philippians 2:2-4*

5. Welcome lulls of silence.

Sometimes during times of silence, we may tend toward restlessness. Instead of rushing to fill a void with speech or to push a decision, take this opportunity to focus more intently on Christ's presence. Don't go forward until you hear His next step.

Actionable Principles

1. Seek spiritual, intellectual, and relational clarity.

The chair or group leader establishes a rhythm of discussion, discernment, prayer, and worship during the meeting. As we listen, Christ will draw out the gifts, experience, knowledge, and expertise of each member.

2. Establish clarity by identifying the core question.

For example, Lisa Hosler describes a board discussion about finding a way to increase the number of clients who made personal commitments to Jesus.

"We thought the issue was finding the right method of presenting the Gospel. But after prayer, we sensed that we weren't asking the right question. Instead, we discussed: 'What really is the Gospel?'"

They sensed God redirecting them to understand the Gospel as a "life-long process of knowing Christ and living for God's glory," rather than focusing only on how to begin a relationship with Christ. That shift in focus revitalized the impact Lisa's team has in helping clients learn to know Christ.

3. Build upon what each is offering.

A simple switch to "Yes…and…" rather than "But…" practically affirms and further develops team oneness. Build on what others have said. "Yes, I see your point… *and*, let's also…"

CHAPTER FOURTEEN PRACTICAL ELEMENTS OF A DISCERNMENT MEETING

4. Discern how various perspectives fit into the whole.

Building our consensus on what Christ is saying differs from the majority vote, compromise, or the weight of the decision being on one person. Rather than polarizing elements of a decision, we find the harmony of complementary perspectives—the interdependent truths innate in the wisdom of God.

We have no specific, practical procedures or steps to building a consensus of God's wisdom. No one "procedure" applies to all situations. PBL is the Art of yielding moment-by-moment to the direction of Christ. We trust Christ to share His leadership genius—His mind—with us.[18]

5. Recognize the power of tension.

Rather than avoiding or fearing conflict, we understand that in a community of diverse individuals, conflict is inevitable and a natural part of a functioning team. If we respond to conflict in a healthy way, the tension helps to move us forward.

Without tension, a rubber band would lay on the desk useless. Without tension, the muscles in our bodies would exist only as limp mounds of protein. Complementary muscles pull and push against each other to create movement. One muscle trying to act without counter-pressure could move nothing. Exercising this tension causes muscles to grow stronger. But if handled in an unhealthy way, instead of moving forward, tension can digress into division, confusion, or atrophy.

Instead of polarizing truths, Christ gives us balanced wisdom. He may use a complementary perspective to tweak an attitude or strategy slightly. Other times, a different angle may turn the whole discernment another direction.

We can choose to argue over whether blue is better, or red is better, but if we submit our perspectives to Christ, He reveals how together they form a purple solution. We need both blue and red to complete the final picture. If either one is missing, we don't gain the fullest understanding of Christ's perspective.

---

18 *1 Corinthians 2:16*

6. Recognize that the *process* of implementing a decision is part of the decision.

The elder team where Pastor Erick serves once made a major decision that took the congregation in a very different direction. All of the elders sensed consolation (peace) for a decision that had been confirmed in numerous ways, so they whole-heartedly approved the new direction. They assumed the congregation would follow suit, but they were wrong.

"The decision caused a lot of anger and anxiety, and many people left the church. It never occurred to us that the congregation would react this way."

Though they had correctly discerned the Lord's direction, the elders had launched change without considering the members' needs.

"We moved too quickly," Pastor Erick said. "We underestimated the necessity of communication and helping people process change. They needed us to shepherd them through it."

The elders repented and asked the Lord for grace to rebuild. "This time, we discerned a healthier strategy for walking the people through the changes," Erick said.

Then, a few years later, they faced another significant change—the transition of the senior pastor. They sought Christ's wisdom for the whole process and worked with the congregation every step of the way. This time they experienced peaceful, smooth progress.

7. Remain decisive and attentive to the Spirit's peace to bring closure to each item.

As the leader draws discernment to a close, look for a collective sense of consolation or desolation. Does the discernment align with the criteria for godly wisdom in James 3:17? "…pure, peaceable, gentle, willing to yield to reason, full of mercy and good fruits, without partiality or hypocrisy, or self-seeking against truth?"[19]

---

19 From James 3:17

8. Remain in an attitude of oneness, even if consensus is still pending.

What if, after sufficient time, or before the deadline, the team doesn't arrive at a consensus? One mark of mature believers is the capacity to live in the tension between two complementary truths. Exercising the attitude of oneness (identity in Father God rather than in a vision), while at the same time holding a differing point of view. If even one perspective doesn't fit with what the rest of the group hears, prayerfully consider:

   a. Avoid a circular discussion. Again, identify the core question. *What question should we ask Christ?*
   b. It may be time to investigate the issue more fully. *Are we missing any necessary pieces of information? Does God have more to reveal at a later time? Is it the right timing?*
   c. *Should we take time out to pray?*
   d. Each person prayerfully examines his or her heart and recommits to a posture that is "willing to yield to reason."[20] *Are there issues in my life that affect the clarity in hearing?*

9. When we don't reach consensus before time limits.

We accept our limitations, "endeavoring to keep the unity of the Spirit..."[21] Though we all seek to discern Christ's answer, sometimes we simply acknowledge that human factors may cloud discernment. From a PBL perspective, this is *not* the time to "agree to disagree." This stance implies that "we will probably never agree." It underestimates the power of the Holy Spirit to work His truth among us eventually.

When time is a factor beyond our control, we continue "endeavoring to keep the unity of the Spirit in the bond of peace."[22] In this case, the chair makes the final decision, documenting his or her reasons for the decision if warranted. For example, "This is what we believe to be the mind of the Lord…"

---

20 *James 3:17*
21 *Ephesians 4:3*
22 *Ephesians 4:3*

With a humble heart, a dissenting member can choose to embrace an attitude of honor: "I recognize God at work in those participating in the group, even though I hold a different perspective. I may have a strong conviction that I don't perceive as being fully honored yet in the group discernment, but I defer to and honor what the rest of the group has discerned."

10. When you don't know what to do next.

Stop, pray, discern how Christ is leading in the moment.

11. Declare and Celebrate.

Through our declaration, we commit to obedience and embrace Christ's promise in the wisdom we discerned. Together, we affirm the power of our agreement, "…if two of you *agree* on earth concerning anything that they ask, it will be done for them by My Father in heaven."[23] In declaring the direction on which we agree, we set into motion a spiritual power to accomplish Christ's will.

God set a precedent for the power of the spoken word when, in the beginning, He used words to take dominion over chaos. To bring into order things that were without form and empty.[24] "…whoever says to this mountain, 'Be removed and be cast into the sea,' and does not doubt in his heart, but believes that those things he says will be done, he will have whatever he says."[25]

As we proclaim His will that we've discerned, we also celebrate the great privilege God has given us, in His mercy, as partners with Him in this situation. We celebrate the peace of His presence, which affirms His will. We praise Christ for the work that He has already begun and will continue as we embrace His grace and guidance in implementing the discernment.

---

23 *Matthew 18:19, italics mine*
24 *Genesis 1:2-5*
25 *Mark 11:23*

CHAPTER FOURTEEN PRACTICAL ELEMENTS OF A DISCERNMENT MEETING

LASTING LEGACY

Leaving a legacy[26] means far more than "reproducing ourselves in others," a phrase we sometimes hear. A lasting legacy means directing people to know Christ, who reproduces His life in them toward their unique purpose in His eternal plan.

The meaning of our lives reaches far beyond anything we could accomplish within a short century or so here on earth. We can't even try to comprehend the extent of our part in God's eternal purpose—the reason why we were born—to rule and reign with Christ as His bride and partner forever.

When we experience the holiness of Face-to-face communion in unveiled Trinity Presence, "we shall be like Him, for we shall see Him as He is."[27] Our self-serving motives will dissipate in His holy presence. We shall be fully transformed into His image—engaging in life-exchanging towardness that enables us to create like He does, in the purity of beauty and wisdom.

In this life, we learn to overcome. As Jesus modeled, we learn obedience through the things we suffer.[28] "To him who overcomes," Jesus said, "I will grant to sit with Me on My throne, as I also overcame and sat down with my Father on His throne."[29]

Christ has already blazed the overcoming trail by His example. He isn't asking us to sacrifice anything He hasn't already sacrificed for us. As we follow Jesus, we learn to overcome fear, shame, sin, deception, and selfishness, just as He overcame. In willing vulnerability, we learn to trust our Father's love, to enter His presence with confidence as His beloved sons.

---

26 Read an excellent online document that describes research done on leaders who finished well and the legacy they left behind: Three Articles About Finishing Well, by Dr. J Robert Clinton, from the Clinton Biblical Leadership Commentary CD, ©1999. This commentary is available from the Clinton Resources at http://BobbyClinton.com
27 1 John 3:2; Revelation 22:17
28 Hebrews 5:8
29 Revelation 3:21

PART FOUR COMMUNITY DISCERNMENT IN PRACTICE

This is how to leave a lasting legacy: to learn to know Christ, to sacrificially follow Him toward His purpose and empower others to do the same. We minister Christ's transforming life to others, so His Presence and overcoming power ignites in their own lives. Christ Himself is the legacy, past, present, and future, the "Alpha and Omega, the Beginning and the End… Who is and Who was and Who is to come."[30]

CHALLENGE

1. Review again the list you made after Chapter One of the characteristics of godly leadership. Prayerfully consider how your understanding of leadership may have developed. For each characteristic, answer two questions:
   a. *In what ways have you demonstrated this quality in your leadership in the past year?*
   b. *In what way is the Lord challenging you to grow in this characteristic?*
2. *If you were to leave this earth today, what legacy would you leave for others? What areas of your life and leadership is the Spirit leading you to change to more fully leave the legacy of Christ's Presence and power to others?*
3. Individually or with your team, complete the *Presence-Based Leadership Assessment* on pages 226–228.

For further leadership development in the PBL model, Keith Yoder is available for workshops and mentoring. You may also find information for conducting interactive teaching sessions with your team on our website. Use the passcode PBL on our Presence-Based Leadership webpage. Find access information on page 8.

---

30 *Revelation 1:8*

CHAPTER FOURTEEN PRACTICAL ELEMENTS OF A DISCERNMENT MEETING

PRESENCE-TO-PRESENCE.

Life-to-life.

Transformation.

Our presence into His.

Our leadership into His government.

Losing life to fullness in Jesus' life.

Emerging unique identity in identity with Father.

Flourishing as valued members of community.

Thriving in responsibility, surrendering to Christ's authority.

Change.

Loss of self-focus.

Finding sanctuary in the heart of Consuming Fire.

Pressing through resistance toward Presence-Based intimacy.

The only way, to rest in identity to produce fruit to fulfill purpose.

Satisfaction in the circle of Trinity fellowship.

....

> *...till we all come to the unity of the faith*
> *and of the knowledge of the Son of God,*
> *to a perfect man,*
> *to the measure of the stature of the fullness of Christ.*[1]
> *Yet indeed I also count all things loss*
> *for the excellence of the knowledge*
> *of Christ Jesus my Lord,*
> *for whom I have suffered the loss of all things,*
> *and count them as rubbish,*
> *that I may gain Christ and be found*
> *in Him.*[2]

---

1 Ephesians 4:13
2 Philippians 3:8-9a

Presence-Based Leadership Assessment

Use this assessment to help your team discern Christ's wisdom for developing a Presence-Based Leadership culture.

First, ask each member to rate the team separately, and then prayerfully consider the questions together as a group. You may discuss one or more evaluation topics during the "Equipping" time in your leadership sessions, or take an afternoon, a day, or more away for a team retreat. Throughout the process, depend on the Holy Spirit's guidance.

1. Develop a clear picture of where your team currently stands in the journey of maturing in PBL. As you discuss each topic, ask the questions:
   a. What are strengths or opportunities for growth?
   b. What are specific examples of how we already walk in this Attitude or Act of PBL? *(Be truthful but avoid dwelling on the "why's and how's" of falling short. Keep an attitude of grace that looks for opportunities to grow.)*
2. Together, prayerfully discern a strategy for growth.
   a. *To develop a growth strategy, we find it helpful to use the "5C Growth Strategy,"[1] which assists in discerning a well-rounded approach for leadership growth in five areas: Christ, Community, Character, Calling, and Competence. Find instructions on our website:* 5C Growth Plan.[2]
   b. *Develop activities you can use during the "Equipping" time in your staff meetings for empowering your team toward growth. Find ideas on our website.*[3]

---

[1] ConneXions Model for Leadership. *See* Webber, Malcolm, Healthy Leaders: SpiritBuilt Leadership 2, *Strategic Press,* strategicpress.org.

[2] *For an in-depth explanation of* **the 5C Growth Plan,** *use passcode PBL on our website to access our resources. See the information on page 8.*

[3] *Use the information in footnote #2 above.*

Presence-Based Leadership Assessment

Note that though these questions address group situations, you may also use them to guide individual self-assessment. You can find PDF copies of this assessment to print for your group on our website.

Mark boxes: 1 = always; 2 = almost always; 3 = sometimes; 4 = once in a while; 5 = never	1	2	3	4	5
1. The culture in our group is one of towardness and honor. We seek to validate each one's identity in Father God and affirm each one's purpose in Christ.					
2. All members of our group are developing their own Presence-Based Lifestyle (chart page 163) and sensitivity to the Shepherd's voice (pages 151–171).					
3. Members intentionally prepare their hearts before discernment meetings, dealing with any hindrances that may disrupt sensitivity to the Shepherd's voice (pages 151–171).					
4. Members come to discernment meetings prepared to intelligently discuss issues, but without pre-conceived expectations, fully open and yielded to discern Christ's wisdom and direction.					
5. We begin each meeting by focusing our hearts and minds together on worshipping and hearing Christ.					
6. The culture of our group is one of prayer. We easily and organically defer to Christ's Spirit for moments of thanksgiving, request, worship and quiet listening.					
7. In our leadership sessions, we often pause to acknowledge Christ and what He's presently doing in the moment so we can follow Him in it.					
8. During the process of discernment, we remain sensitive to the Spirit's peace (consolation) or discordance (desolation).					
9. We regularly experience Christ's revelation of wisdom, even in situations that seem impossible.					
10. When conflicts arise, we speak truth in love with honest transparency and respectful attitude.					

PRESENCE-BASED LEADERSHIP ASSESSMENT

Mark boxes: 1 = always; 2 = almost always; 3 = sometimes; 4 = once in a while; 5 = never	1	2	3	4	5
11. When conflicts arise, we receive each other's perspectives as complementary and seek to hear Christ-in-the-midst of us as He builds discernment.					
12. When confronted by others with truth and love, members respond with an attitude of honest vulnerability and security in Christ.					
13. When we sense anxiety, accusation or revenge in our hearts or discussion, we immediately surrender to Christ to embrace His stance of trust and forgiveness.					
14. In discernment, we seek the perspective of Christ's government and how our situation fits into His eternal plan, rather than grasping for a temporary fix.					
15. When our discernment concerns dealing with specific people, we prayerfully recognize Christ's perspective of both mercy and righteousness.					
16. We test our discernment with the biblical criteria of James 3:17 (see pages 214–216).					
17. We delegate authority that fits the responsibility level of the position.					
18. We honor each other's metrons, with clear boundaries of responsibility and authority.					
19. We recognize our leadership responsibility as one of releasing others to use their gifts to fulfill their God-given purpose in the organization, rather than to serve us.					
20. We seek the posture of oneness in our group as each member identifies with Christ's purpose for the group.					

©2016 TEACHING THE WORD MINISTRIES

Glossary of PBL Terms

Act of PBL: Christ-in-the-midst discernment; stewarding the metron of sonship within the ecclesia, 36

Anointing: the power of influence that comes by leading in and from the presence of the Holy Spirit, 95

Art of PBL: Presence; leading from a posture of rest in and from the circle of Trinity fellowship, 36

Attitude of PBL: Towardness; culture of prayer and honor, 36

Authority: entrusted as a steward in Father God's household with anointing to establish Christ's government in the sphere He assigns, 95

Authority, submitted: the degree to which we align with the measure of truth that the Father entrusts to us to discern and enact Christ's will within our spheres of responsibility, 115

Authority, usurping: unlawfully seizing authority through control or manipulation, 117

Bipolar ecclesiology: the balance of two perspectives of truth, where we find Christ and His wisdom in the center, 120

Complementary truth: instead of considering differing perspectives as "opposing" we submit them to Christ and consider them as "complementary," 119

Consolation: the sense of moving toward God, or God's peace for moving in a certain direction, 181

Desolation: the sense of moving away from God or lack of God's peace in moving in a certain direction, 181

Ecclesia: Greek term translated as "church," presented by Christ as His decision-making body of believers, 46

Flattery: complimenting someone out of a self-centered motivation, such as for people-pleasing or manipulation; misses the freedom of giving godly "honor," 195

Government, Christ's: God's economy, kingdom rule of mercy and righteousness, 37

Honor: to validate and affirm the identity and authority that Christ has assigned and is fulfilling in someone, 112

Illumination: direct guidance of the Holy Spirit to interpret Scripture, 120

Interdependent truth: Hebraic mindset of wisdom that views an issue from many perspectives, 123

Interpenetration: describes the relationship among Trinity members, separate beings moving toward each other and at the same time filling each other's place, 85

Leadership: influencing people to move from one point to another by making effective decisions, 43

Legacy: directing people to know Christ, who reproduces His life in them toward their unique purpose, 223

Logical deduction: interpreting Scripture by logically deducing truth from it, 121

Mastering PBL: accepting the responsibility to discern wisdom in the power and partnership of the Trinity, 45

Maturity, spiritual: our habitual surrender to Christ and His attitude as the Spirit prompts or convicts us to respond, 157

Metron: Greek word for measure or portion; sphere of influence; a leader's boundaries of responsibility and authority, 126

Oneness: members of a group experience sameness in group identity with purpose in Christ, 175

Panim: Hebrew term translated as "face" or "presence," 80

PBL: Presence-Based Leadership; Guiding others with a posture of submission to wisdom discerned from Christ's presence, 33

Perceived Leaders: a person who holds sway over a group's decisions, even if they're not in the position of leadership, 43

Perichoresis: Greek word to describe the relationship among the members of the Trinity, like a circle dance; interpenetration, 85

Presence: the invisible impact we feel when we're around certain people, places or things, whether positive or negative (R. Dobbins), 142

Prosopon: Greek term meaning "face" or "presence," 80

Responsibility: submitted in obedience to Christ, the Firstborn of Father's household, to His call and purpose, 105

Retain: kingly authorization to remove the power of the control, or root, behind the sin and establish the government of Christ in its place, 135

Rule: to carry the government of the Trinity into an area that falls short of His design, 52

Sonship: our identity as adopted sons of Father God, given a measure of responsibility and authority to fulfill a purpose under Christ, the Firstborn and Head, 93

Stewardship: taking responsibility in the Father's household to lead in the metron He has assigned, 96

Submission: in the biblical sense, willful subjection of self to Christ by honoring a person in authority, 113

Towardness: reflecting the Trinity characteristic of being other-focused; assisting and promoting each other's purposes in Christ, 81

Truth, complementary: instead of considering differing perspectives as "opposing," we submit them to Christ to consider them as "complementary," 119

Truth, interdependent: Hebraic mindset of wisdom that views an issue from many perspectives, 123

Union: embracing identity in Father God as His adopted child and joint heir with Christ, 96

Unity: unvaried or uniform character, focus, and goals among members of a group, 175

General Index

Abell, Ben, 91, 105
Act of PBL, 36, 43
actionable principles, 218
active choices, 143
affection, 97
affirmation, 97, 146
affirmation, Father's, 97
affirmation, God's presence, 146
anointing, 146
anointing, in God's Presence, 146
anointing, prophetic, 147
Apollos, 152
appreciation, reflection, 208
approval, 97
Araminta Freedom Initiative, 92
Art of PBL, 36, 46, 48
assignment review, agenda, 207
Attitude of PBL, 36
attitudinal principles, 217
authority, 97
   Christ's governmental, 117
   competence, 197
   delegated, 79
   delegated, *exousia*, 114
   dominating, 117
   forgiving sin, 135
   four types of, 196
   in sonship, 95
   metron, 126
   police officers, 125
   positional, 196
   principles of, 113
   relational, 199
   retaining sin, 135
   spiritual, 113, 115, 198
   submitted, 115, 116, 124, 125, 126
   suffering, 128
   usurping, 117
authority and responsibility, balance of, 129
authority and submission, 115
authority, definition, 105
authority, positional, 194
Barnabas, 162
Barton, Ruth Haley, 45
Ben Abell, 100
bind, 70
bind and loose, 62
bind, definition, 62
bipolar ecclesiology, 120
building community, activities, 177
business leadership. *See* Jared
business methods, 91
Caesarea Philippi, 56, 61
called out ones, 58
Cappadocian church fathers, 80
Carl and Amber, 37
cat, 156
Charts
   Jesus/Abba Union, Sonship, 98

GLOSSARY OF PBL TERMS

Characteristics of Team Cohesiveness, 188
Orphan Mentality vs. Son Mentality, 108
Presence Scale, 142
Presence-Based Living, 163
Sons Evaluation Continuum, 109
Spiritual Maturity compared to Hearing God's Voice, 157
childhood feelings, 169
choices, reactive and active, 143
Christ, preeminence, 58
Christ-in-the-midst, 36, 67, 73, 75, 125, 178, 179, 187, 191, 201, 209, 212, 228
church, definition, 58
circumspectly, walk, 160
clarification, reflection, 208
closure, 220
community, discernment, 174
community, hearing God in, 159
complementary truths, 119
confession, 169, 192, 210
conflict management, 184–186
congregational leadership, 42, 71 See Pastor Erick
consensus, 221
consensus, building, 219
consolation, 181
consolation and desolation, 182
core question, 218, 221
culture of honor, 194
culture of prayer, 189, 191
culture of respect, 197
daughters and sons, 95
David, King, 155
decision-making body, 70
Deeper Still, 111

definition
  krateo, 135
  metron, 126
  pros, 79
  servant leadership, 117
desolation, 181, 182
discern Christ's will, 69
discernment meeting, 202
discernment process, 220
discernment, agenda item, 207
discernment, group, 162
discernment, principles, 216
Dobbins, Richard, 142
dominating authority, 117
ecclesia, 62, 74
ecclesia, church, 55
elder team meeting, 156
Ellison, Karen, 111, 126
equipping, agenda item, 205
Erick, Pastor. *See* Pastor Erick
eternal time, 138
false humility, 214
father
  relationship with, 97
fear and shame, 83
feminine, perspective in leadership, 95
filter God's voice, 154
flattery, 195
forbid, 62
forgiving sin, 135
Gates of Hades, The, 57, 59
gathered together, 179
Geegh, Mary, 73
God Guides, Geegh, 73
government, Christ's, 51, 52, 59, 75, 95, 105, 112, 116, 132, 136, 139, 141, 165, 197, 228

GLOSSARY OF PBL TERMS

Graphics
   Cycle of Discerning Shepherd's Voice, 159
   Cycle of Transparency and Vulnerability, 161
   Dynamic/Static Poles, 120
   Essence of Sonship, 94
   Integration of Presence-Based Leadership Principles, 173
   Issues of the Heart, 155
   Issues of the Heart and Group Discernment, 158
   Keys to Wisdom, 180
   One with God, Each Other, 177
   PBL - Art, 140
   PBL - Attitude, 76
   PBL - The Act, 13
   Priestly Ministry, 134
   Speaking Truth in Love, 183
   Spirit illumination/Logical deduction, 122
Gregory of Nazianzus, 85
group discernment, 162
guarding the heart, 165, 168
harmonize, 69
Hearing God, 152, 162
HIV pandemic, 91
Holy Spirit, heirs of, 104
Holy Spirit, sensitivity to, 212
Holy Spirit, within us, 147
honor, giving, 194
Hope Springs, 92, 101, 105
Hosler, Lisa. *See* Lisa Hosler
household, Father God's, 98
household, Father's, 105
human trafficking, 92
humility, posture of, 210

Humphrey, Edith, 85
hupotasso, submission, 113
identity, 102
identity of the father, 99
Ignatius, 181
image, of God, 79
image-bearing, 96
immersion days, 212
implement Christ's will, 69
improvement, reflection, 209
in My name, 179
inheritance, 96, 103
intercessors, 211
interdependent truth, 123
interpenetration, 85
interpreting Scripture, 119
Invisible Imprint, Dobbins, 142
invited to Trinity fellowship, 83
issues of the heart, 154
Jared, 50, 55, 60, 77, 104, 124, 131, 144, 189
John, 81
John of Damascus, 85
John the baptizer, 96, 152
John, Apostle, 79, 97
Keith Yoder, 71
keys of the kingdom, 56, 61, 62, 64, 178
kingdom mindset, 137
kings, 132
krateo, retain, 135
leadership, effective, 44
Lisa Hosler, 46, 66, 86, 99, 137, 151, 174, 177, 178, 179, 194, 218
listening prayer, 166, 184
loose, definition, 62
love, definition, 184
male and female, 79, 81, 95

GLOSSARY OF PBL TERMS

manipulation, 156
marketplace leadership, 50
meekness, 214
meeting preparation, 209
Mercy Seat, 133
metron, 217
Metron, 126
mind of Christ, 159
ministry, agenda item, 205
mosaic, 77
Moses, 87, 144
Mulinde, John, 84
My beloved Son, 97
naked, 82
non-profit leadership. *See* Lisa Hosler
Nouwen, Henri J.M., 77, 212
obedience, 167
obedience through suffering, 128
observation, reflection, 208
oikodomeo, 105
oneness, 175, 221
oneness/unity, 175
orphan mentality, 107
Orphans or Sons?, 107
paperclip principle, 198
Paradigm Shift in the Church, Schwarz, 120
Pastor Erick, 42, 84, 137, 210, 213
Paul, Apostle, 46, 95, 103, 122, 127, 129, 145, 152, 159, 175, 194
peace, lack of, 182
peace, sense of, 182
perceived leaders, 43
perichoresis, 84, 89
permit, 62
Peter, Apostle, 57, 70, 72, 93, 97, 215
Peterson, Eugene, 37, 68, 152

petra, 57
police, badge of authority, 125
positional authority, 194, 196
posture of rest, 86
Praise and Thanksgiving, 165
prayer and worship, agenda, 205
prayer culture, 190
prayer, from Scripture, 193
prayers, Paul's, 193
preeminence, Christ, 58, 68, 105
preparation for meeting, 205
preparation, discernment meeting, 210
presence, definition, 49, 142
Presence-Based Discernment, 15, 75, 92, 123, 176, 204
Presence-Based Leadership
  authority, 114
  core principle, 64
  definition, 33, 37
  essence of, 78
  how Jesus modeled, 99
  relational substance, 81
Presence-Based *Lifestyle*, 162
priests, 132
Priscilla and Aquila, 152
process, of discernment, 220
prophetic anointing, 147
prophetic teacher, 147
pros, with, 79
prosopon, presence, 80
purpose statement, 100
purpose, knowing, 100
puzzle piece, 179
reactive choices, 143
reflections, agenda item, 207
reporting, agenda item, 206
resolution, reflection, 208

respect, culture of, 197
responsibility, definition, 105
responsibility, in Father's house, 106
responsibility, in sonship, 94
rest, God's, 86
retaining sin, 135, 136
review of agenda, 206
Rock of revelation, Christ, 57
roots, knowing, 100, 101
rule, to, 52
sabbatical, 38
sacred/secular, 59
Schwarz, Christian, 120
scriptural truth, 118
Scripture prayer, 193
serendipity, agenda item, 207
servant leadership, 117
shame and fear, 83
Shepherd's voice, 154, 157, 179
silence in meeting, 218
son mentality, 107
sons and daughters, 95
sonship, 91
   essence of, 95
   inheritance, 103
   legal characteristics of, 95
speaking truth in love, 182
Spirit interpretation, 118
spiritual authority, 115
spiritual maturity, 157
stewardship, 96
still, small voice, 164
strongholds, 71
study of Scripture, 168
submission, 113
submission, willing, 113, 112
submitted authority, 116, 125, 126

temple of God, 149
tension, power of, 219
thanksgiving, 165, 192, 197
time out for prayer, 192
towardness, 77, 78, 86, 186, 195, 217
   definition, 81
towardness and oneness, 176
transformation
   confirmation, 146
   discernment, 146
   general leadership, 145
   strength, encouragement, 145
   succession, 145
transparency, 160
transparent community, 160
transparent fellowship, 170
Trinity, 79
   dance, 85
   substance, 80
   towardness, 80
Trinity presence, 144, 195
Trinity Presence, transformed in, 145
truth in love, speaking, 182
truth, complementary, 119
truth, definition, 184
truth, scriptural, 118
truth, three ways to know, 118
two or three, 67
two or three witnesses, 179
Uganda, 84
unbelievers, discerning, 72
union, 96
union, in sonship, 93
unity, 175
unity/oneness, 175
usurping authority, 117
validation, 97, 146

validation, in God's Presence, 146
vision, 212
vision, knowing, 100, 102
vulnerability, 160
wait, 167
wait, Hebraic definition, 167
weariness, 46, 87
Weaver, Stephen, 12
wholeness, God's Presence, 146
Willard, Dallas, 141
willing submission, 112
wisdom from above, 215

wisdom, recognizing, 214
wisdom, Hebraic mindset, 123
with, *pros*, 79
World Trumpet Missions, 84
worship, 88
Worship, 165
worship, lifestyle of, 174
writers of Scripture, 152
WWJD, 47
yes…and approach, 195
Zizioulas, John D., 80

Scriptural Reference Index

1 Chronicles 26:29	99
1 Corinthians 1:10	162
1 Corinthians 1:24, 30	69
1 Corinthians 2:9–16	148
1 Corinthians 2:10–12	123
1 Corinthians 2:10–16	149
1 Corinthians 2:14–16	148
1 Corinthians 2:16	37, 159, 219
1 Corinthians 6:11	148
1 Corinthians 6:19	149, 165
1 Corinthians 12:4–11	148
1 Corinthians 12:13	153
1 Corinthians 13:9, 12	123
1 Corinthians 13:12	82
1 Corinthians 14:40	112
1 Corinthians 16:15–16	129
1 John 1:9	169
1 John 3:1	93
1 John 3:1 (KJV)	93
1 John 3:1a	84
1 John 3:2	82, 223
1 John 3:8	184
1 John 4:18	83, 161
1 John 5:6	149
1 John 5:15	206
1 Kings 3:9	152
1 Kings 18:39	147
1 Kings 19:12	164
1 Peter 1:2	148
1 Peter 1:4	104
1 Peter 1:8	71
1 Peter 1:22	206
1 Peter 2:4–5	37
1 Peter 2:5	133
1 Peter 2:13–15a	196
1 Peter 2:17	194
1 Peter 2:18	196
1 Peter 3:7	104
1 Peter 5:5	199
1 Peter 5:7	166, 191
1 Samuel 1:17	133
1 Thessalonians 1:6	149
1 Thessalonians 5:17	190
1 Thessalonians 5:18	144, 206
1 Timothy 4:14	145
1 Timothy 5:17–18	122
1 Timothy 5:19	179
2 Corinthians 1:18–20	118
2 Corinthians 3:6	122, 148
2 Corinthians 3:17	149
2 Corinthians 3:18	145
2 Corinthians 4:17	147
2 Corinthians 5:20	52
2 Corinthians 10:4–5	71, 137
2 Corinthians 10:5	70
2 Corinthians 10:12–16	127
2 Corinthians 10:18	163
2 Corinthians 13:11	162
2 Peter 1:20–21	118, 122
2 Thessalonians 2:13	148
2 Timothy 1:6	145, 193
2 Timothy 2:12	46

SCRIPTURAL REFERENCE INDEX

2 Timothy 2:15. 121
2 Timothy 3:5 167
2 Timothy 3:15–17. 118
2 Timothy 3:16–17;
   2:15–16 . . . . .122, 168
Acts 1:5; 19:5 153
Acts 1:8. 149
Acts 2:4, 17–18; 6:3; 7:55; 10:38 148
Acts 5:32. 148
Acts 6:3, 10. 149
Acts 9:1–25. 145
Acts 10:19; 11:28; 13:2; 21:11 148
Acts 13:2. .162
Acts 13:4. .149
Acts 18:28. 152
Acts 19:2, The Message 153
Acts 20:28. 149
Colossians 1:9–12 193
Colossians 1:15–18 105
Colossians 1:15–20, The Message. . 68
Colossians 1:18 . . . . .58, 94, 103, 105
Colossians 2:3 163
Deuteronomy 17:6 179
Deuteronomy 21:17. 99
Deuteronomy 31:14–23. 145
Ecclesiastes 3:11 138
Ecclesiastes 12:13 206
Ephesians 1:10. 176
Ephesians 1:15–23. 193
Ephesians 2:14. 206
Ephesians 3:16. 149
Ephesians 4:3. . . . . 104, 149, 175, 176, 221
Ephesians 4:3–4 149
Ephesians 4:13. 225
Ephesians 4:14–15. 176
Ephesians 4:15, 25. 184
Ephesians 4:30. 104

Ephesians 5:8–10, 15–17 52
Ephesians 5:9. 148
Ephesians 5:15. 160
Ephesians 5:19–21. 165
Ephesians 5:21. . . . . 112, 113, 217
Ephesians 5:31. 81
Ephesians 6:18. 190
Exodus 3:6; 33:11 145
Exodus 33:2–3 87
Exodus 33:11 87
Exodus 33:12–13, 14 87
Exodus 33:15 145
Galatians 3:24–28 94
Galatians 3:26, 28 95
Galatians 4:1–2 103
Galatians 4:6 154
Galatians 4:6–7 107
Galatians 4:7 103
Galatians 4:22–28 122
Galatians 5:18 . . . . .122, 148
Galatians 5:22 . . . . .148, 182
Galatians 6:7 198
Galatians 6:9 46
Genesis 1:2–5. 222
Genesis 1:26. . . . . .78, 81
Genesis 1:27–28. 58
Genesis 1:28. . . . . .51, 79
Genesis 1:31. 163
Genesis 2:25; 3:7, 10. 83
Genesis 3:7–8. 82
Genesis 24:27. 184
Hebrews 1:2. 103
Hebrews 2:6. 68
Hebrews 2:10. 106
Hebrews 2:11. 105
Hebrews 4:9–12. 86
Hebrews 4:12. 168
Hebrews 4:16. 167

SCRIPTURAL REFERENCE INDEX

Hebrews 5:8 . . . . 106, 223
Hebrews 5:8–9 . . . . 106, 128
Hebrews 5:14 . . . . 152, 164
Hebrews 6:1a, The Message 37
Hebrews 9:11 132
Hebrews 9:15 104
Hebrews 10:5 148
Hebrews 10:20 83
Hebrews 12:2 . . . . 100, 128
Hebrews 13:15 166
Isaiah 9:6–7 . . . . 37, 45, 139, 182
Isaiah 9:7 169
Isaiah 42:1 98
Isaiah 53:12 166
James 1:22 . . . . 154, 167
James 2:5 104
James 3:13 214
James 3:14–16 214
James 3:15, NASB 72
James 3:17 . . . . 153, 163, 164, 200, 216, 220, 221, 228
James 3:17–18 48
James 3:18 . . . . 72, 216
Jeremiah 10:23 152
Jeremiah 17:9 168
Jeremiah 30:21, NASB 48, 146
Job 12:2 11
John 1:1 . . . . 80, 119
John 1:1–2 79
John 1:1–4; 5:38–40; 14:6 118
John 1:32 104
John 2:15 100
John 4:23–24 . . . . 82, 165
John 4:34 167
John 5:19 99
John 5:30 80
John 5:39 . . . . 118, 119, 153
John 6:63 . . . . 122, 148
John 6:63: 16:13; 3:8 122
John 7:38 162
John 8:26 116
John 8:28–29 163
John 8:29 80
John 8:32 71
John 10:3, 14, 27 150
John 10:7–9 83
John 10:10 86
John 10:30–39; 19:7 100
John 12:32 40
John 14:6 116
John 14:16, 26 148
John 14:17 . . . . 118, 148
John 14:17; 16:13 149
John 15:2 167
John 15:15 145
John 15:26 . . . . 81, 118, 148
John 16:13 . . . . 118, 148
John 16:13; 3:8 122
John 16:28 101
John 17 . . . . 166, 193
John 17:2 . . . . 100, 116
John 17:4b 105
John 17:21 175
John 17:21–24 36
John 17:21, 24, 26 84
John 20:22 118
John 20:22–23 135
John 38:11 100
Joshua 1:5, 9, 17 145
Joshua 18:1, 8; 19:51 146
Jude 1:20 144
Leviticus 16:16 133
Luke 2:49; 4:1–13 100
Luke 3:22 97
Luke 4:1 122
Luke 4:16–30 100

SCRIPTURAL REFERENCE INDEX

Luke 5:21–24 135
Luke 5:22–24 133
Luke 9:1–2 114
Luke 9:35 (NIV) 97
Luke 15:31 103
Luke 16:10 198
Luke 17:21 . . . . 37, 104, 169
Luke 22:42 106
Luke 22:42; 9:53 100
Luke 23:34 100
Mark 1:11 97
Mark 1:22, 27 114
Mark 2:5 100
Mark 2:7 135
Mark 2:9–10 133
Mark 9:7 97
Mark 10:35–40 128
Mark 10:42 114
Mark 11:23 222
Mark 11:25 135
Mark 12: 30–31 193
Mark 12:35–37 122
Matthew 3:11 . . . . .128, 153
Matthew 3:17 . . . . .97, 103
Matthew 4:1 122
Matthew chapters 5–7 52
Matthew 5:13–16 52
Matthew 5:17 122
Matthew 6:8 .167
Matthew 6:9–13 193
Matthew 6:10 64
Matthew 7:29 114
Matthew 9:11 62
Matthew 11:5; 9:35 100
Matthew 12:34 143
Matthew 14:22 182
Matthew 14:23–32 93
Matthew 16:13–19 57
Matthew 16:15–19 56
Matthew 16:18 . . . . .54, 56, 70, 105
Matthew 16:19 61
Matthew 16:19; 18:18 63
Matthew 16:23 70
Matthew 17:5 . . . . 80, 97
Matthew 18:15–17 62
Matthew 18:16 121
Matthew 18:17 . . . . 56, 62
Matthew 18:18 . . . . 62, 63
Matthew 18:19 222
Matthew 18:19–20 . . . . 67, 178
Matthew 18:20 . . . . .45, 159
Matthew 18:20b 65
Matthew 18:21 67
Matthew 19:8–9 122
Matthew 20:25 114
Matthew 20:25–26 . . . . 115, 117
Matthew 25:21 167
Matthew 26:53 215
Matthew 27:51 83
Matthew 28:18 . . . . .116, 128
Nehemiah 8 133
Numbers 14:5; 16:22; 20:6 147
Numbers 16:5 146
Philippians 1:3–6 193
Philippians 2:1–2 149
Philippians 2:2 162
Philippians 2:2–4 217
Philippians 2:3 197
Philippians 2:3–4 206
Philippians 2:3–5 163
Philippians 2:5 163
Philippians 2:10–11 128
Philippians 2:22 163
Philippians 3:8 145
Philippians 3:8–9a 225
Philippians 3:14–15 163

SCRIPTURAL REFERENCE INDEX

Philippians 4:6 . . . . 144, 192, 213
Philippians 4:7 . . . . 166, 182, 216
Philippians 4:8 144
Proverbs 1:7 206
Proverbs 3:5–6 . . . . 1, 209
Proverbs 4:23 . . . . 154, 157
Proverbs 16:6; 20:28 184
Psalms 8:4; 144:3 68
Psalms 16:11 139
Psalms 22:3 . . . . 165, 211
Psalms 22:3, KJV 211
Psalms 22:3, NRSV 197
Psalms 25:10; 61:7; 85:10; 89:14 184
Psalms 27; 40:1–16; 71:1–6 193
Psalms 42:7 154
Psalms 100: 1–5 163
Psalms 109:9; 23:3 155
Psalms 119:160 . . . . 118, 122
Psalms 119:99, 130 168
Psalms 131:2, The Message 88, 163
Revelation 1:5 90
Revelation 1:6 132
Revelation 1:6; 5:10 138
Revelation 1:8 224
Revelation 3:21 223
Revelation 5:10 46
Revelation 7:11 147
Revelation 22:17 223
Romans 1:20–24 165

Romans 5:5; 15:30 149
Romans 8:2 148
Romans 8:9 104
Romans 8:14 . . . . 122, 148, 163
Romans 8:14–17 . . . . 94, 96
Romans 8:15–17 93
Romans 8:17 90
Romans 8:26 166
Romans 8:26–27 . . . . 134, 149
Romans 8:27 148
Romans 8:28 . . . . 139, 155
Romans 8:34 166
Romans 9:1 149
Romans 12:1 . . . . 163, 174, 191
Romans 12:1 (NIV) 165, 191
Romans 12:2 . . . . 168, 170
Romans 12:3–4 127
Romans 12:5 81
Romans 12:6–8 136
Romans 12:10 200
Romans 13:1 . . . . 114, 196
Romans 13:2 . . . . 197, 198
Romans 13:7 196
Romans 14:17 . . . . 104, 166
Romans 15:16 148
Ruth 4:10–11 60
Titus 3:5 148
Titus 3:7 104

Other Books by Keith Yoder

ORDER THESE AND FIND OTHER RESOURCES AT *TTWM.ORG*

Healthy Leaders, 3rd Edition
Expand your leadership with a clear sense of identity and direction

Thousands of readers have experienced greater maturity and strength in their leadership through the principles of this book. Increase your godly influence by understanding and establishing your identity in Father God and direction in Christ.

Navigating Your Sabbatical: Purpose, Plan, Support

The art of balancing work and rest as God modeled and intended leads to a healthy life and leadership. Learn to understand sabbatical, and plan intentional, workable times of rest that touch God's heart and draw strength from Christ and His body.

OTHER BOOKS

Foundation Stones
Clarify Your Calling and Direction

BY KEITH YODER, DON RIKER, BARRY STONER

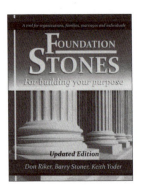

A practical tool that guides individuals, organizations, and business teams, married couples, and/or families through the meaningful process of discerning and writing statements for your: Purpose, Mission, Vision, and Core Values. Through a step-by-step process, heart-searching questions, helpful tips, and supportive encouragement, *Foundation Stones* leads you through the investigation, implementation, and evaluation stages of discerning your statements. Great for processing with a group.

Gifts of Grace
BY KEITH & MARIAN YODER

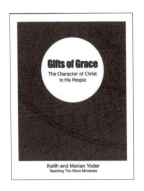

Discern your gift mix and how that works in your sphere of influence. Widely used in business, congregations, nonprofits, and counseling for building relationships, team harmony, and insight into God's purposes. Based on Romans 12: Prophecy, Serving, Exhortation, Teaching, Giving, Ruling, Mercy.

- Spiritual Gifts Questionnaire
- The Character of Christ in His People

Giving to Worship Devotional
Encounter the delight of The Giver through sacred expressions of worship
BY KEITH YODER AND CINDY RIKER

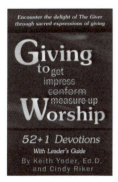

Readers appreciate how these devotions give them a deeper understanding and attitude for what giving really means. Is it just a habit to plunk our change and checks into the plate each week? Why do we give? To worship God. We know the right answer, but do we always intentionally turn on the flow of worship from our hearts? Whether individual, family, offertory leader, pastor, teacher, or group facilitators, these meditations help you honor God with your offerings for powerful spiritual fruit in Christ's kingdom.

- 52+1 thought-provoking, meaningful meditations
- Lesson plans for adults and children
- Suggestions for moderators of worship services
- Meaningful ideas for application
- Suggestions for household dedication

Endorsements

Mastering the Art of Presence-Based Leadership is a paradigm shift in leadership education. From a deep scriptural foundation, applied to vivid and practical examples, Keith Yoder offers a leadership approach that humbly seeks the presence and guidance of Christ for both the day-to-day and the seemingly impossible decisions. I encourage every leader, marketplace, or ministry to integrate the qualities and practices of Presence-Based Leadership within their teams.

— **Sarah F. Davies,** Head of Data & Analytics, NovaCredit.com, President, Teaching the Word Ministries

---

Mastering the Art of Presence-Based Leadership is based upon two basic truths. First, all of life and eternity are the result of relationships. Everything we have and experience is the consequence of relationships. Secondly, the most important relationship we will ever have is with the Lord Jesus Christ. Keith states that the act of presence-based leadership is stewarding Christ's presence in the midst of us. This requires intentional action on our part. To act appropriately, we must develop an attitude of *towardness* to God and each other. We soon discover that Presence-Based Leadership is more than a method; it is an *art* born out of a culture of honor and love.

We all face the challenge and constant pressure to conform to culture in a post-modern age. There are countless books on leadership. But this book is different! Presence-based leadership is not only possible; it is essential in every aspect of life. Whatever sphere of responsibility you have, be it family, business, work, or ministry, this is the perfect guidebook. I encourage you to read it, recommend it, and implement it.

— **Dr. Dale A. Fife,** Author, *The Secret Place: Passionately Pursuing God's Presence*

ENDORSEMENTS

I have known Keith Yoder for more than 40 years. His wisdom and insight have been a great blessing to me. The truths shared in this book are what have guided Keith's pattern of helping countless leaders in finding their place in life, ministry, and leadership. Inviting and acknowledging the presence of God in leading meetings results in spontaneous discernment that brings freedom and wisdom.

—**Pastor Sam Smucker**, The Worship Center Ministers Network, Lancaster, PA

....

Dr. Keith Yoder has lived his life modeling a personal, intimate relationship with the GODHEAD. This has qualified him to write *Presence-Based Leadership*. If you desire a life centered in Christ and His wisdom for living and desire to fulfill GOD'S plan/purpose for you, then this book is for you!!! Other benefits include true personal rest in GOD and His abiding peace, which will lead to accomplishment in all areas of life.

Keith is a gifted professor/teacher, and the material is based on years of personal study and life experience. If you are a leader of or member of a team in the home, church/ministries, marketplace, and/or government, I enthusiastically recommend this book as your practical guide.

—**Ken Mullen,** former Executive Vice President, Cardone Ind.

About the Author

You don't judge a book by its cover; you judge it by its author. I know Dr. Keith Yoder personally and have the distinct privilege of ministering with him as an apostolic consulting team. We serve a significant, world-changing church in Tennessee. This congregation and its leaders are an exemplary testimony of *Presence-Based Leadership* and Worship. Judging by the person and the fruit produced through Keith's life, I know of no one better qualified than he is to write a book on Presence-Based Leadership.

Keith is much like the Scribe Ezra; he loves the word of God, he seeks to live the word of God, and he teaches the scriptures with anointed and studied knowledge and experience. When you combine these attributes with Keith's absolute passion for God's presence, you have the perfect combination: biblical wisdom and experiential insight.

—**Dr. Dale A. Fife**

KEITH YODER IS AVAILABLE FOR LEADERSHIP DEVELOPMENT, WORKSHOPS, AND SEMINARS. CONTACT:

*For Jesus' sake,
Cultivating healthy leaders
Who transform their world and finish well*

EMAIL: MAIL@TTWM.ORG | TTWM.ORG